From Text to Context

Stylistics, in parallel with similar trends in language studies and literary theory, has widened its scope of investigation from a close reading of texts to considering texts in context. This broadening-out has greatly increased the literary critical potential of stylistics.

This book makes new insights from linguistic and literary scholarship accessible to students in their daily practice of reading, analysing and evaluating poetry. The twelve chapters are written by an international team of leading figures in the field. They provide a firm foundation for the development of language and context-based literary criticism, allowing students to increase their creative responsiveness to the interplay between text and context, and between language and social situation. Each chapter contains a set of suggestions for further activities.

Based on extensive teaching experience, the book is designed specifically for use by students of language, literature, and English as a foreign language.

The editor, Peter Verdonk, is a Reader in English at the University of Amsterdam.

The INTERFACE Series

A linguist deaf to the poetic function of language and a literary scholar indifferent to linguistic problems and unconversant with linguistic methods, are equally flagrant anachronisms.   (Roman Jakobson)

This statement, made over twenty-five years ago, is no less relevant today, and 'flagrant anachronisms' still abound. The aim of the INTERFACE series is to examine topics at the 'interface' of language studies and literary criticism and in so doing to build bridges between these traditionally divided disciplines.

Already published in the series:

NARRATIVE
A Critical Linguistic Introduction
Michael J. Toolan

LANGUAGE, LITERATURE AND CRITICAL PRACTICE
Ways of Analysing Text
David Birch

LITERATURE, LANGUAGE AND CHANGE
Ruth Waterhouse and John Stephens

LITERARY STUDIES IN ACTION
Alan Durant and Nigel Fabb

LANGUAGE IN POPULAR FICTION
Walter Nash

THE LANGUAGE OF JOKES
Analysing Verbal Play
Delia Chiaro

LANGUAGE, TEXT AND CONTEXT
Essays in Stylistics
Edited by Michael Toolan

THE DISCOURSE OF ADVERTISING
Guy Cook

The series editor
Ronald Carter is Professor of Modern English Language at the University of Nottingham and was National Coordinator of the 'Language in the National Curriculum' Project (LINC) from 1989 to 1992.

Twentieth-Century Poetry:
From Text to Context

Edited by Peter Verdonk

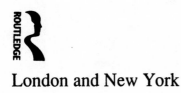

London and New York

First published 1993
by Routledge
2 Park Square, Milton Park, Abingdon, Oxon, OX14 4RN

Transferred to Digital Printing 2005

Simultaneously published in the USA and Canada
by Routledge
270 Madison Ave, New York NY 10016

Typeset in 10/12 point Times by
Ponting–Green Publishing Services, Chesham, Bucks

British Library Cataloguing in Publication Data

A catalogue record for this book is available from the
British Library

Library of Congress Cataloging in Publication Data

Stylistic criticism of twentieth-century poetry : from text to
    context / [edited by] Peter Verdonk.
        p.   cm. – (Interface)
    Includes bibliographical references and index.
    1. Poetry–20th century–History and criticism.   2. Style,
Literary.   I. Verdonk, Peter, 1935– .   II. Series: Interface
(London, England)
PN1271.S87   1993
                                809.1'04–dc20   92-47061

ISBN 0–415–05862–7   ISBN 0–415–05863–5 (pbk)

Contents

Series editor's introduction to the Interface series

There have been many books published this century which have been devoted to the interface of language and literary studies. This is the first series of books devoted to this area commissioned by a major international publisher; it is the first time a group of writers have addressed themselves to issues at the interface of language and literature; and it is the first time an international professional association has worked closely with a publisher to establish such a venture. It is the purpose of this general introduction to the series to outline some of the main guiding principles underlying the books in the series.

The first principle adopted is one of not foreclosing on the many possibilities for the integration of language and literature studies. There are many ways in which the study of language and literature can be combined and many different theoretical, practical and curricular objectives to be realized. Obviously, a close relationship with the aims and methods of descriptive linguistics will play a prominent part, so readers will encounter some detailed analysis of language in places. In keeping with a goal of much work in this field, writers will try to make their analysis sufficiently replicable for other analysts to see how they have arrived at the interpretative decisions they have reached and to allow others to reproduce their methods on the same or on other texts. But linguistic science does not have a monopoly in methodology and description any more than linguists can have sole possession of insights into language and its workings. Some contributors to the series adopt quite rigorous linguistic procedures; others proceed less rigorously but no less revealingly. All are, however, united by a belief that detailed scrutiny of the role of language in literary texts can be mutually enriching to language and literary studies.

Series of books are usually written to an overall formula or design. In the case of the Interface series this was considered to be not entirely appropriate. This is for the reasons given above, but also because, as the first series of its kind, it would be wrong to suggest that there are formulaic modes by which integration can be achieved. The fact that all the books address themselves to the integration of language and literature in any case imparts a natural and organic unity to the series. Thus, some of the books in this series will provide descriptive overviews, others will offer detailed case studies of a particular topic, others will involve single author studies, and some will be more pedagogically oriented.

This range of design and procedure means that a wide variety of audiences is envisaged for the series as a whole, though, of course, individual books are necessarily quite specifically targeted. The general level of exposition presumes quite advanced students of language and literature. Approximately, this level covers students of English language and literature (though not exclusively English) at senior high-school/upper sixth-form level to university students in their first or second year of study. Many of the books in the series are designed to be used by students. Some may serve as course books – these will normally contain exercises and suggestions for further work as well as glossaries and graded bibliographies which point the student towards further reading. Some books are also designed to be used by teachers for their own reading and updating, and to supplement courses; in some cases, specific questions of pedagogic theory, teaching procedure and methodology at the interface of language and literature are addressed.

From a pedagogic point of view it is the case in many parts of the world that students focus on literary texts, especially in the mother tongue, before undertaking any formal study of the language. With this fact in mind, contributors to the series have attempted to gloss all new technical terms and to assume on the part of their readers little or no previous knowledge of linguistics or formal language studies. They see no merit in not being detailed and explicit about what they describe in the linguistic properties of texts; but they recognize that formal language study can seem forbidding if it is not properly introduced.

A further characteristic of the series is that the authors engage in a direct relationship with their readers. The overall style of writing is informal and there is above all an attempt to lighten the usual style of academic discourse. In some cases this extends to the way in which notes and guidance for further work are presented. In all cases, the style adopted by authors is judged to be that most appropriate to the mediation of their chosen subject matter.

We now come to two major points of principle which underlie the conceptual scheme for the series. One is that the term 'literature' cannot be defined in isolation from an expression of ideology. In fact, no academic study, and certainly no description of the language of texts, can be neutral and objective, for the sociocultural positioning of the analyst will mean that the description is unavoidably political. Contributors to the series recognize and, in so far as this accords with the aims of each book, attempt to explore the role of ideology at the interface of language and literature. Second, most writers also prefer the term 'literatures' to the singular notion of literature. Some replace 'literature' altogether with the neutral term 'text'. It is for this reason that readers will not find exclusive discussions of the literary language of canonical literary texts; instead the linguistic heterogeneity of literature and the permeation of many discourses with what is conventionally thought of as poetic or literary language will be a focus. This means that in places as much space can be devoted to examples of word-play in jokes, newspaper editorial, advertisements, historical writing, or a popular thriller as to a sonnet by Shakespeare or a passage from Jane Austen. It is also important to stress how the term 'literature' itself is historically variable and how different social and cultural assumptions can condition what is regarded as literature. In this respect the role of linguistic and literary theory is vital. It is an aim of the series to be constantly alert to new developments in the description and theory of texts.

Finally, as series editor, I have to underline the partnership and cooperation of the whole enterprise of the Interface series and acknowledge the advice and assistance received at many stages from the PALA Committee and from Routledge. In turn, we are all fortunate to have the benefit of three associate editors with considerable collective depth of experience in this field in different parts of the world: Professor Roger Fowler, Professor Mary Louise Pratt, Professor Michael Halliday. In spite of their own individual orientations, I am sure that all concerned with the series would want to endorse the statement by Roman Jakobson made over twenty-five years ago but which is no less relevant today:

> A linguist deaf to the poetic function of language and a literary scholar indifferent to linguistic problems and unconversant with linguistic methods, are equally flagrant anachronisms.

In this collection of essays of stylistic criticism, Peter Verdonk has brought together a wide range of well-known international contributors and ensured a tightly focused commentary on a wide range of twentieth-century poetry. The book provides a guided, carefully structured introduction to the close reading of modern poetry and should be found especially useful by teachers and students of modern English language and literature, particularly as a result of the suggestions for further activity and study provided by the editor and contributors. The collection is, however, more than one with a careful pedagogic design; it also pushes back a number of descriptive and theoretical frontiers by the way in which text and context are interwoven. This ensures that there is a focus on language but the focus also guarantees that language is not the sole carrier of significance. Texts are produced in contexts and analysis of language always takes place in relation to a wider social and cultural environment. Such a focus avoids the danger of text-immanence in the stylistic analysis of literature and reinforces the importance of an approach to literary language which is consistently 'contextualized'.

Notes on contributors

Ronald Carter is Professor of Modern English Language at the Department of English Studies, University of Nottingham. He has published widely in the fields of stylistics, literary theory, and linguistics, and has particular interests in the applications of linguistics to the teaching of language and literature, both for students of English as a mother tongue and as a second or foreign language. He is the series editor of the Routledge Interface series.

Richard D. Cureton is an Associate Professor of English Language and Literature at the University of Michigan, where he teaches courses in English language, poetry, linguistic stylistics, and stylistic criticism. He has published many articles on these topics and has just completed a major study of English verse rhythm, *Rhythmic Phrasing in English Verse* (1992). Currently, he is working on three other books: a pedagogical survey of the language of poetry, a theory of English metre, and a volume of rhythmic analysis.

Balz Engler is Professor of English at the University of Basel. He has published a critical edition of *Othello* (1976), which includes a German prose translation of the play. He has written books on Shakespeare translation, on how poetic texts may indicate the way they should be performed (*Reading and Listening*, 1982), and on literature as performance, its theoretical basis and cultural implications (*Poetry and Community*, 1990). He has also edited two collections of essays, on community drama and on the links between writing and culture. His interests currently focus on theoretical aspects of the relationships between literature and the theatre.

Walter Nash is Emeritus Professor of Modern English Language at the University of Nottingham. He has earned an international reputation as a lecturer and writer, culminating in an honorary doctorate from the

University of Lund. His academic interests include English usage, composition, stylistics, the language of literature and rhetoric, and in addition to numerous articles, his recent publications in these fields include *The Language of Humour: Style and Technique in Comic Discourse* (1985), *English Usage: A Guide to First Principles* (1986), *Rhetoric: The Wit of Persuasion* (1989), *Language in Popular Fiction* (in the Interface series, Routledge, 1990), and *An Uncommon Tongue: The Uses and Resources of English* (1992). He has also written a novel, *Kettle of Roses* (1982). Currently, he is engaged in writing a book on 'the games of literature'.

Mary Louise Pratt is Professor of Latin American and Comparative Literature at Stanford University. Her work in the area of linguistics and literary analysis includes the books *Toward a Speech Act Theory of Literary Discourse* (1977) and *Linguistics for Students of Literature* (co-authored, 1980). In more recent years her work has focused on questions of discourse and ideology, particularly in relation to the subjects of race, gender, nationalism, and imperialism. Her essays on these topics have appeared in *Race, Writing and Difference* (1985), *Writing Culture* (1986), *Literature and Anthropology* (1987), *The Linguistics of Writing* (1989), and *Women, Culture and Politics in Latin America* (1990). Her most recent book is *Imperial Eyes: Travel Writing and Transculturation* (1992), a study of how ideologies of expansionism are deployed, questioned, and appropriated in writings on Africa and South America from the eighteenth century to the present.

Roger D. Sell, formerly Professor of English Literature at the University of Gothenburg, is currently Professor of English Language and Literature at Åbo Akademi University, and also teaches at Helsinki University. His publications range over English and American literature from Chaucer to the present day, and he is particularly concerned to promote the study of literature by interdisciplinary methods drawing on linguistics and sociocultural history. He has guest lectured on this theme in many countries and is a member of the Bureau of UNESCO's Fédération Internationale des Langues et Littératures Modernes. He is Director of the Academy of Finland's Literary Pragmatics Project, has recently edited a collection of literary pragmatic papers for Routledge (*Literary Pragmatics*, 1991), and is at present completing a general introduction to literary pragmatics for Longman. Forthcoming publications also include a collection of papers on interdisciplinary approaches to literature, and a Macmillan New Casebook on *Great Expectations*.

Mick Short is a Senior Lecturer in the Department of Linguistics and Modern English Language at Lancaster University. He is chair of the Poetics and Linguistics Association (PALA), and editor of the association's new journal, *Language and Literature*, published by Longman. In addition to numerous articles on stylistic analysis, he wrote *Style in Fiction* with Professor Geoffrey Leech in 1981, and edited *Reading, Analysing and Teaching Literature* in 1989. He and Geoffrey Leech are general editors of two book series for Longman, 'Learning About Language' and 'Studies in Language and Linguistics'. He is currently working on an introduction to stylistics, and is planning a book on the stylistics of drama.

Michael Toolan is Professor of English at the University of Washington, Seattle. He has published books on narratology and stylistics, recently authoring *Narrative: A Critical Linguistic Introduction* (in the Interface series, Routledge, 1988), *The Stylistics of Fiction* (1990), and editing *Language, Text and Context: Essays in Stylistics* (1992). His current research interests include pragmatics and linguistic theory, culminating in the completion of a book-length manuscript provisionally entitled *Taking Language in Context Seriously.*

Peter Verdonk is a Reader in the Department of English Language and Literature at the University of Amsterdam. He is international secretary of the Poetics and Linguistics Association (PALA) and a member of the editorial board of the association's journal, *Language and Literature*. He has published articles on literary stylistics and criticism in books and journals, and his forthcoming publications include a book on English syntax and a collection of papers on the literary stylistic criticism of nineteenth- and twentieth-century prose (co-edited with Jean Jacques Weber of the University of Luxembourg). Most recently he has co-edited and contributed to a television and radio course in twentieth-century British and American literature.

Katie Wales is a Senior Lecturer in English in the University of London (Royal Holloway and Bedford New College) with special interests in stylistics and English language. She has published over thirty articles and the first ever *Dictionary of Stylistics* (1990); most recently, *The Language of James Joyce* (1992). She has guest lectured widely on stylistics, English language, and James Joyce in Cairo, East Berlin, Milan, Florence, Zurich, Monte Carlo, Turkey, Seville, and South Africa. Since October 1992 she has been a British Academy Senior Research Fellow. Previously, she was treasurer of the international Poetics and Linguistics Association (PALA) and assistant editor of its journal *Language and Literature*, launched by Longman in June 1992.

Ruth Waterhouse is an Associate Professor of English at Macquarie University, New South Wales, Australia. Together with John Stephens, she has recently published *Literature, Language and Change: From Chaucer to the Present* (1990). With two other colleagues she is at present compiling (for Boydell and Brewer) an exhaustive annotated bibliography of medieval chronicles written in English, having just completed work on another jointly compiled annotated bibliography on Chaucer's *Monk's Tale*. She has published numerous articles on Old English literature and children's literature, and is currently working in these areas and on aspects of literary discourse and theory.

H. G. Widdowson holds a double appointment of Professor of Education at the University of London and Professor of Applied Linguistics at the University of Essex. He has written widely on language education and has a particular interest in the discourse of literature. His publications include the highly influential *Stylistics and the Teaching of Literature* (1975), and his most recent book is *Practical Stylistics* (1992), published by Oxford University Press.

Acknowledgements

I have only been able to achieve the aims of this collection with the help of its contributors and I wish to express my sincere thanks for their keen appreciation of my ideas and their inspiring papers. Furthermore I am grateful to Ronald Carter, the series editor, for his encouragement to undertake this project and for having the benefit of his wide experience.

Acknowledgement is due to the copyright holders of the following poems for their kind permission to reprint them in this book:

Cecil Day Lewis: for 'Last Words' from *The Complete Poems*, 1992. Reprinted by permission of Sinclair-Stevenson.

Thomas Stearns Eliot: for 'A Game of Chess' from *The Waste Land*. Reprinted by permission of Faber & Faber Ltd, London, from *Collected Poems 1909–1962*; and Harcourt Brace Jovanovich Inc., Florida.

Dave Etter: for 'Summer of 1932' from *Electric Avenue* (Spoon River Poetry Press, 1988). Copyright © by Dave Etter. Used by permission of the author.

Robert Frost: for 'Nothing Gold Can Stay' from *The Poetry of Robert Frost* edited by Edward Connery Lathem. Copyright 1923, © 1964 by Holt, Rinehart, & Winston. Copyright 1951 by Robert Frost. Reprinted by permission of Henry Holt and Company, Inc., New York, and by permission of Random Century Ltd, London, on behalf of the Estate of Robert Frost, and Jonathan Cape Ltd, London.

Tony Harrison: for 'Long Distance II' and 'Books Ends I' from *Selected Poems* (King Penguin edition, 1984). Reprinted by permission of the author.

Gwen Harwood: for 'In the Park' from *Selected Poems*, © 1975 by Gwen Harwood. Reprinted by permission of Collins Angus & Robertson, North Ryde, NSW, Australia.

Seamus Heaney: for 'Punishment' from *North*, 1975. Reprinted by permission of Faber & Faber Ltd, London.

Geoffrey Hill: for 'Of Commerce and Society' from *Collected Poems* (King Penguin edition, 1985). Reprinted by permission of André Deutsch Ltd, London.

Ted Hughes: for 'To Paint A Water Lily' from *Lupercal*, 1960. Reprinted by permission of Faber & Faber Ltd, London.

Philip Larkin: for 'Church Going' from *Collected Poems*, 1988. Reprinted by permission of the Marvell Press, England and Australia.

Naomi Quiñonez: for one stanza of 'Trilogy', from *Sueño de Colibri/ Hummingbird Dream*, Boulder, Colorado: West End Press. Reprinted by permission of West End Press, Albuquerque, New Mexico.

Helen Silvas: for 'Malinche Reborn', from *Irvine Chicano Literary Prize, 1985–7*, Irvine, California: Department of Spanish and Portuguese, University of California. Reprinted by permission of the Department of Spanish and Portuguese, University of California at Davis.

Carmen Tafolla: for 'La Malinche' from *Five Poets of Azlán* edited by Santiago Daydí-Tolson, 1985. Reprinted by permission of Bilingual Press/Editorial Bilingüe, Arizona State University, Tempe, AZ.

Figures 8.1 and 8.2 are reprinted by kind permission of Routledge from J. Stephens and R. Waterhouse (1990) *Literature, Language and Change: From Chaucer to the Present*, London: Routledge.

We have been unable to trace the copyright holder of Adaljza Sosa-Riddell's untitled poem from *El Grito* 7, p. 76.

Introduction

Peter Verdonk

TWO SCHOOLS OF STYLISTICS: DIVISION OR CONCORD?

When in the 1960s stylistics was introduced into many school and university curricula, it had close links with American New Criticism and British Practical Criticism.[1] Both critical movements advocated, and so did stylistics, what was in essence a formalist approach, that is, literature was to be looked upon as a self-contained enterprise. Extra-textual matters such as biographical details, the author's intention, or socio-historical and cultural influences were to be disregarded; the meaning was only to be found in the words on the page. This language-centred theory of meaning happened to fall in with the then dominant linguistic models on which stylistics took its bearings. Though it seems that this formalist tradition is still pretty strong in English literary studies, critical approaches derived from New and Practical Criticism, and in consequence also text-oriented stylistics, have been exposed to a lot of criticism in recent years for failing to recognize that the meaning relationship between words and the things in the world they denote is by no means unproblematic.

This criticism is justified, but judging from several publications, I have the impression that most, if not all, practising stylisticians are in the meantime well aware of the theoretical limitations of this school of stylistics, which, is often referred to as pedagogical stylistics. Actually, it is the qualification 'pedagogical' which provides the answer to the question why this text-intrinsic stylistic approach still has a good many supporters in English literature teaching, either separate from or in relation to the language, and in the teaching of English as a foreign or second language. As a matter of fact, it is their experience, and mine, that an effective and sensitive analysis of textual structure and its semantic implications provides a sound basis for a rewarding and aesthetic interpretation of literary texts. After all, such analyses by learners often appear to show what Mick Short (1986: 161) called 'the inferential approach to language', that is, the meanings they attach to salient formal features are greatly affected by their own intuitions, and their own social and cultural backgrounds.[2]

All the same, in the last two decades, concurrently with similar trends in literary theory, linguistic models have been developed which hold that the meanings of linguistic expression are to be found in a real world context. And since stylistics has a long tradition of being a strongly interdisciplinary field, and has always profitably drawn on an eclectic mixture of both literary and linguistic theories, these socio-logical trends gave rise to another school of stylistics which does recognize the existence of that messy world outside. These stylisticians regard all speech and writing as primarily dialogic, that is, as social discourse in which the words used and the meanings of the words used cannot be divorced from their relevant contexts (Macdonell 1986). Accordingly, they also view literary texts as part of a complex social and cultural process (Fowler 1981). There is no doubt that from a theoretical point of view, this contextualized model has greatly in-creased the literary critical potential of stylistics and will give more satisfaction in advanced literary studies.[3]

Now, in recognizing the limits and limitations of text-oriented stylistics, I do not wish to suggest that there is a rift between this school and that of contextualized stylistics. On the contrary, I think that the two are interdependent, for the simple reason that successful communi-cation is the combined effect of textual (linguistic) competence and contextual (pragmatic) interpretation. Furthermore, I agree with Michael Toolan (1992: xiv) that theoretical study and practical analysis must be complementary, and that stylisticians have built up a particular expertise in this respect, which should never be cast off.

THE BASIC PRINCIPLES AND METHODOLOGY UNDERLYING THIS BOOK

It is along these lines that I wrote my editorial brief to the contributors. Actually, I started with the following quotation from Hans-Georg Gadamer's philosophical study *Truth and Method* (1975: 165–6):

> Insofar as utterance is not merely an inner product of thought, but is also communication and has, as such, an external form, it is not simply the immediate manifestation of the thought, but presupposes reflection. This is true, of course, of what is written down, and hence of all texts. They are always presentation through art. But where utterance is an art, so is understanding.

... every act of understanding is ... the inverse of an act of speech, the reconstruction of a construction.

This statement is a fair summary of the basic principles and methodology underlying this book. Thus, it is assumed that communication is the dominant function of all texts, literary and non-literary. Any text has 'an external form', usually a verbal structure which 'presupposes reflection', that is, the text encodes a verbal interaction or discourse between writer and reader, in which the former, directly or indirectly, invites (or, as the case may be, persuades, provokes, motivates, etc.) the latter to make sense of the formal structure and to create conceivable contexts for it ('the reconstruction of a construction'). From this it follows that the contributors were asked to adopt a functional approach to their linguistic descriptions, that is, to take a pragmatic view of language as discourse or social interaction. This implies that the common levels of linguistic analysis (phonology/graphology – grammar – lexis – semantics) should also include a kind of extension (which, as such, is not a level of formal linguistic organization) accommodating the facets of language in use, which is the business of pragmatics. In other words, pragmatics attempts to explain the facts in the use of language which have a motivation and operation independent of language, but which at the same time function in combination with that language to effect communication (Graham 1992: 185–7).

So my conception of the book was inspired by the desire to arrange a 'marriage of true minds': to match analysis with theory, text with context. Therefore I asked my co-authors to perform an analysis of a twentieth-century poem, following the mainstream of language-oriented literary criticism, and showing at the same time their responsiveness to the current issues in modern literary and linguistic theory.

WHY POETRY OF THE TWENTIETH CENTURY?

Good poetry is always rooted in ordinary daily speech from which, of course, it is at the same time different through its intensified meaning potential. If the language of poetry is to retain its vitality, it has to tap the sources of contemporaneous, everyday speech. In this way the language of poetry will create a place to accommodate the reader, who will thus be tempted to unravel the myriad of meanings concealed in a language s/he is familiar with.

If all this is true, there is a lot to be said for a selection of twentieth-century texts, the more so as the book is aimed at a level where students usually have not yet developed an historical sense of language and style.

ORDERING THE CHAPTERS

There is of course a great deal of cross-linking among the chapters, but I have tried to order them in such a way that there is a progression in the widening of, what I call in my own chapter, the text's contextual orbit. In the first eight chapters this progression is gradual and varied, while in the last four chapters it gathers full momentum. The only exception to this ordering principle is Richard D. Cureton's chapter 'The auditory imagination and the music of poetry' in which he applies his new theory of verse rhythm to Robert Frost's 'Nothing Gold Can Stay'. While rhythm itself is not specifically linguistic, our rhythmic responses to language cross-cut all of the levels of linguistic structure. To indicate this all-embracing role of rhythm, I have placed the chapter right in the middle. Furthermore, I have put Mick Short's chapter first for pedagogic reasons. He answers some preliminary questions often asked by students taking up literary stylistics and shows how to structure a profusion of analytical details in a well-argued and coherent written account.

TARGET GROUP AND ADVICE ON USING THIS BOOK

This books intends to offer an extensive introduction to literary stylistic criticism and is aimed at senior school students of English, under-graduate students of English language and literature, students of applied linguistics, and upper-intermediate and advanced students of English as a second or foreign language.

In view of the educational level aimed at, the book contains a detailed subject index telling the student where to find the explanation of the main linguistic and literary terms. Furthermore, there is a list of references at the end of each chapter which enables the student to read up on particular topics.

By way of introduction, I have supplied a preface to each of the chapters. In most cases these prefaces try to give the reader an idea of what the chapter is about, and sometimes they volunteer a piece of information which helps to put the poem under discussion in a par-ticular literary or linguistic perspective.

From a pedagogic point of view, the classroom model for teaching literary stylistics is very important. I have found that the seminar format and working in groups ensures maximum involvement of the students while the teacher's role is less dominant. As a result the students feel more inclined to share their views and ideas and to cooperate on oral and written assignments.[4]

Finally, I asked the contributors to include a set of assignments in the form of 'suggestions for further work'. I firmly believe that their chapters in combination with these suggestions will foster the students' linguistic awareness as well as their creative interpretation of salient formal and pragmatic features, and that they will be given a very firm foundation for the development of a receptive and sensitive language- and context-based literary criticism.

NOTES

1 Readers wishing to learn more about the intellectual genesis of stylistics and its growth in the last three decades can do so by consulting Carter (1982: 1–17), Carter and Simpson (1989: 1–20), and Toolan (1990: 1–53).
2 For instance, Carter and Walker (1989: 2–4) cite a great many benefits of pedagogical stylistics, listing at the same time its theoretical limitations. Other recent publications stressing the usefulness of this kind of stylistics in education but also recognizing its theoretical incompleteness, include Carter (1989: 10–21), Verdonk (1989: 262–3), and Toolan (1990: 42–3).
3 In addition to Fowler (1981), some other recent books containing con-textualized, i.e. discoursal, stylistic analyses of texts include Carter and Simpson (1989), Pallotti (1990), Sell (1991), Toolan (1992), Van Peer (1988), and York (1986).
4 See Verdonk (1989: 242–5) for a detailed account of a teaching project in literary stylistics carried out with upper-intermediate and advanced students of English as a foreign language.

REFERENCES

Carter, R. (ed.) (1982) *Language and Literature: An Introductory Reader in Stylistics*, London: Allen & Unwin.
—— (1989) 'Directions in the Teaching and Study of English Stylistics', in M. Short (ed.) *Reading, Analysing and Teaching Literature*, London: Longman.
Carter, R. and Simpson, P. (eds) (1989) *Language, Discourse and Literature: An Introductory Reader in Discourse Stylistics*, London: Unwin Hyman.
Carter, R. and Walker, R. (1989) 'Literature and the Learner: Introduction', in R. Carter, R. Walker, and C. Brumfit (eds) *Literature and the Learner: Methodological Approaches*, London: Modern English Publications in association with The British Council.
Fowler, R. (1981) *Literature as Social Discourse: The Practice of Linguistic Criticism*, London: Batsford.
Gadamer, H.-G. (1975) *Truth and Method*, trans. G. Barden and J. Cumming, New York: Seabury Press.
Graham, J.F. (1992) *Onomatopoetics: Theory of Language and Literature*, Cambridge: Cambridge University Press.
Macdonell, D. (1986) *Theories of Discourse: An Introduction*, Oxford: Blackwell.
Pallotti, D. (1990) *Weaving Words: A Linguistic Reading of Poetry*, Bologna: Cooperativa Libraria Universitaria Editrice Bologna.
Sell, R.D. (ed.) (1991) *Literary Pragmatics*, London: Routledge.

Short, M. (1986) 'Literature and Language Teaching and the Nature of Language', in T. D'haen (ed.) *Linguistics and the Study of Literature*, Amsterdam: Rodopi.

Toolan, M. (1990) *The Stylistics of Fiction: A Literary-linguistic Approach*, London: Routledge.

—— (ed.) (1992) *Language, Text and Context: Essays in Stylistics*, London: Routledge.

Van Peer, W. (1988) *The Taming of the Text: Explorations in Language, Literature and Culture*, London: Routledge.

Verdonk, P. (1989) 'The Language of Poetry: The Application of Literary Stylistic Theory in University Teaching', in M. Short (ed.) *Reading, Analysing and Teaching Literature*, London: Longman.

York, R.A. (1986) *The Poem as Utterance*, London: Methuen.

1 To analyse a poem stylistically: 'To Paint a Water Lily' by Ted Hughes

Mick Short

EDITOR'S PREFACE

This chapter by Mick Short begins by answering some preliminary questions often asked by students taking up literary stylistics. He rightly argues that their first and most urgent question: 'Which comes first, the analysis or the meaning?' is prompted by a misguided view of 'objectivity'. First of all, the question reflects a chicken and egg situation because any analysis, however formal or informal, of the language of a text requires our reading and interpreting it, while conversely reading and interpreting a text is a kind of analytic exercise. So being objective is not a matter of the order in which these activities take place but of monitoring their interplay: the interpretation should be constantly checked against the linguistic evidence produced by the analysis.

The remaining questions are more practically oriented, in that they are concerned with the problem of how to structure a profusion of analytical details in a well-argued and coherent written account.

The second part of this essay is devoted to a revealing stylistic analysis of 'To Paint a Water Lily' by Ted Hughes. Here Short puts into practice the answers he has given to the above questions, structuring his interpretative analysis of the poem as follows: (1) overall interpretation, (2) overall text structure, and (3) more detailed stylistic analysis. Wishing to keep his analysis and his interpretation in step with each other, he does not allow his reading of the poem to be snowed under by an abundance of linguistic evidence. Instead he first points to those linguistic levels which bring out the overall structuring of the poem's meaning. Thus, it appears that viewed from an interactional situation of speaker to listener or, more technically, in speech act terms, the poem is composed of a marked pattern of statements and commands, which turn the text into a strongly goal-oriented utterance. This tactical structure of the text is found to confirm Short's preformulated literary hunch about the poem's overall meaning.

Furthermore, this dominant pattern of statements and commands divides the poem into a number of clear-cut sections which prove to converge with the various preparatory phases the aspiring painter of the water lily has to go through. It is these sections that Short subjects to a more detailed stylistic analysis, examining also the linguistic levels less directly connected with the production of meaning such as phonetics and metrics. Consistent with his method, he keeps relating his analytical data to his interpretation of these 'steps to artistic perfection', thereby also filling out his initial literary hypothesis.

Though this chapter, as Mick Short says, is not a formula for analysing every kind of poetic text, it does show in a lucid and systematic way how to perform a stylistic analysis in general terms and how to present its results in a well-argued and readable account.

P. V.

INTRODUCTION

In this chapter, I will demonstrate one way of performing a stylistic analysis of a poem. This activity is a bit like providing instructions for assembling a machine, or a recipe for baking a cake. So it is appropriate that I will use as my demonstration text a poem which purports to be a set of instructions for painting a picture: 'To Paint a Water Lily', by Ted Hughes. Before I discuss the poem, however, I will address some general, preliminary questions about how to do stylistic analysis. These remarks will provide the background to my analysis of 'To Paint a Water Lily'.

WHICH COMES FIRST, THE ANALYSIS OR THE MEANING?

Stylistic analysis involves examining carefully the linguistic structure of a text and showing the role which that linguistic structure plays in helping a reader to arrive at an interpretation of that text. Students often ask me whether they should start by analysing the text linguistically or by reading the text thoroughly in order to understand it. My answer is that it does not matter, as long as both things are done thoroughly. What is most important is that there is a clear and strong relationship between the interpretation proposed and an accurate account of the language of the text. My students worry about where to start because they feel that unless they do the linguistic analysis first they will be acting in an unobjective way – their reading will in part determine their analysis. But the pristine purity they are in search of rarely, if ever, exists. If you analyse a text linguistically, you have to read it in order to perform the task. And if you read it, you can't help but understand it. You could, of course, get one person to analyse the language and another to interpret it. But even then, someone (a third person?) would have to spell out the relationship between the linguistic structure and the reading, because all the linguistic features of a text are not equally relevant to interpretation.

In any case, to be objective does not mean, as the man in the street often assumes, only to say things which are true for all time. Scientists often change their minds about the 'facts' of the world around us as new analytical evidence comes to light. To be objective really means to take all the available evidence into account in arriving at conclusions. In this sense, interpretations of poems are like hypotheses, which can be checked by analytical work. Scientists often form hypotheses and then do work to test them. Again, what counts is not the order in which you do things, but the *relationship* between them and the accuracy of the testing.

DOING THE RESEARCH AND WRITING IT UP

Working at the poem to understand and analyse it is one thing. Writing up what you discover for someone else to read is another. There is no *necessary* connection between the form that these two activities take. If I am inventing a recipe for a new curry, I may try all sorts of alternative ingredients, cooking processes, and sequences in which to do things, discarding and rearranging in the light of experience. But when I write the recipe, this experimentation disappears from the account, as I try to produce a text which is easy for someone else to follow and come out of the kitchen with a decent curry. The same is true for writing up scientific experiments and stylistic analyses. What counts in writing an analysis up is making it well-argued, coherent, and transparent for your reader. So, even if I have done my linguistic analysis first in my research phase, I always start a written analysis with a summary of my interpretation. This allows my reader to be able to relate what I say later to that initial interpretative hypothesis. Then, as my paper unfolds, my summary analysis is fleshed out and becomes more detailed through my stylistic analysis.

Another question which I am often asked is what general form the written analysis should take after the initial interpretation has been spelled out. Is it best to go through the text line by line, or take one linguistic level (for example, grammar, phonetics, metrics) at a time, or what? The answer to this apparently simple question is, in fact, quite complicated. It depends partly on what you are trying to achieve in your paper and partly on the nature of the text you are analysing. However, making things clear and accessible for your reader must be the paramount consideration. For this reason, a line-by-line analysis (the first thing the unwary attempt), is almost always a mistake, unless your overall strategy demands it (see, for example, Short and van Peer 1989). It is very difficult in most cases to control the details of each line in relation to your overall writing strategy and your summary interpretation. Taking a linguistic level at a time is a good thing if you are trying to convince your tutor that you are being systematic, for example, but this structure may make it difficult to bring out the interpretation you are arguing for. So, think out the writing structure your overall strategy appears to demand *and* the structure of the text and your interpretation suggests, and see if they match. If they do, fine. If not, then *either* you have to come up with a compromise structure, *or* you have to choose the structure dictated by one overall consideration and then mitigate, in the detail of your writing, the problems caused to your other overall aim(s).

As it happens, the structure of the interpretation I am going to propose for 'To Paint a Water Lily' relates quite well to a division of the text into sections, and so I will treat the text a section at a time. Because I will be wanting to relate my analysis to my interpretation all the time, I will not work systematically through the description of the text a linguistic level at a time. Instead, I will bring the linguistic evidence to bear when it is relevant to my interpretation. I will tend, though, to examine first those linguistic levels most closely connected with the overall structuring of the poem's meaning (for example, textual cohesion and lexis); those levels less directly connected with meaning (for example, phonetics, metrics) will tend to come later in the description of each part of the poem. This will enable me to relate most easily the less directly meaning-bearing items to my interpretation at each stage, as, by the time I examine them, my interpretation will have been specified in more detail.

THE POEM

To Paint a Water Lily

A green level of lily leaves
Roofs the pond's chamber and paves

The flies' furious arena: study
These, the two minds of this lady.

5 First observe the air's dragonfly
That eats meat, that bullets by

Or stands in space to take aim;
Others as dangerous comb the hum

Under the trees. There are battle-shouts
10 And death-cries everywhere hereabouts

But inaudible, so the eyes praise
To see the colours of these flies

Rainbow their arcs, spark, or settle
Cooling like beads of molten metal

15 Through the spectrum. Think what worse
Is the pond-bed's matter of course;

Prehistoric bedragonned times
Crawl that darkness with Latin names,

Have evolved no improvements there,
20 Jaws for heads, the set stare,

Ignorant of age as of hour –
Now paint the long-necked lily-flower

Which, deep in both worlds, can be still
As a painting, trembling hardly at all

25 Though the dragonfly alight,
Whatever horror nudge her root.

(Ted Hughes)

OVERALL INTERPRETATION

The title of the poem has a syntactic form ('to'-verb-object) conventionally associated with sets of instructions or recipes. So at first
sight the poem looks as if it will be a mechanical set of instructions to

paint the water lily, rather like painting by numbers. There is thus a potential clash between the associations of this title-form and an activity which, when done well, at least, is more often associated with the mystery of artistry and genius. This clash turns out to be the key to the poem. Hughes suggests that in order to *paint* the water lily you must first *understand* it. This understanding, in turn, involves a complex appreciation of what lies beneath the surface, an appreciation of the distinction between appearance and reality. In other words, the painting by numbers approach is bound to fail: you can't paint just what can be seen by the eye if you want to capture the essence of the flower. And painting the unseeable reintroduces the genius of great art. Lastly, because there is a possible analogy, often used by writers, between writing and other forms of art, it is also possible to see the poem as one which is telling us about the nature of poetry as well as of painting. To describe the water lily well, you would need the same sort of understanding which is necessary to paint it well.

OVERALL TEXT STRUCTURE

In speech act terms, the poem is a mixture of statements and commands realized grammatically by declarative and imperative forms respectively. The speech act patterns in conjunction with a pattern of sentence-initial sequence-adverbs can be used to divide the text up:

1 general description of the lily, living in two opposed worlds, the serene lower world and the busy upper world, plus a general command to study these two aspects of the lily (declarative structures plus imperative structure, sentence 1, lines 1–4);
2 command to study the upper world, plus a description of it, which involves an appearance/reality distinction (sentence-initial 'first' plus imperative structure plus declarative structures, sentences 2 and 3, lines 5–15);
3 command to study the lower world, which also involves an appearance/reality distinction (imperative structure plus declarative structures, sentence 4, lines 15–21);
4 final general command to paint the lily with a summary description of the two worlds it inhabits, correlating with (2) and (3) but contrasting with (1) (sentence-initial 'now' plus imperative structure plus declarative structures, sentence 5, lines 22–26).

The description I have given here helps us to see how the text is constructed tactically. Note that there is a symmetry to this sentence/ speech act analysis. Each section begins and ends at a sentence boundary, and contains an imperative and some declarative structures (I am assuming that each clause contains such a structure). The second and third sections are parallel to one another (imperative plus declaratives), and the first and last sections are mirror images of one another (declaratives plus imperative/imperative plus declaratives). This structuring accords well with the appearance/reality meaning pattern which I outlined above.

MORE DETAILED STYLISTIC ANALYSIS

I will now describe in detail each of the above sections of the poem in turn.

General description plus general command (lines 1–4)

The initial description has two clauses with stative verbs ('roofs', 'paves'). 'A green level of lily leaves' is subject to both clauses, and they both have the same underlying syntactic structure, SVO. This parallelism helps bring out the janus-faced lexical contrast between 'roofs' and 'paves', and the contrast between 'chamber' (enclosed, and associated with quiet) and 'arena' (open, and associated with activity and noise). This contrast is underlined by contrasting patterns of /l/ and /f/ alliteration in lines 1 and 3. There is a collocational clash between 'furious' and 'arena', and so through the maxim of relation (Grice 1975; Sperber and Wilson 1986) we associate the implied activity with the flies, not the arena. The imperative structure in stanzas 2–3 indicates an interactive discourse structure, and invites readers to imagine themselves in some context where the poet is talking directly to them. This interpretative move is reinforced by the use of near deictic demonstrative pronouns ('these', 'this') most easily understood by reference to some particular water lily in the situational context. Although lilies are inanimate, this lily is strongly personified in the NP in apposition to 'these', directly by the use of 'lady', and by implication through the use of 'minds', which suggests that the two worlds are as much a matter of perception as reality. The cataphoric use of 'these' is typical of speech, reinforcing the assumption of a situated conversational context.

Command to study the upper world of the lily, plus its description

The use of the sentence-initial 'first' at the beginning of line 5 indicates that we should be looking as we read for an enumerated textual structure. 'Observe' is also a partial synonym for 'study', and so we are likely to interpret this command as a more detailed extension of the earlier one. The word 'dragonfly' forms a cohesive chain with the 'fly' of line 3, and, as we shall see later, the fish that live under the water. 'Dragonfly' is premodified unnecessarily by 'air's' (flying things must, by definition, belong to the air), and so the modification will probably be interpreted by the reader as helping to bring out the upper/lower world contrast. 'Dragonfly' is postmodified by three relative clauses, each of which exhibits an internal alliterative or assonantal pattern involving the last word of the clause ('*eats meat*'; '*bullets by*'; '*space . . . aim*'). These phonetic patterns help to foreground the unusual semantic relations between each of these relative clauses and the head noun they postmodify. Meat-eating is usually associated with carnivorous animals, not insects, 'bullets by' involves a functional conversion of the noun 'bullet' to a verb, and brings in connotations of war usually associated with human beings, an interpretation supported by the idea of the dragonfly taking aim (to fire a gun?) in the next line. A high incidence of nasal sounds ('da*n*gerous', 'co*m*b', 'hu*m*', 'u*n*der') in association with the lexical content of 'comb' and 'hum' will almost certainly be given an onomatopoeic interpretation by readers (as the /f/ alliteration in line 3 may also have been), leading to the inference that the others referred to are wasps, hornets, etc. Sentence 3 continues the cohesive chain of words with human-warlike associations through 'battle-shouts' and 'death cries'. The usual implications of noise associated with these items (and indeed with earlier terms associated with the flies) are then explicitly cancelled at the beginning of line 11. This is done by the use of contrastive 'but' ('But inaudible') in an extension structure (Sinclair 1972), which creates a surprise, 'flip flop' interpretative effect because the clause to which the 'but' clause is opposed ends at the end of the previous line, making it look as if the propositional structure is complete at that point. It thus becomes clear, at this point, that the noise of battle (and by implication the nature of what is going on?) is not normally perceived correctly by human onlookers. This interpretation explains the series of lexico-semantic deviations which occur in the next few lines. 'Praise' is normally a transitive verb which takes a human subject. But here the definite generic plural 'the eyes' (associated with perception) is the subject, and 'praise' is intransitive. The lack of an object here could be claimed to be mimetic of our lack of understanding. Presumably the eyes praise because they cannot perceive the terrible things that are actually going on. They see not the carnage of reality, but an apparently beautiful sight: 'the colours of these flies/Rainbow their arcs, spark, or settle/Cooling like beads of molten metal/Through the spectrum'. The lexico-semantic deviations here are particularly dense. The abstract noun 'colours' is the head noun of the phrase which is subject to the active transitive verb 'rainbow' which is itself a neologism. The object of 'rainbow' is, however, the abstract phrase 'their arcs'. Similarly, colours cannot spark, or settle (though flies can), and if they do all these strange things anywhere, we would expect it to be in a sensible place-location, not through the abstract 'spectrum'. There are other features which add to the foregrounding (for example, the semi-dead metaphor 'beads of . . . metal', which may well become re-enlivened in this context, and the sound patterns associated with 'arcs spark', 'molten metal', and others. What we have here is a highly foregrounded verbal firework display, with lots of activity (four of the six words of line 11 are dynamic verbs) and a high density of words implying colour and light. We see, then, an extraordinary, highly active, and beautiful colour display from the flies. What we fail to perceive is the noise, the death, and the destruction.

Command to study the lower world, plus its description

There is no sentence-initial sequence adverb at the beginning of sentence 4, but because of the 'first' at the beginning of sentence 2 and the new imperative structure, we perceive this sentence as the beginning of the next structural phase. The 'pond bed's matter of course' is obviously opposed to the world above the surface of the water, and the way in which this underwater world is depicted contrasts dramatically with the world of the air. Note the use of remote deixis ('that darkness', 'there') in contrast with the close deixis we saw associated with the world of the flies. The beings referred to in the upper world (fly, dragonfly) were initially realized lexically by concrete nouns, but the underwater creatures are introduced abstractly with the noun 'times':

Prehistoric bedragonned times
Crawl that darkness with Latin names

The associations here are with slowness, not speed. This can be seen in the use of the verb 'crawl' but also in the modification of 'times' with a four-syllable and a three-syllable word. 'Prehistoric' and 'bedragonned' have associations with the ancient past, and the possible associations with dinosaurs are consistent with associations of slow and ponderous movement. But there is an interesting ironic cohesive link between 'bedragonned' and the earlier 'dragonfly'. There is considerable semantic deviation here, as there was in lines 11–14. 'Crawl' demands a concrete, animate subject, but 'times' is abstract. Because 'times' is abstract, it is deviant to modify it with 'bedragonned'. 'Crawl' is normally an intransitive verb but is used transitively here, and in any case, you can't normally crawl a darkness because of the concrete/ abstract inconsistency. There is also an ambiguity over the syntactic role of 'with Latin names', which in analogous constructions could refer to some instrument object being carried (cf. 'he walked the streets with his gun').

The implications of slow movement are continued in the use of the verb 'evolved' and the verbless (and hence stative) constructions in line 21: 'Jaws for heads, the set stare' which themselves contain lexical items implying no movement. The world under the water, which we cannot normally see, is apparently one where there is little movement, and where change takes place hardly at all. As we have just seen, this sharp contrast with the world above the water is controlled mainly by lexical and grammatical means. The world under the water is also terrifying in its own right, full of beings associated with lumbering size which appear to consist mainly of jaws, which, of course, are used for biting.

The final command to paint the water lily, plus description

The sentence beginning in line 22 has another initial adverb 'now' immediately before the imperative verb. This use helps us to see that it is part of the pattern of sentence-initial sequence-adverbs already noted, and given the implicit contrast between 'now' and the 'then' of the rest of the poem and its position only five lines before the end, it clearly bears a climactic interpretation. The imperative verb 'paint' is an action word, in contrast with the other cognition imperatives, 'study', 'observe', and 'think'. It also repeats the verb of the title, indicating that we have come full circle. 'The long-necked lily flower' echoes the first line in both phonetic (/l/ alliteration) and associative (beauty, still, quiet) terms. With this echo, the last section recapitulates the full personification of the lily through the pronoun 'her' and the indication that she is a sentient being capable of movement. 'Trembling hardly at all' implies that she *is* trembling to some degree, and this in turn implicates fear on her part. The use of the poem's only modal verb 'can' in 'can be still as a painting' also implies a possibility that in some other circumstances she might *not* be able to be 'still as a painting' (with its obvious ironic relation the title – it is, of course, easier to paint things which do not move).

The last two lines of the poem also recapitulate the descriptions of the two contrasting worlds which the lily lives in, repeating the linguistic features we have come to associate with those worlds. This is achieved by the two paralleled and contrastive conditional clauses beginning with 'though' and 'whatever'. 'Dragonfly', which is a repetition from line 5, at the beginning of what I have called section (2), is a concrete noun, and is subject to 'alight', which connotes the fast, light movement associated with the world of the flies. The verb 'nudge', on the other hand, connotes slower and less precise movement, and has for its subject the abstract noun 'horror' which reminds us of the abstract 'times' used to refer to the underwater creatures near the beginning of section (3).

CONCLUSION

I have not, of course, referred to every aspect of the linguistic structure of 'To Paint a Water Lily'. For instance, I have done very little work on Hughes's interesting use of metrical form and off-rhyme scheme. So, the analysis is by no means complete. Instead, I have tried to concentrate on the aspects of the poem's language which are relevant to my interpretation. 'Relevant' here means anything which bears on that interpretation, either supporting it or going against it. Note that the interpretation of a text cannot just 'pop out' of its linguistic structure. Understanding involves a reader, and hence an analyst, in inferring meaning, and the relation between aspects of meaning on the basis of the text's structure. The best we can do is to make our interpretations, and the evidence on which they are based, clear for others to consider.

In fact the interpretation does rather well. There is lots of evidence to support it, and it is difficult to find evidence which counts against the reading I have proposed. Note, however, that you are open to challenge my view of the text, perhaps by bringing other evidence to bear, as long as you also take into account the important (usually foregrounded) linguistic features that I have considered.

What I have not done, however, is to bring linguistic evidence to bear on the aspect of my interpretation which suggests that the poem could be about writing poems as well as painting. It is clear that this sort of additional meaning, if you see it, comes about not as a result of particular linguistic features in this text, but because of a generalized analogy between writing and other forms of description, and an alertness of particular readers at particular times to 'see' such readings (they happen to be rather popular in our present, postmodernist world). Not every aspect of textual meaning, by any means, is controlled by linguistic structure. This is because meaning comes about as a consequence of the interaction between a reader (who brings along all sorts of assumptions) and a text. This is another reason why stylistic analysis cannot have the sort of 'objectivity' associated with '2 + 2 = 4' or 'water has two hydrogen atoms and one oxygen atom'. But I would want to claim that my reading of this poem is objective in the sense that a clear basis can be found in the text to support it, and that stylistic analysis can be extremely useful in demonstrating that relationship between text and meaning. This chapter is not a 'recipe' for analysing each and every text, but hopefully it will have helped you to see how to go about doing a stylistic analysis in general terms, and how to adjust your own ways of performing and writing up stylistic analyses to particular circumstances and particular texts.

SUGGESTIONS FOR FURTHER WORK

(Note: it is often profitable to work together with another student on these exercises. You will each notice different things, and you will find the ensuing discussion helpful.)

1 Read carefully one of the following poems, and summarize in a few sentences what you think it is about: 'Ariel' by Sylvia Plath, 'Death of a Son' by Jon Silkin, 'Going' by Philip Larkin. Then, analyse the poem stylistically and compare your understanding of the poem before and after analysis. Has your understanding changed in any way? Do you understand the poem more deeply, or in more detail? Lastly, compare your analysis with that described by Peter Verdonk (1989: 241–66). Finally, write up that analysis into an essay, taking into account the advice for structuring your work mentioned in this chapter.

2 The Ted Hughes poem analysed on pp. 11–18 relies for its meaning and effect on your intuitive understanding of a variety of language, the language of instruction. Explore how, within the following poems, the variety of language used changes, and how those variations in style can be related systematically to meaning and effect: 'Adlestrop' by Edward Thomas, 'Naming of Parts' by Henry Reed.

3 Stylistic analysis depends on the notion of choice. Meanings and effects are produced by writers making a series of linguistic choices, as opposed to others they might have made. Often, to understand the choices writers make, we have to consider them in the abstract, for example, by comparing a word used with a synonym which might have been used (for example, 'shut' instead of 'close'), or a construction actually used with an alternative which could have been used (for example, a passive construction in place of its active equivalent). One tangible way of seeing linguistic choice in action is to compare carefully different versions of the same text. Below is the normally published version of 'The Tyger' by William Blake, followed by another version (actually an amalgam from a number of different drafts which Blake produced before

settling on the final version). Carefully chart the differences between the two versions (noting that choices at one linguistic level (for example, lexis) might have knock-on consequences at other levels (for example, phonetics – cf. alliterative, assonantal, and rhyme patterns)). Then try to work out the differences in meaning and effect for each choice, deciding which version you prefer, and why.

The Tyger (final version)

Tyger! Tyger! burning bright
In the forests of the night,
What immortal hand or eye
Could frame thy fearful symmetry?

In what distant deeps or skies
Burnt the fire of thine eyes?
On what wings dare he aspire?
What the hand, dare seize the fire?

And what shoulder, & what art,
Could twist the sinews of thy heart?
And when thy heart began to beat,
What dread hand? and what dread feet?

What the hammer? what the chain?
In what furnace was thy brain?
What the anvil? what dread grasp
Dare its deadly terrors clasp?

When the stars threw down their spears,
And water'd heaven with their tears,
Did he smile his work to see?
Did he who made the Lamb make thee?

Tyger! Tyger! burning bright
In the forests of the night,
What immortal hand or eye
Dare frame thy fearful symmetry?

The Tyger (amalgam of earlier versions)

Tyger! Tyger! burning bright
In the forests of the night.
What immortal hand and eye
Dare frame thy fearful symmetry?

Burnt in distant deeps or skies
The cruel fire of thine eyes?
Could heart descend or wings aspire?
What the hand dare seize the fire?

And what shoulder and what art
Could twist the sinews of thy heart?
And when thy heart began to beat
What dread hand forged thy dread feet?

Where the hammer? where the chain?
In what furnace was thy brain?
What the anvil? What the grasp
Could its deadly terrors clasp?

And dare he laugh his work to see?
Dare he who made the lamb make thee,
When the stars threw down their spears
And water'd heaven with their tears?

Tyger! Tyger! burning bright
In the forests of the night,
What immortal hand and eye,
Dare form thy fearful symmetry?

REFERENCES

Grice, H.P. (1975) 'Logic and Conversation', in P. Cole and J.L. Morgan (eds) *Syntax and Semantics, Volume 3: Speech Acts*, New York: Academic Press.

Short, M.H. and van Peer, W. (1989) 'Accident! Stylisticians Evaluate: Aims and Methods of Stylistic Analysis', in M. Short (ed.) *Reading, Analysing and Teaching Literature*, London: Longman.

Sinclair, J. McH. (1972) 'Lines about "Lines"', in B.B. Kachru and H.F.W. Stahlke (eds) *Current Trends in Stylistics*, Edmonton, Alberta: Linguistic Research Inc.

Sperber, D. and Wilson, D. (1986) *Relevance: Communication and Cognition*, Oxford: Blackwell.

Verdonk, P. (1989) 'The Language of Poetry: The Application of Literary Stylistics Theory in University Teaching', in M. Short (ed.) *Reading, Analysing and Teaching Literature*, London: Longman.

2 Person to person: relationships in the poetry of Tony Harrison

H.G. Widdowson

EDITOR'S PREFACE

'You weren't brought up to write such mucky books!' is the final line in italics of Tony Harrison's poem 'Bringing Up'. It refers to what his mother said when he showed her his first volume *The Loiners*, and it epitomizes the social dislocation of a working-class boy who won a scholarship to Leeds Grammar School and subsequently graduated in Classics.

In this chapter Henry Widdowson demonstrates in a sensitive reading that the way in which the grammatical categories of person (first, second, and third) are distributed across Harrison's poem 'Long Distance II' throws into relief its basic theme of estrangement; of loss of contact, person to person.

Widdowson points to a significant distinction between the pronouns of the first and second person (*I* and *you*) on the one hand and those of the third person on the other (*he, she, they*): the former are terms of address used to talk *to* people, while the latter are terms of reference used to talk *about* people. To put it differently: it is only the first and second person that are actually participating in a speech event. They are equals in terms of communication, in that their roles are potentially transferable as the speech event proceeds. The third person is not associated with any positive participant role; it has a distancing effect and people referred to in this way are cut off from communication.

Starting from this fundamental distinction, Widdowson soon recognizes that at crucial junctures in the poem the use of certain second- and third-person items is artfully blurred. As a matter of fact, this linguistic ambiguity appears to reflect that in his relationship with his parents the poet feels both intellectually detached and emotionally involved. Widdowson also points out some other formal and linguistic features dramatizing this state of mind, and comes to the poignant conclusion that this patterning of language, this casting of emotions in a poetic mould, would have been lost on his parents. Both the ambivalence and the estrangement will persist.

This chapter is an excellent example of how seemingly insignificant linguistic details can be related in such a way that they confirm and expand our initial responses to a poem. It also demonstrates that *language* as such is 'innocent', but that it loses this innocence and becomes a 'loaded weapon' (Bolinger 1980) as soon as it is used in communication, that is, in social *discourse*. This social ground of language, to which Harrison has shown to be highly sensitive, has been a key issue in much recent literary theory (Rylance 1991: 53–67).

P. V.

First a general comment to set the scene. The particular poem I want to analyse is one of a pair among a number of poems in the volume *'The School of Eloquence' and Other Poems* (1978) which are about the relationship between the poet and his parents. A recurring theme is one of disparity of values and guilt that his scholarship has estranged him from them and their working-class ways. Even his portrayal of them is betrayal of a kind, since it can only be based on the dissociation of his experience and expressed in a poetic idiom they cannot understand.[1] He cannot talk about his parents in the way he talked to them. What comes across in these poems is a sense of exile and uncertainty of self. They are expressive of an ambivalence of position, a dilemma of identity: they are intellectually detached with descriptions distanced in the third person, the poet apart from what he describes, but at the same time he is emotionally involved in the first person, a part of it all as well.

This, then, is the poem: one of several variations on a theme of estrangement; of loss of contact, person to person.

Long Distance II

Though my mother was already two years dead
Dad kept her slippers warming by the gas,
put hot water bottles her side of the bed
and still went to renew her transport pass.

You couldn't just drop in. You had to phone.
He'd put you off an hour to give him time
to clear away her things and look alone
as though his still raw love were such a crime.

He couldn't risk my blight of disbelief
though sure that very soon he'd hear her key
scrape in the rusted lock and end his grief.
He *knew* she'd just popped out to get the tea.

I believe life ends with death, and that is all.
You haven't both gone shopping; just the same,
in my new black leather phone book there's your name
and the disconnected number I still call.

At the most obvious referential level of paraphrase summary this poem is about family relations and their severance by bereavement. It is about communication and its loss in two senses, physical contact and emotional ties, telephone connections and human relationships, the one expressed in terms of the other. It is about being cut off, disconnected, distanced.

Linguistically, human relationships are mediated through the grammatical category of person, and in particular the personal pronouns. To quote from the recent *Collins Cobuild English Grammar*: 'You use **personal pronouns** to refer to yourself, the people you are talking to, or the people or things you are talking about' (Sinclair 1990: 29). It is through the categories of person (first, second, and third) that we make a connection between self and others and establish positions of identity. We might expect, therefore, that, given the obvious theme of the poem, the category of person should repay closer study. This, then, can serve as the starting point for our analysis.

A word or two to begin with about pronouns and person in general. The first- and second-person pronouns ('I' and 'you') identify participants and provide the necessary terminals so to speak, whereby people are connected in communicative interaction. They coexist in the same plane of involvement. Thus they are, in principle, interchangeable in the turn-taking of talk: the second person is a potential first person, and each presupposes the existence of the other. The same human person shifts role into the different grammatical persons of 'I' and 'you', addresser and addressee. And these pronouns are, of course, independent and self-contained. In spite of the term we give them they are not pro-nouns. We can of course use them in assocation with nouns, as when they are specifically identified ('I, Claudius'; 'Me Tarzan, you Jane'), but they have no proxy function. They are terms of address, not terms of reference.

The third-person pronouns, on the other hand, indicate a non-participant role; they are terms of reference rather than of address. When people are referred to in third-person terms they are distanced, put at a remove from involvement with first-person self, no longer interactants. When you talk about people in the third person, rather than to people in the second person, you in effect disconnect them from communication: 'Does he take sugar?'

So what, then, of the pronouns and persons in this poem? The first two lines establish the relationships of child (let us assume son in this case) as first person with parents as third persons: 'my mother', 'Dad': me, the poet, and them. There is a difference, though, between these two expressions. The first of them is a straightforward term of reference. The second 'Dad', however, can serve as a term of address also, a vocative (for example, 'Sorry, Dad') so although it is used here in the third person, it carries the implication of involvement, indeterminate, so to speak, between reference and address. He is not just being talked about in detachment but is also marked as a potential participant. 'Dad' seems appropriate as suggesting a continuing relationship: he is still alive. 'My mother', already two years dead, is distanced as a third-person entity by the use of the standard referential phrase. One might consider the difference of effect if the lines had been otherwise:

Though mother was already two years dead,
My father warmed her slippers by the gas . . . .

There is a further observation to be made about the distancing effect of these terms. 'Dad' is not only to be distinguished from 'my mother' because of its address potential, it is also a less formal term and expresses closer familial ties, more personal involvement. The version which is unmarked for such affect is 'Father', just as the marked versions for the address term 'Mother' are 'Mummy' or 'Mum' or (in Harrison's dialect) 'Mam'. And, of course, these affectively marked terms can also be used for reference as well as address. Indeed, they are so used by Harrison himself in other poems. For example:

I asked mi mam. She said she didn't know.
                    ('Wordlists')

Since mi mam's dropped dead mi dad's took fright.
                    ('Next Door')

Here too, of course, the use of dialect forms is a further device for reducing distance, expressing empathy, identifying the first person with third-person description.[2]

What we seem to have here, then, is a kind of fusion of participant address and non-participant reference perspectives. We might suggest that there is a set of three terms of reference of increasing affective involvement in Harrison's poetry:

```
my mother  my father
mi mam     mi dad
mam        dad³
```

If we use these possible alternatives in the first two lines of the poem we are considering, with other modifications to retain the metrical pattern, we can propose a number of variants:

Though mam was then already two years dead,
Dad kept her slippers warming by the gas . . . .

Mi mam was then already two years dead,
But dad still warmed her slippers by the gas . . . .

Though mi mam was already two years dead,
Mi dad still warmed her slippers by the gas . . . .

And so on.

Each variant, I would argue, represents a different relationship with the parents. And so it is with the original lines. The father, unlike the mother, is still, as it were, affectively connected, the relationship is alive as a potential participation. And yet to some degree distanced by third-person reference. The writer is connected in a way, and yet, in another way, disconnected. The ambivalence I referred to earlier is already present in the first two lines of the poem, represented, I would suggest, by the very choice of referential expression. In this sense, the end of the poem is anticipated by its beginning.

But what of the lines in between? They too, I suggest, are expressive of this ambivalence. And again, it is the grammatical category of person that is crucial. Consider the second-person pronoun in the first two lines of the second verse. It occurs three times. But it does not have a participant sense. It is the informal equivalent of the third-person impersonal pronoun 'one':

One couldn't just drop in, one had to phone . . . .

And this is the non-participant equivalent of the first-person pronoun 'I':

I couldn't just drop in, I had to phone . . . .

Again, there is distancing, but at the same time some retention of affective involvement represented by the residual participant force of the second-person pronoun 'you'.

Consider now how the third person is used to talk about the father in the poem. In the first verse, there is an account of what he actually does, his physical actions, expressed as a series of objective statements of observable fact. In the second verse, there is an *interpretation* of his action. It is not a matter simply of what he does, but why he does it. The first person intervenes to give reasons and adduce motives. He is drawn into subjective involvement. And in the third verse he is drawn even further in. Here it is not just a matter of interpreting action but attributing feelings and attitudes to the third person which cannot possibly be accessible to observation, and which would normally, therefore, be associated only with first-person expression:

I couldn't risk his blight of disbelief . . . .

I'm sure that very soon I'll hear her key . . . .

I knew she'd just popped out to get the tea.

There is, then, in these three verses an increasing involvement, a gradual identification of the first person with the third person until they at times in effect fuse one into the other and the son articulates the feelings of the father in the father's idiom ('. . . just popped out to get the tea'). And yet he retains some detachment and separate identity: expressions like 'my blight of disbelief' and 'end his grief' are of his thoughts in his idiom carried over from the last line of the second verse: 'as though his still raw love was such a crime'.[4]

These verses, then, represent an ambivalence of position of the first person: he is both apart from and a part of what he describes, detached from the actions, and able to comment on them, but drawn into empathy with the feelings. Then in the first line of the last verse this ambivalence disappears with a definite assertion of separate and independent identity with the first occurrence (as the first word) of the first-person pronoun:

I believe life ends with death, and that is all.

This is clear and straightforward enough: a change of tone, a first-person assertion of present reality in contrast to the paternal illusions of the past that he has been recounting. And this shift is also marked, we might notice by a change in rhyme scheme in this last verse: a different form for a different kind of statement. Life ends with death: that is all, and that is that: no ambivalence or uncertainty here. But that is not all. Consider the next line. Here the second-person pronoun makes another appearance. This time, however, it is used not as before (in verse 2) but in its full participant sense: he is addressing his parents. They are both dead, and life ends in death and that is all, and yet he is talking to them nevertheless, reviving the relationship by this direct address. The line is disconnected, but he is making a call all the same. The ambiguity of his relationship as represented in the earlier verses is resolved into the definite distinction between first and second persons 'I' and 'you'. But this only serves to create the poignant anomaly of addressing the dead, as if there were a possibility of continuing relationship. The uncertainty persists, in spite of the assertion of belief in the first line of this last verse.

And it persists, we should note, in spite of the assertion of actuality expressed in the phrase 'my new black leather phone book'. This elaborate noun phrase (by far the most elaborate in the poem, with all its adjectives) seems, we might suggest, to insist on objective reality. Here is my phone book, new, black, made of leather, a real and tangible object, here and now. And yet it is black, suggestive perhaps of mourning, and though emphatically new and present, it contains the old and the past: your name and number are in it, even though you are dead and disconnected. Notice that this ambivalence is suggested even by the phrase 'there's your name' not 'here's your name': distal, not proximal; there (and then) not here (and now). And notice too that the number is 'there', as if it appeared on its own. There is no indication of human agency. The line does not after all read:

In my new phone book I write down your name . . . .

The line is disconnected, then, the parents dead. He still calls, just the same.

'Just the same': the concessive phrase that ends the poem itself relates to those that precede ('though' makes an appearance in each verse). Although . . . yet. Concession runs throughout: the very first word of the poem sets the key ('Though my mother'). This much is certain, and yet . . . . And the poem ends on the same note. Ultimately, what the son believes is also undermined by concession. His certainty has no more substance than his father's. In spite of his assertion, he behaves like his father, and so is subject to the same disbelief in spite of what he claims to believe. There is even a recurrence of lexical items to link them: 'still/(re)new' in the last line of the first verse, 'new/still' in the last two lines of the poem: appropriately enough a kind of mirror image. The father still got a new transport pass for his dead wife, the son still puts a disconnected number of dead parents in his new phone book. So the father's resistance to the reality of severed relationship is shared by the son, and this itself represents a continuity of their relationship. Life in a way, then, does not end in death. And yet . . . the number is nevertheless disconnected.

The ambivalence remains unresolved, except in the resolution that its representation provides in the very patterns of language of the poem. For although the poem is referentially about disconnection, the patterns, the prosodic regularities, the links, and correspondences, represent the opposite. The end of the poem paradoxically connects up with the beginning, and one might almost propose combining words from the first and last lines to provide a summary:

Though dead and disconnected, I still call.

This patterning of language though, this casting into poetic form, is a mode of communication which his parents would not have understood or recognized as significant. As the ambivalence persists, so does the estrangement. The persons, parents and son, first, second, and third, ultimately remain distinct.

And yet . . . . Just the same . . . .

SUGGESTIONS FOR FURTHER WORK

1 Compare the original poem with the following variant. What do you think the effect is of the different changes that have been made?

Though Mam was then already two years dead,
My father warmed her slippers by the gas,
put hot water bottles her side of the bed,
and still went to renew her transport pass.

I couldn't just drop in. I had to phone.
He'd put me off an hour to give him time
to clear away her things and look alone,
as if his still raw love was such a crime.

He couldn't risk my blight of disbelief.
He *knew* she'd just gone out to get the tea,
and sure that very soon he'd hear her key
scrape in the rusted lock and end his grief.

I believe life ends in death, and that is all.
They haven't both gone shopping; just the same,
in my new phone book here I write their name,
and the disconnected number that I call.

2 The following is another poem by Tony Harrison, again one of a pair, about his parents:

Book Ends I

Baked the day she suddenly dropped dead
we chew it slowly that last apple pie.

Shocked into sleeplessness you're scared of bed.
We never could talk much, and now don't try.

You're like book ends, the pair of you, she'd say,
Hog that grate, say nothing, sit, sleep, stare . . .

The 'scholar' me, you, worn out on poor pay,
only our silence made us seem a pair.

Not as good for staring in, blue gas,
too regular each bud, each yellow spike.

A night you need my company to pass
and she not here to tell us we're alike!

Your life's all shattered into smithereens.

Back in our silences and sullen looks,
for all the Scotch we drink, what's still between 's
not the thirty or so years, but books, books, books.

Consider these questions:

a Personal pronouns are much in evidence in this poem as well: first person ('me', 'we', 'us'), second person ('you'), third person ('she'). What relationships do you think they express in this case? Do you think they represent the same attitudes as in the other poem?

b How would the effect of the poem differ (i) if the second person was replaced by the third, (ii) if the two persons were interchanged, or (iii) if the address terms 'mam' and 'dad' were used? For example:

   i   Shocked into sleeplessness, he's scared of bed . . . .

       The 'scholar' me, him, worn out on poor pay . . . .
       etc.

   ii Baked the day you suddenly dropped dead . . . .

       A night he needs my company to pass
       and you not here to tell us we're alike . . . .

   iii Baked the day mam suddenly dropped dead . . . .

       The 'scholar' me, dad worn out on poor pay . . . .

c Both of the poems consist of sixteen lines. They are, however, arranged differently. The first consists of a series of four-line verses, this one consists of six two-line verses, then a single line, and then a final verse of three. What significance, if any, do you think this arrangement has? Is it in any way suited to the theme of the poem?

d Verses 5 and 6 have the appearance of sentences. But they lack a main verb and so are grammatical fragments. In what way does this linguistic feature relate to the arrangement of lines as expressive of the poem's theme?

e What do you think the effect would be if the first lines of the poem were altered to read as follows?

   We slowly chew mi mam's last apple pie,
   Baked the day she suddenly dropped dead.

f What do you think the effect is of:
   i   The use of direct speech, the mother's actual words, in verse 3?
   ii The inverted commas round the word 'scholar' in verse 4?
   iii The repetition of the word *books* in the last line of the poem?

30   H.G. Widdowson

NOTES

1   Sorry, dad, you won't get that quatrain
    (I'd like to be the poet my father reads!)
                              ('The Rhubarbarians')

See also Harrison's poem 'Confessional Poetry'.

2 Dialect forms are frequent in Harrison's poetry. They sometimes occur as the representation of direct speech (typographically marked in italics), as for example in the first of the 'Long Distance' poems:

Ah can't stand it no more, this empty house!

Carrots choke us wi'out your mam's white sauce!

They sometimes occur unmarked in a text of otherwise standard English:

Mi aunty's baby's still. The dumbstruck mother.
The mirror, tortoise-shell-like celluloid
held to it, passed from one hand to another.
No babble, blubber, breath. The glass won't cloud.
                              ('Study')

And, again, sometimes the forms are set aside in single inverted commas:

Mi mam was 'that surprised' how many came
to see the cortege off and doff their hats –
All the 'old lot' left gave her the same
bussing back from 'Homes' and Old Folk's Flats.
                              ('Next Door I')

The variation in representation itself perhaps indicates an ambivalent attitude. We should note too that although the use of dialect can be interpreted as an indication of sympathy or empathy, an identifying with what is described (as I have suggested) it can also be interpreted as mockery, an ironic distancing of self. This again suggests the uncertainty of position that I have traced in this particular poem, and which seems to me to run through all of Harrison's work.

3 There are variants of 'Mam' and 'Dad' as terms of address in other social dialects, of course: 'Ma(ma)' and 'Pa(pa)', 'Mater', 'Pater'. Some people (but not Harrison) use the unmarked referential terms 'mother' and 'father' for address as well, in which case we of course only have a two-term system of third-person reference:

my mother   my father
mother   father

With regard to the terms that Harrison uses, all six make their appearance in his poetry (together with the minimal referential pronouns 'he' and 'she'). It would be interesting to explore the significance of their alternation. Consider, for example:

My writing desk. Two photos, mam and dad.

Dad's in our favourite pub, now gone for good.
My father and his background are both gone.
                              ('Background Material')

My mother said: *It suits you, your dad's cap.*

Dad was sprawled beside the postbox (still VR).

('Turns')

4 As I suggest in note 2, Harrison seems to be especially sensitive and uncertain about this difference of idiom. See the pair of poems 'Them & [uz] I, II'. See also 'Wordlists II', a poem about the 'tongues I've slaved to speak or read', which ends with the lines:

but not the tongue that once I used to know
but can't bone up on now, and that's mi mam's.

REFERENCES

Bolinger, D. (1980) *Language – The Loaded Weapon*, London: Longman.

Harrison, T. (1978) *'The School of Eloquence' and Other Poems*, London: Rex Collins (reprinted in idem. (1984) *Selected Poems*, London: Penguin).

Rylance, R. (1991) 'Tony Harrison's Languages', in A. Easthope and J.O. Thompson (eds) *Contemporary Poetry meets Modern Theory*, Hemel Hempstead: Harvester Wheatsheaf.

Sinclair, J. (ed.) (1987) *Collins Cobuild English Grammar*, London: Collins.

3 Approaching Hill's 'Of Commerce and Society' through lexis

Michael Toolan

EDITOR'S PREFACE

In her recent monograph on Geoffrey Hill, Elisabeth Knottenbelt rightly observes that his poetry appears elevated and coldly austere as well as closed and dense, particularly in comparison with the verse of many contemporary poets who tend to shun the formal style and aim at plainness and openness (Knottenbelt 1990: 1).

Indeed many a reader, when confronted with Hill's 'Of Commerce and Society', will have the disheartening experience that the poem is almost impenetrable and refuses to open up. To prevent these readers from falling by the wayside, Michael Toolan provides in this chapter a key to the poem in the form of an analysis of its main lexical patterns.

Lexical patterning is one of the principal resources for 'cohesion', which is a blanket term for the linguistic devices by which a text is made to cohere or hang together intersententially. The other major source from which we can draw elements to perform this function is the grammar. For instance, the cohesion of the following brief text from a computer manual is achieved partly by lexical patterning ('WordPerfect', 'computer program', 'set of instructions', 'computer', 'programs', 'WordPerfect', and 'computer') and partly by grammatical items ('your', 'like', 'your', 'you', and 'it'): 'WordPerfect is a computer program, a set of instructions that tells your computer how to act. Like all programs, WordPerfect must be purchased separately and installed on your computer before you can use it.' It will be noticed that the lexical items in this text are closely related either through mere repetition or simple variation ('computer program'/'set of instructions'). Evidently, lexical relations appear to have some psychological validity because we expect a manual to be highly cohesive, that is, very much to the point. Similarly, at the other end of the scale, so to speak, we expect a totally different kind of behaviour of lexical relations in poetry. Here we are prepared for a wide variety of 'loaded' lexical items suggesting a rich imagery. Consider, for instance, the two lexical patterns formed by the verbal phrases 'do not go gentle', 'burn and rave', and 'rage, rage', and the nominal phrases 'that good night', 'close of day', and 'the dying of the light' in the first three lines of Dylan Thomas's poem 'Do not go gentle into that good night':

Do not go gentle into that good night,
Old age should burn and rave at close of day;
Rage, rage against the dying of the light.

It will be obvious that in terms of stylistic choice, the grammar provides a fixed number of possibilities and draws a clear dividing line between what is possible and what is not. By contrast, lexis offers a much wider choice, the only limitation being that some lexical items are more probable and some less probable. It is precisely this 'probabilistic' nature of lexical patterning which makes it such a creative device to weave a closely knit and evocative text. 'Evocative' indeed, because lexical patterns generate two kinds of context: an internal context built up by their own textual surroundings as well as an external context drawing us to ideas and experiences in the world outside. This creates the play of connotative references so convincingly demonstrated in Toolan's analysis of the richly associative network of the lexical relations in Geoffrey Hill's poem.

P. V.

SEARCHING FOR WORDS

How can the less well-armed reader 'break into' a difficult poem (and carry off its jewels)? That is the kind of question I shall try to give a kind of answer to here. By a less well-armed reader I mean someone who may be a non-native speaker, with a relatively limited experience with the range of written and spoken genres of a language (it has to be said that quite a few native speakers, in our technologized world, driven more and more by the computer chip and less and less by the book, also fit this description); or someone who has read little poetry, and who therefore approaches a difficult modern poem very much as a novice. Or it might be someone who *thinks* they are less well-equipped to handle poetry. In the United States teachers talk of students whose brains shut down at the prospect of a calculus problem as suffering 'math anxiety'. Something very similar seems to afflict many people, of all ages, when confronted with a poem: desperate to retrieve the message, to be able to 'see what the poem is about', they scan the text in search of a continuous thread of argument about a major topic. Often, no such thread of sense presents itself and, disappointed and resigned, such readers give up on poems and poetry as things which they themselves could never cope with (as distinct from coping with the surrogate readings provided by literary criticism). 'I've always been scared of poetry, especially modern poetry', they explain. 'I always felt sure I wouldn't get it, and couldn't get it.'

Of course one stock teacherly response is to reassure the pessimistic reader that there is no particular thing to get, no single point or message to extrapolate, from a good poem; but that sort of reassurance can sound rather hollow to the reader who feels that their problem is not a failure to see a particular thing in the poem, but anything. In any event, to the extent that this engendered sense of incompetence at poetry persists, among otherwise intelligent and literate individuals, it is a minor tragedy within the literary culture. Anything that may break its hold is worth trying; and in my view attention to lexical patterning in poems fits that category. By noting some of the more prominent lexical patterns in a poem you are 'getting' some of the poem, while putting yourself in a position, of inward knowledge of the text, from which very much more of the poem can be 'got'.

The basis for what I am calling a lexical pattern (and what might alternatively be called lexical cohesion, as in Halliday and Hasan (1976), or aspects of the associative axis of language, as in Saussure (1983)), is simple: it is the judgement, supportable by empirical tests, that two or more words are linked in either some logical way, or on the basis of frequent co-occurrence (perhaps in an idiom). Examples of linkage of the former kind (which may involve antonymy, or part–whole relations, or an implicit hierarchy of a general term and more specific ones) are 'parent' and 'child', 'deep' and 'shallow', 'tree' and 'elm' and 'branch'; examples of linkage of the latter kind are 'spill' and 'beans', 'oil' and 'water', 'salt' and 'pepper', and 'salt' and 'wound'. These two kinds of associative bonds between words in the language represent sense and usage tendencies, of a more-than-random likelihood of particular words co-occurring, that any proficient user of a language is aware of: it is part of what constitutes proficiency in a language. A proficient language-user knows the vocabulary not as an alphabetized list, as in a dictionary, but more intelligently as a network of multiple cross-referenced items.

Enough preliminaries. I shall assume the reader has read Geoffrey

Hill's poem 'Of Commerce and Society' (see Appendix, pp. 41–4) and, as I certainly was after a first reading, is quietly floundering. Rescue from floundering can commence anywhere. Let us assume that the poem is indeed, as the title promises, about commerce and society in some sense – perhaps about how society depends upon commerce, or about how certain societies have so depended. More broadly understood, perhaps commerce is definitional of any society? A first lexical exercise, particularly since the subtitle announces that here are 'Variations on a Theme', might be to bear in mind some terms that associate with *commerce* and *society*, as near-synonyms of them:

> *commerce*: 'trade', 'exchange', 'barter', 'bargain', 'buying and selling', 'money transaction' . . . .
> *society*: 'nation', 'culture', 'community', 'tribe', 'civilization', 'élite' (as in the 'society' page of a magazine).

COMMERCE

Let us begin, for no particularly compelling reason, with section 2, 'The Lowlands of Holland'. Notwithstanding its title, this section is immediately oriented more broadly, to 'Europe': perhaps Holland is representative of a wider European experience. Even before we try to make continuous sense of the section, we can see a lexical pattern around the idea of fullness. The 'hub' of the pattern is perhaps 'replete' in stanza 2: 'its [Holland's or Europe's: does it matter which?] replete strewn Cities such ample monuments to lost nations and generations'. Even in this proposition, 'replete' is echoed four words later by 'ample', and the image of the well- or over-fed gourmand, who sits back replete, having consumed 'an ample sufficiency' may come to mind. Armed with 'ample' and 'replete' the reader can scan back to the final line of the first stanza, where two further associatable terms are used: '*Stuffed* with artistry and *substantial* gain' (my emphases). Again, the image is of something (Europe itself?) packed, but also overpacked, bloated. The 'gain' (another near-synonym of commerce?) is substantial, and that emphasis on material prosperity, even exploitation, is frankly yoked, in the same line, to the acknowledged artistry.

But there's no deflecting that sharply double-edged phrase, 'stuffed with artistry'. Along with the focus on substantial gain it helps us to see lines 2 and 3 of that first stanza as lexically related to the theme of the commercialization of art, and culture, by a society. Europe, line 1 declares, is a much-scarred, much-scoured terrain. Although compactly expressed, the claim seems clear enough: Europe's 'terrain' (an appropriately military and alienated nuance there: who thinks of their own native region as 'terrain'? Imagine Blake's 'Jerusalem' ending 'on England's green and pleasant terrain'!) has often suffered the scars of, especially, war. 'Scour' seems to apply in both its transitive and intransitive senses (i.e., the terrain has been many times cleaned or purged, and many times rushed over for the purposes of quest or pursuit). We may note in passing the lexical link between 'scoured' Europe here and '*hollowed* Europe' of 1:6, and history 'scraped clean' of 6:7 (here and henceforth, numbers indicate the section and line in which a cited expression can be found).

But now how, interpretively, might we traverse to line 2 of this section? Are the attested liberties the independent states of Europe themselves, achieved at the cost of much scarring and scouring – countries such as 'poor little Belgium', over whose liberty, allegedly, the great powers pursued the war whose epilogue was the scene depicted in section 1 ('Versailles, 1919')? Or perhaps the European liberties alluded to are more abstract and general: democracy, freedom from slavery, freedom of association and expression, and so on. Of such vaunted European liberties, which post-Second World War political rhetoric repeatedly spoke of 'exporting' to benighted corners of the globe, two things are noted. First, the liberties are 'attested': they have been witnessed to, 'certified' – a description which provokes a countercurrent of uncertainty of the kind that any such recourse to official docu-mentation triggers (additionally the use of 'attested' here helps con-textualize the three occurrences of 'witness', as a verb, in the final lines of this same section). Second, the liberties are 'home-produce'. This may mean that Europe's liberties are not brought in from outside, not a foreign import or imposition, nor the output of a large-scale industrial enterprise, nor produced for the purposes of 'commerce': 'home-produce' is local, indigenous, an organic and spontaneous flowering.

And yet, in the transition to line 3, this home-produce seems to be not so innocent as this. For in line 3 it is blatantly commodified: 'Labelled and looking up, invites use'. Here the home-produce is evidently not simply for home-consumption: as material labelled and inviting use, it 'looks up' and seems to say 'buy me', with Hill using words that evoke the commercial catchphrase of the postwar generations: 'business is looking up'. And now the final word in line 3, 'use', while partly congruent (in the sense of 'worn, much-used') with the 'much-scarred' and 'much-scoured' of line 1, more importantly forms links with words in following lines, most noticeably its synonym 'custom', which itself may be intended in several of its main senses: custom as respected cultural practice, as habitual activity, and as the buying of goods and services. In these respects, the word 'custom' is as eloquent a go-between for the twin pillars of Commerce and Society as we are likely to find: the ambivalent status of custom is masterfully pursued in lines 9–10, where the skeletons are 'cultural or trade'. A fourth sense of custom, we might note, is the imposing of duties upon imports or exports: as it were, an extraneous duty charged upon the very activity of international commerce. In all these respects, the poem is right to see Europe as 'profiting from custom'. Thus we have seen how a relatively simple lexical pattern in section 2, comprising and linking the words 'much-scarred', 'use', 'custom', and 'cultural or trade', can be enormously helpful in the weaving of an interpretive response to match the complex artistry of Hill's weavings.

SOCIETY

But we have hardly begun to chart the lexical patternings of this section, nor, deliberately, have I yet broached its darkest evocations, for which the trade and profit imagery forms a background – arguably, a necessary and enabling background. I am thinking here of a line such as 2:5 –

Shrunken, magnified (nest, holocaust)

where the final word's allusion to the genocidal onslaught on Europe's Jews, taken from Holland as much as elsewhere, dominates our attention. Something there is that has been both shrunken and magnified, or has involved both, yielding, as the parenthetical gloss suggests, both nest and holocaust. Perhaps 'nest' and 'holocaust' are antonymically intended, particularly if we link 'nest' up with the mention of 'home' three lines earlier: a nest is small and compact (like Holland in relation to Europe?), domestic, familial, a protection. And yet 'nest' has other idiomatic links too: 'a nest of vipers', 'a wasp's nest'. And on another tack, focusing on the terrible commodification of the Jews in Nazi Europe, the 'trading' of them, 'stuffed' into cattle-trucks, to the Polish death camps, the shrunken compactness of the 'nest' could well allude to the nature of day-to-day conditions in a concentration camp, while 'holocaust' confronts their conclusion.

Nevertheless, the earlier suggestions linking 'nest' with domestic self-protection seem to be the reading that fits the general progression of the poem best. This might be paraphrased in the following way: the pursuit of private (home) profit from trade and commerce can be for the purposes of 'feathering one's own nest' – perhaps a not entirely dishonourable activity. On the other hand, a 'magnified' and generalized protection of selfish interests and a culpable disregard of others' humanity can and did lead to genocide. In the years following the Second World War, it was often falsely asserted that anti-Semitism was entirely a (German) Nazi affair, but the speaker knows otherwise, and judges Europe (and its exemplar, Holland) to be

> Not half innocent and not half undone;

I take the first phrase in this line literally: Europe's nations were more guilty than innocent, in their preoccupation with feathering their own nests while other 'nations and generations' – archetypically the Jews, but colonized, exploited, and persecuted communities generally – are 'lost' (2:8–9). But the second phrase, partly in virtue of being a repetition of the phrase 'not half' and thus inviting an accelerated reading, may provoke a contradictory idiomatic interpretation alongside the literal one. Literally, Europe has not been even half undone or ruined by its selling of its products for trade and profit; but in the British English ironic slang usage, Europe has in fact been totally undone by such debased trading. If this suggested reading seems plausible, it means the latter half of the line is a dramatic example of how two contrary voices and viewpoints may inhabit, and be heard, within a phrase sometimes – particularly where assessing a situation truthfully requires divergent answers. Such equivocations belie guilt. Some people in Europe during the war suffered terribly even as others, quite clearly, did not.

What gives us the licence even to consider such a double reading is the seeming appearance of other such outrageous punnings, in Hill's poetry, of phrases in both their standard, respectable senses and in some local, vernacular application. We do not need to search far for such putative puns: in line 13 of this section reference is made, in support of the idea that even the finest people or things are flawed and may need to be brought down, to '*classic* falls'. Here the allusion seems to be not merely to the tragic end of so many of the heroes of the classical period of Greece and Rome, nor the falls of those heroes remembranced in Europe's classic works of art. In addition, the again-ironical demotic use (that great leveller, that bringer-low) of *classic*, to mean 'perfect or ideal in its dysfunctionality', seems to shadow the line. Other examples of outrageous co-presence of a literal and an undercutting idiomatic interpretation include the observation, in 6:2, that the naked Saint Sebastian 'catches his death' from the arrows piercing his body, and that (6:4) his situation is 'priceless'. A particular characteristic of these two-valued expressions, where a high serious sense is undercut – or made more poignant – by a low mocking one, is that the ironizing

Babel-toppling effect is instant: no sooner is the idea of pricelessness invoked than it is undercut; no sooner is the magnificent Titanic launched than it is sunk. Here in section 2, the jarring clash of serious and mocking tones in the word 'classic' – and, two lines later, in the words 'decently' and 'decent' – only reflects how the whole section is wracked with brutal ironies, to match the sheer dishonesty and cruelty, in view of the holocaust, of Europe's 'attested liberties' mentioned in line 2.

BRANCHING OUT

By this stage of word-pattern annotation and interpretation, we should feel confident about branching out from section 2 to other ones. A simple first link to acknowledge is that between the 'half's of 2:6 and those of stanza 3 of section 4. There, Auschwitz, with its chambers 'half-erased', is said to be 'half-dead' – in the sense, surely, of half-forgotten (cf. the idiom 'dead and gone'). The lexical link seems to confirm the theme of evasion of the facts of the holocaust adumbrated in the earlier line.

Before examining section 4 further, we can note that the idea of Europe doing things by halves persists to the close of the poem, 6:13, where Europe 'half-under a cloud' is contrasted with deep-oiled America enjoying its day in the sun. Doing things by halves suggests being half-hearted (cf. 2:14, 'The dead subtracted; the greatest resigned' – possibly echoic of Yeats's observation in 'The Second Coming' that 'the best lack all conviction, while the worst/Are full of passionate intensity'); perceiving things 'through a glass, darkly' rather than with 'face to face' fullness, as Paul's letter to the Corinthians, quoted in the preface to section 6, promises; or doing things at half-cock (cf. the 'estranged' and passive 'apostles' of section 1).

Returning to section 4, notice that it continues with the comment that, looking back, Auschwitz and all its horrors seem not only 'half-dead' but 'unbelievable':

> . . . a fable
> Unbelievable in fatted marble.

In this insidiously bland line and a half, patterns and overlaps operate not only on word-senses and usage, but also at the level of sounds and word-forms. To begin with the latter, there are the similar but differently-pronounced unstressed word-endings, *-able*, *-able*, *-arble*, which must be a deliberately unfeeling contrivance, along with the 'breaking', at word level, of 'fable' into 'fatted marble' – anagrammatic crossword ingenuity which suggests a flippancy of mental attention at appalling variance with the shame and evil which are the line's subject-matter. As for the sense, the holocaust is termed a fable, unbelievable as all fables are: as such, it could be the stuff of legend (or poem . . .), to be framed and set apart from us, as a Greek myth might be on a marble monument (cf. 3, i:3–4: 'There's Andromeda/Depicted in relief, after the fashion' – with its fine pun on 'relief', denoting both Andromeda's rescue from the sea by Perseus, and the raised projection of the sculpted depiction; and, in 'fashion', another synonym of 'custom'). The odd phrase 'fatted marble' surely calls to mind (besides its near-synonyms, noted in section 2) the only common collocate of 'fatted', in 'fatted calf'; and the latter expression's association with (propitiatory?) sacrifice has a complex relevance both to this stanza and the whole poem. A physical referent for the 'fatted marble', however, could be such a memorial to the holocaust as the monument in Israel. Further, the connections between this marble and the Auschwitz lime pits (4:10) in which holocaust victims were buried are brutally direct, beyond the chronological sequence in which the outrage leads to the grieving memorial. For 'marble', as my *Chambers Twentieth Century Dictionary* puts it, is 'a granular crystalline limestone'. Out of the '*crystalline*' (Hill's quotation marks: section 6, stanza 2) suffering – of the Jews, of Saint Sebastian, of the oppressed everywhere – comes art, fable, beauty. From lime and be-liming comes marble, just as from grit comes pearls (3, ii:3). Or so the poem, at certain points, seems to concede. But it would be wrong to say the poem subscribes to such a verdict as the brutal truth: rather the poem probes the implications of such a verdict, and so questions whether it is the brutal truth. 'Suffering for art' takes various forms, including, in section 5, that of the Titanic (that horizontal, nautical Tower of Babel, carrier of high 'society', expression of boundless commercial ambition), sunk by an enormity of crystalline water. On all such suffering the ironist of 6:9–10 observes 'the . . . gods/Destroy only to save'.

Again, a lateral connection should be made: the granular, crystalline nature of marble can be set alongside that other granular crystal that plays such a major lexical and thematic role in this poem: salt. Salt is the very essence of the sea (the word is descended from the Greek *hals*, which can denote either 'salt' or 'sea'). Salt as curative, purgative, and preservative, as 'the residues of refined tears' (3, i:1), as invaluable commodity and cargo ('the gods of coin and salt' (1:7), as the Roman empire's wealth-measure (whence 'salary'), as the profitable crop of Holland's lowest Lowlands (in whose salt-beds the earth is 'decently drained' – 2:15 – a reference to which procedure is perhaps the best way of making literal sense of line 3 of the first section, where 'water curdles from clear'); in all these ways salt seasons the poem, as it were, even as it introduces a pervasive bitterness.

END OF THE BEGINNING

This beginning upon a lexically-driven voyage through 'Of Commerce and Society' must now close. I have been arguing for an extended, open-minded, open-ended brainstorming among the complex reticulations of associatively-charged expressions that comprise the text. I do not pretend that anything more than a start has been made here on the enriching and inspiring activity (let us not call it a 'task'!) of making sense of the poem. But a start has been made, and themes, motifs, and arguments have begun to emerge. We are already in a position to be able to suggest that the poem concerns art-production, trade, colonialism and post-colonialism, exploitation, suffering and sacrifice, commercialism and materialism, the wars of land and sea, prestige language and slang, and art or belief as liberator. Though over-used, and so much-scarred, Walter Benjamin's reminder that 'there is no document of civilisation which is not at the same time a document of barbarism' (Benjamin 1970: 258) seems compellingly apposite. On the same page Benjamin writes 'The cultural treasures [an historical materialist] surveys have an origin which he cannot contemplate without horror.' The reader is urged now to continue lexical brainstorming and sense-making with this poem; I will close with the suggestion that we all (poetry-lovers, or poetry-phobes) have more knowledge in matters lexical than we sometimes remember to use.

APPENDIX

Of Commerce and Society

Variations on a Theme

Then hang this picture for a calendar,
As sheep for goat, and pray most fixedly
For the cold martial progress of your star,
With thoughts of commerce and society,
Well-milked Chinese, Negroes who cannot sing,
The Huns gelded and feeding in a ring.
ALLEN TATE: *More Sonnets at Christmas, 1942*

1 THE APOSTLES: VERSAILLES, 1919

They sat. They stood about.
They were estranged. The air,
As water curdles from clear,
Fleshed the silence. They sat.

They were appalled. The bells
In hollowed Europe spilt
To the gods of coin and salt.
The sea creaked with worked vessels.

2 THE LOWLANDS OF HOLLAND

Europe, the much-scarred, much-scoured terrain,
Its attested liberties, home-produce,
Labelled and looking up, invites use,
Stuffed with artistry and substantial gain:

Shrunken, magnified (nest, holocaust)
Not half innocent and not half undone;
Profiting from custom: its replete strewn
Cities such ample monuments to lost

Nations and generations: its cultural
Or trade skeletons such hand-picked bone:
Flaws in the best, revised science marks down:
Witness many devices; the few natural

Corruptions, graftings; witness classic falls
(The dead subtracted; the greatest resigned);
Witness earth fertilized, decently drained,
The sea decent again behind walls.

3 THE DEATH OF SHELLEY

i

Slime; the residues of refined tears;
And, salt-bristled, blown on a drying sea,
The sunned and risen faces.
                              There's Andromeda
Depicted in relief, after the fashion.

'His guarded eyes under his shielded brow'
Through poisonous baked sea-thing Perseus
Goes – clogged sword, clear, aimless mirror –
With nothing to strike at or blind
                              in the frothed shallows.

ii

Rivers bring down. The sea
Brings away;
Voids, sucks back, its pearls and auguries.
Eagles or vultures churn the fresh-made skies.

Over the statues, unchanging features
Of commerce and quaint love, soot lies.
Earth steams. The bull and the great mute swan
Strain into life with their notorious cries.

4

Statesmen have known visions. And, not alone,
Artistic men prod dead men from their stone:
Some of us have heard the dead speak:
The dead are my obsession this week

But may be lifted away. In summer
Thunder may strike, or, as a tremor
Of remote adjustment, pass on the far side
From us: however deified and defied

By those it does strike. Many have died. Auschwitz,
Its furnace chambers and lime pits
Half-erased, is half-dead; a fable
Unbelievable in fatted marble.

There is, at times, some need to demonstrate
Jehovah's touchy methods that create
The connoisseur of blood, the smitten man.
At times it seems not common to explain.

5 ODE ON THE LOSS OF THE 'TITANIC'

Thriving against façades the ignorant sea
Souses our public baths, statues, waste ground:
Archaic earth-shaker, fresh enemy
('The tables of exchange being overturned');

Drowns Babel in upheaval and display;
Unswerving, as were the admired multitudes
Silenced from time to time under its sway.
By all means let us appease the terse gods.

6 THE MARTYRDOM OF SAINT SEBASTIAN

Homage to Henry James

'But then face to face'

Naked, as if for swimming, the martyr
Catches his death in a little flutter
Of plain arrows. A grotesque situation,
But priceless, and harmless to the nation.

Consider such pains 'crystalline': then fine art
Persists where most crystals accumulate.
History can be scraped clean of its old price.
Engrossed in the cold blood of sacrifice

The provident and self-healing gods
Destroy only to save. Well-stocked with foods,
Enlarged and deep-oiled, America
Detects music, apprehends the day-star

Where, sensitive and half-under a cloud,
Europe muddles her dreaming, is loud
And critical beneath the varied domes
Resonant with tribute and with commerce.

SUGGESTIONS FOR FURTHER WORK

1 In section 1, consider the following crucial but seemingly disparate verbs: 'estranged', 'curdles', 'spilt', and 'creaked'. If a simplifying paraphrase of 'estranged' might be 'relationship gone wrong', can you offer parallel paraphrases, highlighting the element of 'things going wrong', for the other verbs here? With what interior scene in the New Testament, where too the apostles at first stand about inert and estranged, does this scene glaringly contrast?

2 Line 10 of section 2 refers to 'hand-picked bone', but like other phrases of fused multiple associations this seems to mean something more or other than 'bone picked by hand'. Attempt to explicate this phrase within its context here, referring (if you find it appropriate) to the meanings and associations of the following expressions:

'hand-picked', 'bone china', 'bone picked' ('clean').

3 In section 3, ii the sea 'voids, sucks back, its pearls and auguries'. As so often in this poem, an obscure line becomes less opaque if a local incongruous pairing is first considered. Here, consider 'pearls and auguries'. What verb, idiomatically, frequently partners both 'pearls' and 'auguries', taken separately? Now how does that verbal process applied to pearls differ in meaning from the same process as applied to auguries? The pearls and auguries are, in a sense, paired opposites. Now draw up a list of all the other paired opposite terms, or opposite processes, or opposed implications, contained in this section. Could these all be subsumed under the heading 'Processes of giving and taking'?

4 In tandem with lexical cohesion it is usual to think about grammatical cohesion, that is the grammatical means by which the sentences of a text are cross-linked and organized into a coherent message. Pronouns are one common form of grammatical cohesion (for example, we assume that the 'they' of lines 1, 2, 4, and 5 of section 1 are all linked, by co-reference, to 'The Apostles' of the title); sense-signalling sentence-introducers, such as 'So', 'Nevertheless', and 'On the other hand', are another. But in this poem the colon seems a rather prominent cohesive device, though just what it might signal is open to debate.

State your own thoughts on what the colons here seem to signal. Consider also the use of 'witness' towards the close of section 2: how would you paraphrase these 'witness's' is 'witness' a lexical counterpart of the colon?

5 In the final section, for the first time, America is mentioned (although Allen Tate, whose poem is used as preface, was American). Here it may be especially important to remember the poem was written in the 1950s. Make a note of all the ways in which America might be said to be 'well-stocked' and 'deep-oiled' (6:10–11). Comment on the lexical association (on the basis of commonest context of use) between 'detects' and 'apprehends', in line 12: what might be being hinted at here?

FURTHER READING

An excellent systematic introduction to using lexical patterning in the analysis of literary texts is Carter and Long (1987). To enlarge one's acquaintance with Hill's poetry, the *Collected Poems* is the obvious place to go, while Hill (1984) reveals much about Hill's aesthetic, his preoccupations, and his sense of the English poetic tradition(s). Ricks (1984) is a brilliant literary–critical response to Hill and his contemporaries.

REFERENCES

Benjamin, W. (1970) *Illuminations*, trans. H. Zohn, London: Jonathan Cape.
Carter, R. and Long, M. (1987) *The Web of Words*, London: Longman.
Halliday, M.A.K. and Hasan, R. (1976) *Cohesion in English*, London: Longman.
Hill, G. (1984) *The Lords of Limit*, London: Deutsch.
—— (1985) *Collected Poems*, London: Penguin.
Knottenbelt, E.M. (1990) *Passionate Intelligence: The Poetry of Geoffrey Hill*, Amsterdam and Atlanta, GA: Rodopi.
Ricks, C. (1984) *The Force of Poetry*, Oxford: Oxford University Press.
Robinson, P. (ed.) (1985) *Geoffrey Hill: Essays on His Work*, Milton Keynes: Open University Press.
Saussure, F. de (1983) *Course in General Linguistics*, trans. R. Harris, London: Duckworth.

4   The lyrical game: C. Day Lewis's 'Last Words'

Walter Nash

EDITOR'S PREFACE

Through a sensitive stylistic analysis, Walter Nash reveals that the playful artifice in C. Day Lewis's poem 'Last Words' is not 'just the game/For a man of words', as the poet claims, but a cloak for what is in fact an ingenious control of design firmly wedded to the poem's theme: how should we face age, and loneliness, and death?

Beginning with the poem's prosodic form, he notes that certain progressions in the acoustic features of its rhyme-scheme as well as in the long–short variation of its metrical lines, seem to mimic the permutations in the poem's dominant 'mood': from hesitation and doubt to reassurance and harmony.

Nash goes on to point out the poem's rhetorical structure with an introduction (the first stanza), a narration (stanzas 2, 3, and 4, with their three arguments), and a conclusion (the final stanza). Each component of this classical layout is found to have its own appropriate style and syntactic structure, while again the alternations of line-length appear to establish recursive symmetrical patterns reinforcing the semantic relationships in the poem.

Coming to the lexicon, he perceives a tendency towards semantic shifts not unlike the permutations in the poem's acoustics, its prosodic design, and syntactic structure. On the whole, these ambivalences, which are generated by puns on single words as well as by some resourceful lexical patterns spanning the whole poem, allow the reader to shift from an obvious reference to some kind of *fact* to a disguised reference to a state of *feeling*.

Probably prompted by the poet's own announcement that the occasion for the poem was just the game for a man of words, Nash brings up the ever intriguing notion of intentionality (see Wimsatt

1954). Are the meanings a reader derives from a form the same ones that the poet intended? Steering a judicious middle course, he argues that in poetic texts we cannot be wholly certain of whether the meaning attached to some allusive formal structure or pattern is a product of the poet's purposeful design or of the reader's inferential activity. Nevertheless, he does not hesitate to conclude that this poem at least contains several instances of deliberate verbal diversions seeking harmony with its elegiac theme.

P. V.

Last Words

Suppose, they asked,
You are on your death-bed (this is just the game
For a man of words),
With what definitive sentence will you sum
And end your being? . . . Last words: but which of me
Shall utter them?

– The child, who in London's infinite, intimate darkness
Out of time's reach,
Heard nightly an engine whistle, remote and pure
As a call from the edge
Of nothing, and soon in the music of departure
Had perfect pitch?

– The romantic youth
For whom horizons were the daily round,
Near things unbiddable and inane as dreams,
Till he had learned
Through his hoodwinked orbit of clay what Eldorados
Lie close to hand?

– Or the ageing man, seeing his lifelong travel
And toil scaled down
To a flimsy web
Stranded on two dark boughs, dissolving soon,
And only the vanishing dew makes visible now
Its haunted span?

Let this man say,
Blest be the dew that graced my homespun web,
Let this youth say,
Prairies bow to the treadmill: do not weep.
Let this child say,
I hear the night bird, I can go to sleep.

I

This graceful and touching lyric is the end-piece in Day Lewis's collection *Pegasus and Other Poems* (1957); the title, 'Last Words' is thus playfully ambiguous, referring to the poem's epilogic role in the volume, as well as to the topic it proposes. That any reader might consider it a profound utterance, much less a difficult one, seems unlikely. Its great charm is in the ease – a kind of discursive suppleness – with which it proposes, elaborates, and resolves a simple and powerful theme. And yet it is a subtle and in some respects complicated poem. Its playfulness is complex. Rereadings bring out eccentricities of form, of content, of syntax and semantics, until it seems to the reader that the words 'just the game' are indeed applicable to these verses; though whether we are entitled to describe them as 'just *a* game' is another matter.

II

Its prosodic form, at first glance quite regular in broad outline, is notably eccentric in two respects. The first of these is its rhyme-scheme, for it is indeed a rhyming poem of sorts. In each six-line stanza, the first, third, and fifth lines are unrhymed, while lines two, four, and six rhyme – or rather 'chime', with half-rhymes or consonances. Thus in stanza 1 we find 'game', 'sum', 'them'; in 2, 'reach', 'edge', 'pitch'; in 3, 'round', 'learned', 'hand'; in 4, 'down', 'soon', 'span'. In 5, there is at first a half-rhyme, 'web'–'weep', but then the poem concludes with its one and only full rhyme, 'weep'–'sleep'. This full rhyme obviously communicates a sense of ending, and of positive ending at that; we close the poem on a major, reassuring, conciliatory harmony, after all the preceding modulations of uncertainty.

Those 'modulations' are worth looking at in more detail. In each rhyming trio it is the consonantal element that is the most obvious: the nasal /m/ in stanza 1, the affricates /tʃ/, /dʒ/ in 2, the nasal + stop cluster /nd/ in 3, the nasal /n/ in 4, the stops /b/, /p/ in 5. The accompanying vowels, it might almost seem, are merely there to shape the syllable. They do, however, make interesting acoustic progressions as we follow them through each stanza – progressions from length to shortness, or from greater to lesser sonority. The progressive diminution of sonority is quite evident in stanza 1, where the vowel-length of 'game' is drastically shortened in 'sum', and where the central vowel of 'sum' gives place to a vowel of even lower resonance, the mere murmur of /ə/ in 'them'. (Unless, of course, we pronounce 'them' in its strong form, /ðɛm/; but this is barely plausible). In 2, the progression runs from the long vowel of 'reach' to the shorter 'edge' and 'pitch'; in 3, the diphthong of 'round' is followed by the long central vowel of 'learned', and then by the short vowel of 'hand'; and in 4 there is a similar acoustic progression from diphthong ('down') to long vowel ('soon') to short vowel ('span'). Only in the last stanza is the general progression from greater to lesser sonority reversed; there, the short 'web' is followed by the long 'weep', in preparation for the full, concluding sonority of 'sleep'.

These responses to the acoustics of the poem are not mere fancies; they are reasonably based on what is demonstrable from textual fact. But is it then fanciful to suggest a connection between such recurrent shifts of vowel quantity or quality and the prevalent 'mood' or 'feeling' of the poem, its conveyed sense of a talkative hesitation and doubt turning at last to epigrammatic certainty? We here confront the problem that so often vexes beginners in the art of literary stylistics: how can we be sure that the writer *intended*, or indeed was aware of, the 'effects' which we, as readers, are so ready to perceive? But creativeness – as the teacher must repeatedly tell his pupils – trades between levels of conscious awareness and a deep, instinctual feel for the right choice, the true harmonic. In 'Last Words', the full rhyme at the close no doubt occurred in clear consciousness, as a matter of purposeful design, but the drifting half-rhymes of the preceding stanzas need not have been so deliberately worked out; they suggest a feeling for 'the true harmonic', grounded in instinct, confirmed in effect.[1]

III

The second respect in which the form of 'Last Words' is eccentric is in the pattern of varying line-lengths from stanza to stanza. There are other poems in the *Pegasus* volume which set out a six-line stanza in regular alternations of short and long lines (that is, either S–L–S–L–S–L or L–S–L–S–L–S). Only in this, the volume's final poem, does Day Lewis apparently play a casual game of permutation with the line-lengths. No two stanzas follow quite the same pattern, as the following representation of the scheme will show:

	1	*2*	*3*	*4*	*5*	*6*
Stanza 1	S	L	S	L	L	S
Stanza 2	L	S	L	S	L	S
Stanza 3	S	L	L	S	L	S
Stanza 4	L	S	S	L	L	S
Stanza 5	S	L	S	L	S	L

We might see this simply as an instance of the poet varying the form to amuse himself. Nevertheless, it prompts interesting speculations about relationships between line-length, stanza pattern, and poetic perspective. For instance, the poem begins with a short, grammatically incomplete line ('Suppose, they asked') and ends with a line that is long and grammatically self-contained ('I hear the night bird, I can go to sleep'). The final stanza, indeed, is the only one to end on a long line. That might suggest an affective correlation of 'short'/'unresolved' and 'long'/'resolved'; but although it is arguable that the fluctuations of line-length do indeed trace some such course from questioning to certainty – corresponding to changes noted above in the acoustic and affective character of the rhyme-words – it is not quite so simple or banal (or demonstrably fruitless) as trying to say what the short line 'equals' or what the long line 'connotes'. The significance of the long–short variations is best considered with reference to the total shape of the poem.

Of the five stanzas, the first propounds a question, or in classical terms a *topos*; the last offers a resolution; and the stanzas in the intervening group present three convergent cases, or 'arguments'. This rather obviously resembles the standard lay-out of Graeco–Roman rhetoric, with an introduction, a narration, and a conclusion. We must notice, however, the quite striking stylistic contrast between the introduction, which is conversational, musing, *pre-poetic*, the evocation of a man talking to himself, and the rest of the poem, which is unabashedly *poetic*, rhetorical, or even – if one wished to suggest an adverse criticism – high-flown. But there is a further internal contrast, between the style of the narration, with its three arguments, each filling the stanza with a different syntactic scheme, and that of the conclusion with its three concise, syntactically parallel declarations, each contained in a short–long pair of lines.

In their alternations of line-length, two stanzas have a mirror-relationship with each other: stanza 2, the first of the narration group, and stanza 5, the conclusion. Stanza 2 has L–S–L–S–L–S, and stanza 5 supplies the reverse pattern with S–L–S–L–S–L. If we accept that the poem proper, at least in its narration, begins with stanza 2, then the mirror turnabout in the patterning of the final stanza must reinforce the impression of an ending, of reaching a goal. It creates a kind of prosodic figure, comparable to verbal schemes like *anti-metabole*, in which a design appears to be turned back upon itself, as if in the accomplishment of a completed argument.[2] Stanzas 3 and 4 (the 'romantic youth', the 'ageing man') seem at first glance to be haphazardly regulated in their divisions of long and short, but they too make a symmetrical pair. In their first four lines they mirror one another. Stanza 3 begins S–L–L–S; stanza 4 has L–S–S–L. In the last two lines they are not mirrors but parallels: each ends L–S.

Four stanzas of a poem in which the management of line-length is apparently random, or possibly geared to syntactic requirements, thus turn out to have recursive symmetrical relationships in their prosodic design, like patterns in wallpaper or carpeting. Only the first stanza, it appears, has no design partner; but this is the odd item out, not only in the numerical sense (there are five stanzas in the poem, and two pairs leave one over), but also in the rhetorical–poetic sense, the first stanza being the prefatory mulling over of a proposition roughly paraphrasable as 'let's write a poem'. It is external to the symmetry which contains the rest of the poem, a symmetry leading, in the final stanza, to a prosodic mirror which is also a mirror of content; for the 'child', 'youth', and 'ageing man' of the narration appear in reverse order in the conclusion, as 'man', 'youth', and 'child'.

Once again, those old questions of intentionality arise. Here we have what seems to be a very ingenious control of prosodic design, linking the management of line-length with the very movement and meaning of the poem, its progression from the hesitant mumbling of its opening to the decisive assertions of its close. Is this a clear case of a poet knowing and consciously choosing?; or of what might be called the permutations of instinct?; or simply of a reader seeing what a reader wishes to find? It is in the nature of things poetic that we cannot be wholly certain about such matters; nevertheless, this text presents more than one instance of the ostensibly casual choice that must in fact be the product of an inherent, controlling intelligence.

IV

There is, for example, the matter of the poem's syntax in relationship to its prosody and to its overall design in the phases of introduction, narration, and conclusion. The first and the last stanzas, are, so to speak, structurally fragmented, albeit in significantly different ways. Stanza 1 rambles over its six lines, but the ramble is interrupted by marks suggesting the vocal features of an 'aside' (the parenthesis), a pause (the dots), a colloquial topic–comment structure (the colon after 'Last words'). The syntax, the dynamics of punctuation, the breaking of lines and overrunning of line-ends, collectively suggest talk, and talk of a hesitant and somewhat muted kind. This is in contrast with stanza 5, which is divided, or 'portioned', rather than 'fragmented'. The portions are of equal size, are parallel syntactic/rhetorical structures, and suggest, rather than the talker, the speaker, and the public speaker at that, convinced of the rightness of his oration. It is almost as though the poem began with Mr Pooter and ended with St Paul.

These 'fragmented' and 'portioned' outer stanzas are to be contrasted with the interior group of three making up the narration. Here in each case there is an elaborate syntactic structure filling the whole stanza, without breaking or portioning. These are non-finite structures, complex noun phrases developing their initial headwords ('the child', 'the romantic youth', 'the ageing man') through qualifying relative clauses ('who . . . heard', 'for whom horizons were') or, in the case of stanza 4, a participle clause ('seeing his lifelong travel . . .'). These qualifiers are in each case extended by additional clauses expressing, in some way, a sense of the unfolding of time. Thus, in stanza 2, 'Heard nightly . . . and *soon* . . . had perfect pitch'; in 3, 'were the daily round . . . *till* he had learned'; and in 4, 'seeing his . . . toil scaled down to a flimsy web . . . dissolving *soon*, and only the . . . dew makes visible *now* its haunted span'.

In that fourth stanza, the present participle and the time adverbs – notably *now* – are tell tales, bringing the narrative up to date, as it were. Stanzas 2 and 3 are perspectives on the past, but 4 tells us emphatically that the standpoint of the story is *now*; which explains and introduces the deixis of the final stanza, where what we read is not '*the* man', suggesting an objective distance, as in 'I am not the man I was', but '*this* man'. Furthermore, 'this man' is emphatically identified with 'this youth' and 'this child'. The question is no longer 'which of me'? The answer is 'each and all of me' – even though it is the child who is given the last tender word.

V

This is a poem of transmutations, not least in the lexicon, where there are shifts of meaning – or perhaps shifts of shades of meaning – comparable with the shiftiness of the acoustic colouring, the prosodic design, and the grammar. Anyone generally acquainted with Day Lewis's work will be aware of his liking for what might be called the serious pun, the play on words that significantly enriches or adumbrates an image. There are several examples of this in 'Last Words'. 'Hoodwinked' is an instance of a word with a dual relationship, referring on the one hand to 'orbit', via the implied image of falconry, and on the other to the notions of 'deception', 'delusion', commonly associated with this term.[3] 'Travel' in stanza 4 is a manifest etymological play on 'travail', a reminder of the close association between journeying, labour, and suffering. 'Stranded' puns on the senses 'stretched out like a strand, or thread', and 'left in helpless isolation'. It is generally characteristic of this poet that the overt allusion to some kind of *fact* is accompanied by a veiled, transmuting reference to a state of mind or *feeling*.

In the cases quoted, the transmutation takes place within a single word; the receptive reader takes these ambivalences into immediate account. But there is another device of transmutation, spanning the poem, linking the three arguments of the narration with the three declarations of the conclusion. This lexical scheme runs as follows:

'an engine whistle'   becomes 'the night bird'
'hoodwinked orbit'   becomes 'treadmill'
'flimsy web'   becomes 'homespun web'

Each of these implies a psychological change for the better, though that might not seem immediately obvious from the bare examples. The instance of 'an engine whistle'–'the night bird' is the clearest; something objective, factual, specific, *worldly*, reappears at the end as something subjective, mythical, *unworldly*. The transmutation of 'flimsy web' to 'homespun web' is also quite clearly a change towards positive affirmation. 'Homespun' suggests the strength of decent effort and craftsmanship. There is truth and honour in what is homespun; 'flimsy' may suggest hapless failure, 'homespun' does not. More puzzling is the transmutation of an 'orbit' into a 'treadmill'. Both may imply repetitive movement, vain circling – but the treadmill is surely a more painful, punitive thing than the hunting bird's orbit. This looks rather like a change for the worse – until we consider the assertion that '*prairies* bow to the treadmill' – meaning that hard labour may have huge rewards; whereas the falcon's flight is an 'orbit of *clay*', a vain, hoodwinked circling over barren ground. The transmutation of 'orbit' into 'treadmill' is the change from profitless yearning to a perception of how golden attainments – Eldorados and prairies – become accessible through common repetitive toil.[4]

VI

'Last Words' is characteristic of Day Lewis's mature (or middle-aged) lyric style: a blend of modern techniques – for example, in the use of half-rhymes – with traditional or classical sentiments and topics. Though he is a poet of great (and generally underestimated) technical accomplishment, his verse is rarely innovative in content; it remembers its own moods, keeps faith with its own past. In the second stanza of 'Last Words', the stanza that so poignantly evokes the image of the wakeful child listening for the melancholy–romantic sound of the engine whistle, readers may perceive the reworking of a motif from 'Cornet Solo', a poem written thirteen years earlier, in which the child lies awake listening to the plaintive music of the cornet in a street-band.[5] That is typical of the retrospective stance of his later work.

It is also typical of him to organize the contents of a volume so that the poems have some kind of hermeneutic relationship with one another; each poem speaks to its neighbours. Accordingly, anyone reading the *Pegasus* volume will detect in 'Last Words' a note of summation. The collection is divided into three sections, the first containing reworkings or psychological transmutations of classical myth, the second a group of mainly elegiac or memorial poems, and the third a miscellany principally devoted to reflections on the past and on personal relationships. The reader who comes to 'Last Words' with these themes freshly in mind will perceive echoes of them, and will be predisposed to read the poem not only as a statement in its own poetic right, but also as an epilogue to the volume. This no doubt makes for a richer, or at least a more complex reading. But the poem will stand on its own, and its strength, it may be said, is in its playfulness, the ludic spirit that almost distracts attention from the sombre *topos* – 'how should we face age, and loneliness, and death?' – and creates a poem of conciliatory elegance, most memorable in the tenderness and grace of its closing line. Just the game for a man of words – but the game is serious, the words well-chosen.

SUGGESTIONS FOR FURTHER WORK

1 But after all, did the poet *intend* these effects? The question of what the author consciously planned and what seemingly came along of its own accord – or came along in the reader's mind – is one that arises over and over again in discussions of literary language. Discuss this matter, with reference to what has been said about 'Last Words', and also in connection with a poem of your own choosing.

2 This chapter attempts to demonstrate a close, 'integral' relationship between form and content, arguing that in a true poem one generates, and is generated by, the other. Are you convinced by the demonstration? If not, would you interpret the formal facts (of rhyme, stanza form, syntax, lexicon) in some other way? Do you think that the form has no essential bearing on the paraphrasable content of the piece?

3 Make a study of half-rhymes in twentieth-century verse, beginning with a poem by Wilfred Owen (for example, his 'Futility') and including two other lyrics by more recent authors. Does the aesthetic of half-rhyme propounded by Blunden (see note 1) apply to your chosen examples? Pay due attention to the effects wrought by mingling half-rhyme and full rhyme.

4 Day Lewis's stanza form in 'Last Words' is both conventional – in being stanzaic, in conforming to the assumption that a lyric poem is presented in sections of a regular length and prosodic design – and yet original, in that it would be difficult to find another modern poem with exactly this scheme. Find and discuss one or two further examples of conventional/original stanza patterns in twentieth-century verse.

5 Here is a possible contribution to an anthology of ludicrously bad poems. Its content, as it happens, is generally comparable to that of 'Last Words'. Make a stylistic analysis of its prosody, grammar, rhyme-scheme, lexicon, and (as the examination papers say) *any other feature that strikes you*; and then attempt to show why 'Last Words' is a good poem and 'Death-bed Confessions' is bad.

Death-bed Confessions

'You are a man of words', they said;
'Suppose your pulse is growing weak;
Which of your former selves should speak
For you upon your dying bed?'

'Perchance that inner voice you'll hear
Will tell of childhood, how at night
An engine-whistle soothed your fright
And seemed to make the future clear?'

'Or else – maybe! – the appropriate word
Belongs to your high-flying youth,
Circling for honour, freedom, truth,
Like some great predatory bird?'

'This aged man, it might befall,
Just half alive, still not quite dead,
Whose days draw out like spider's thread,
Can speak the speech that says it all?'

'Who knows? Confess! Which self to keep?
Greybeard submission, meek and mild?
Youth's lofty pride? Or else that child,
Tucked up in bed, and half-asleep?'

NOTES

1 There is perhaps no need to offer a defence against a possible charge of fancifulness in response to half-rhymes. Wilfred Owen and his commentators established a principle of half-rhyme usage described by Edmund Blunden (1931: 29): 'again and again by means of it he creates remoteness, darkness, emptiness, shock, echo, the last word'. Michael Roberts (1936: 23–4) elaborates: 'In Owen's war poetry, the half-rhymes almost invariably fall from a vowel of high pitch to one of low pitch, producing an effect of frustration, disappointment, hopelessness. In other poets, rising half-rhymes are used, which produce the opposite effect, without reaching out to the full heartiness of rhyme.' (Roberts's reference to 'pitch' is phonetically

inaccurate.) Blunden remarks of Owen's half-rhymes that 'so complete and characteristic is his deployment of this technical resource that imitators have been few'. That, however, was written in 1931; half-rhyme was a regular feature in the poetry of the ensuing decade. Commenting on Owen, Kennet Allott observes: 'His discovery of para-rhyme . . . was an invention of an important order *and its subsequent too indiscriminate use by poets of the thirties* should not blind us to this fact' (1963: 118; my emphasis).

2 A classic example of *antimetabole* (or *chiasmus*) is the assertion 'One must eat to live, not live to eat', where the constituent elements are mirrored a–b–b–a. Such formulations create the impression of a clinching statement – even when nothing is clinched.

3 Here Day Lewis perhaps deliberately unsettles the propriety of his image. The hunting bird is 'hoodwinked' with a small leather cap until the moment comes for it to fly; it does not wear this hood when in 'orbit', and 'hoodwinked orbit' is an oxymoron, or contradiction in terms. However, the poet may have intended just that; the young idealist's free flying is in fact blind flying.

4 When I wrote this, I had primarily in mind the kind of treadmill represented in lithographs of nineteenth-century penal institutions – a kind of stepped drum which was revolved by the endless tramping of the unfortunate prisoners. It has since been put to me that the word 'treadmill' may also denote another kind of device, a millstone fixed on a pole and turned by a horse plodding round and round in circles. This, indeed, may better suit Day Lewis's concept of false and true effort: the barren circuit of the lofty hawk, the profitable circling of the patient horse.

5 'Cornet Solo', from *Word over All* (1943), reprinted in *Collected Poems, 1954*: 215.

REFERENCES

Allott, K. (ed.) (1963) *The Penguin Book of Contemporary Verse*, rev. edn, Harmondsworth: Penguin.

Blunden, E. (ed.) (1931) *The Poems of Wilfred Owen*, (1946 edition), London: Chatto & Windus.

Day Lewis, C. (1954) *Collected Poems, 1954*, London: Jonathan Cape.

—— (1957) *Pegasus and Other Poems*, London: Jonathan Cape.

Roberts, M. (ed.) (1936) *The Faber Book of Modern Verse*, 3rd edn 1965, rev. by Donald Hall, London: Faber & Faber.

Wimsatt Jr, W.K. (ed.) (1954) *The Verbal Icon*, Lexington, KY: University Press of Kentucky.

5 Between languages: grammar and lexis in Thomas Hardy's 'The Oxen'

Ronald Carter

EDITOR'S PREFACE

In his introduction to the Oxford Authors edition of Thomas Hardy's poetry, Samuel Hynes remarks that in the best of Hardy's poems the passage of time is a major theme, and even his philosophical premise. (In this connection, it is important to remember that Hardy's life as a poet really began when he was well over 50.) To some extent, Hynes continues, it is also a *formal* principle (Hynes's emphasis), because the poems are often structured in such a way that the observed present is set in opposition to the remembered past in an equivocal pattern which 'reveals how expectations are defeated, losses suffered, and hope and happiness destroyed, simply because time *does* pass' (Hynes 1984: xxvi).

It is precisely this pattern that manifests itself as a result of Ronald Carter's acute stylistic analysis of Hardy's poem 'The Oxen'. This contrast between present and past, between observation and memory, is found to be captured perfectly by a sharp division between the linguistic features of the first two stanzas involving the past and the last two concerning the present. Thus, the dissimilarity between the relatively simple grammatical structure of the first two stanzas and the much greater grammatical complexity of the last seven lines of stanzas 3 and 4, is felt to be a syntactic metaphor, so to speak, of the disparity between the simple beliefs of the past and the gnawing doubts of modern times. The phrase 'Hardy's grammar of grief' is therefore particularly apt in relation to the emotion reflected by the poet's contorted syntax (Creighton 1977: vii).

In addition to this syntactic contrast, there appear to be similar contrastive patterns in Hardy's use of tenses, modal verbs, and pronouns, and Carter rightly claims that these grammatical patterns too will be experienced by the reader as incentives to broaden their interpretation.

From this it follows, according to Carter, that the poet's syntactic choices are controlled to bring out these semantic contrasts. In other words, Hardy uses syntax as an instrument to create order, establishing, as it were, the pastness of the past and the presentness of the present. However, with regard to the poet's lexical choices, i.e., his diction, things are entirely different, because the obviously deliberate clashes between several lexical patterns are felt to express fragmentation, a loss of order. By refusing to build on the established patterns and certainty of a received poetic diction, but instead juxtaposing words from widely different contexts, Hardy effectively expresses the disharmony he experiences between what is and what might have been.

Throughout his chapter, Carter integrates the poem's formal features with a consideration of relevant contextual factors such as Hardy's rejection of an established poetic diction as well as of the possibility of expressing his emotions through more colloquial everyday language. Carter concludes that as a result of this stylistic choice, Hardy is 'caught between languages', and, widening the context, he extends the discussion of lexis to other modern poets who find themselves in a similar position.

P. V.

INTRODUCTION

In this chapter a stylistic analysis of a key poem by Thomas Hardy, 'The Oxen', is undertaken. The initial focus is on grammar. The analysis seeks to demonstrate that the grammatical choices Hardy makes are crucial to the meanings established in the poem. At the same time we recognize that Hardy's use of grammar is patterned, consistent, and controlled throughout the poem. The same cannot be said for his lexical choices where there is something of a breakdown of harmony between the words. The absence of lexical pattern and consonance is argued to be part of a phase where Hardy is 'between languages' seeking an appropriate poetic diction for the disharmony he experiences at the gradual displacement of long-held beliefs and convictions. After establishing this lexical instability, conclusions are drawn for the discussion of lexis in a number of other modern poets caught between languages. Throughout this chapter there is a constant attempt to draw analogies between Hardy's style and the contexts in which he writes.

The chapter draws on an earlier analysis of Hardy's 'The Oxen' in which the emphasis was on grammatical structure (see Carter and Nash, 1990: 115–19). In its emphasis on lexis and on the relationship between grammar and lexis this chapter aims to go beyond the earlier discussion in a number of important respects.

GRAMMATICAL ANALYSIS

The speaker in 'The Oxen' is looking back to a point in time ('then') when patterns of life appeared to be less complex; when religious belief was less likely to be displaced by rational scepticism and the ritual supports of a community of people were more likely to be securely in place. By contrast, the present time ('In these years') is characterized by self-doubt and a certain spiritual vacillation as well as by an isolation from that past world in which values and beliefs were more stable.

The Oxen

Christmas Eve, and twelve of the clock.
'Now they are all on their knees',
An elder said as we sat in a flock
By the embers in hearthside ease.

5 We pictured the meek mild creatures where
They dwelt in their strawy pen,
Nor did it occur to one of us there
To doubt they were kneeling then.

So fair a fancy few would weave
10 In these years! Yet, I feel,
If someone said on Christmas Eve,
'Come; see the oxen kneel

In the lonely barton by yonder coomb
Our childhood used to know,'
15 I should go with him in the gloom,
Hoping it might be so.

(Thomas Hardy)

ORGANIZATION

What is particularly interesting about this poem is the way in which language is patterned to provide stylistic contrasts which can be read as reinforcing the division between a past and present world. Such a division is reflected in the poem's organization where the linguistic features of stanzas 1 and 2 (the past) contrast effectively with those of stanzas 3 and 4 (the present). There is a clear opposition between how things are now and how they were; and this contrast is patterned in the poem's clause structures, which, in very general terms, shift from simple to more complex structures.

CLAUSE STRUCTURE

The first two stanzas have a relatively simple sentence structure. The predominant structure is one of a main clause followed by a subordinate clause (the latter indicating time, place, or manner of action). Also, no single sentence is longer than two lines of the poem. For example:

> We pictured the meek mild creatures/where
> <   main clause   > / <
> They dwelt in their strawy pen
> subordinate clause   >

Such patterns contrast significantly with the final sentence of the poem, which runs over the last seven lines of stanzas 3 and 4, and has a more complex structure than those in the first two stanzas. This sentence has the following features:

1   The sequence of main clause 'Yet, I feel' (line 10) and object clause 'I should go with him in the gloom' (line 15) is interrupted by a conditional clause (line 11), and this in turn contains reported clauses which are embedded within it (lines 12–14).
2   Line 14 is a defining relative clause which imparts a more precise definition to the coomb, but which also adds to the greater clausal complexity.
3   This clausal structure continues over five and a half lines of the poem to line 15, and is then extended by another clause – here, participial (line 16).

It is not unreasonable to suggest that such contrasting clause patternings underlie differences between a more certain experience (simple main + subordinate clause structure) and one which is more affected by wavering doubt and a measure of vacillation (complex clause structure with interruptions and extensions). By the end of the poem the speaker seems to look back at a disappearing world with some mixed feelings and in a kind of suspension between belief and disbelief, between knowing and unknowing.

TENSE

There is a similar stanza contrast between past and present tenses. With the exception of line 1 (which lacks a main verb, in part at least in order to provide a linguistically economic frame for the action) and line 2 (which is spoken), the remaining clauses are all in the past tense ('said', 'pictured', 'dwelt', 'did occur', 'were kneeling'). However, the tense in which the main clause operates in the second half of the poem is present. Here 'I feel' (line 10) carries the main burden of response to the present situation brought about by the speaker's retrospection.

MODALITY

Another contrast which serves rather more to underline an expression of greater uncertainty is one between degrees of modality. There are no modal verbs in the first half of the poem, while, in the second half, there are three ('would', 'should', 'might'). In general signalling a more subjective view, their presence can be equated with a more subjective alignment to events adopted by the speaker in the second half of the poem. The speaker, in this more complex time, expresses a somewhat less clear-cut view of the world in which oxen, moved by a supernatural force, might kneel at Christmas and thus re-enact the kneeling of animals in the stable at the birth of Christ.

PRONOUNS

A similarly prominent contrastive pattern is displayed by the pronouns. In the first two stanzas the pronoun 'we' is used: in the last two stanzas it is replaced by 'I'. The contrast provides a stylistic corollary for the move from community ('we') to isolated individuality ('I') which is in part a consequence of the speaker's habitation of the uncertain present of 'these years'. A similar effect is created by the parallelism between stanza 1 (line 3) 'An elder' and stanza 3 (line 3) 'someone' where the definite and clearly identifiable elder is replaced by the less discernible and definite 'someone'.

The above analysis should not suggest, of course, that there are no other significant patterns or that they do not have a part to play. What is, however, evident is that a skilful and careful modulation of grammatical patterns is a key contributory factor in recognizing divisions and oppositions in the poem and that such analysis should be a necessary prerequisite for further exploration and interpretation.

LEXICAL ANALYSIS

Precise analysis of the vocabulary of a poem is not possible in the same way as it is possible to analyse precisely the grammar of a poem. The grammar of English is finite. There are only a certain number of possible grammatical combinations. This makes it easier to describe departures from normal or expected choices. However, the lexis of English is infinite. There *are*, of course, some very tightly organized lexical patterns. For example, the words 'hot' and 'cold' and 'slow' and 'fast' are structural opposites; words such as 'front', 'anti-cyclone', 'depression' are linked by a common connection with the register of weatherforecasting. However, there are theoretically endless possibilities of lexical choice open to a writer and it is accordingly difficult accurately to account for and interpret the particular patterns of words across a poem.

In the case of 'The Oxen' the lexical patterns are varied. For an understanding of such patterns readers need to be sensitive to particular literary and cultural associations. For example, in the first stanza words such as 'elder', 'flock', 'meek and mild' are unified by their common co-occurrence in religious and biblical contexts.[1] In this poem they suggest a community with religious beliefs intact, reinforcing at the same time the settled patterns encoded by the syntactic choices Hardy makes in the first two stanzas. Such associations are not, however, continued into the second half of the poem. This contains networks of words which do not automatically relate to those in the first half of the poem. Words such as 'fancy' in:

So fair a fancy few would weave
In these years!

are formal lexical items with their meanings fairly fixed in time. 'Fancy' is a word which is associated with discussions in literature in the Romantic period and refers to an order of poetic creation rather less powerful than that of the imagination itself. In the context of the final two stanzas of 'The Oxen' it contrasts markedly with the distinctively dialect words such as 'yonder' and 'barton' and 'coomb'. In turn, these words do not contract relations with any other similarly dialectal words or phrases elsewhere in the poem, retaining a resonance specific only to two or three lines of the poem. The words hint at the community, its local dialects, and its communal beliefs outlined at the beginning of the poem. They serve to register a sense of belonging which time has eroded and may therefore be deliberately displaced to this part of the poem. But the overall effect is of a lack of fit, a certain incongruity as words from different contexts of use sit alongside one another.

This lack of coherent connection is underlined by the strong association between two words across the stanzaic divide in the poem. 'Gloom' links with 'embers' in a metaphoric reinforcement of a fading light which in turn parallels the disappearance of a strong and clear belief in a world represented by oxen which kneel at Christmas. Such words gently reinforce the irony of words with strong religious associations in the first and second stanzas which are placed against a background of gradually disappearing beliefs and the passing of pattern and order in the lives of the depicted community.

The overall lexical discontinuity and lack of clear pattern and harmony between words contrasts with poems which are characterized by their adherence to a clearer and more consistent poetic order. Several poems conform to a distinct poetic *diction* – a language deliberately marked off from everyday language. At certain points in history there have been tugs between different poetic languages: for example, the poetic decorum of the Renaissance lyric contrasts with the more colloquial and demotic language of Metaphysical poetry; the elevated and ornate but restricted diction of much Augustan poetry contrasts with the attempt to reproduce in some Romantic poetry the more accessible 'language spoken by men'. Here is an example of consistent and homogeneous poetic diction:

> Now the golden Morn aloft
>   Waves her dew-bespangled wing;
> With vermeil cheek and whisper soft
>   She woos the tardy Spring:
> Till April starts, and calls around
> The sleeping fragrance from the ground;
> And lightly o'er the living scene
> Scatters his freshest, tenderest green.

This first stanza from an eighteenth-century poem by Thomas Gray, 'Ode on the Pleasure arising from Vicissitude', manifests a poetic diction unified by vocabulary choices which are both formal and markedly 'poetic' – the kind of diction regularly associated with the poetry of that time and distinct from the everyday language. It was this kind of unitary diction which Wordsworth and Coleridge attempted to challenge at the turn of the eighteenth century.

The case of 'The Oxen' is not, however, quite so straightforward as a simple alternative between one poetic style or another. It is more a case of mixed languages for Hardy has created an altogether more heterogeneous poetic order. There is a breakdown in the relations of consonance and harmony between words. Hardy is seeking neither for the established pattern and certainty of a poetic diction nor for the more direct and personal expressiveness conferred by more colloquial everyday language. He is 'between languages', allowing different lexical layers to coexist and exploiting for creative purposes the disharmonies such styles of vocabulary produce.

This particular development of poetic vocabulary has been identified by the modernist poet and critic Ezra Pound as 'logopoeia'. He defines logopoeia in the following terms:

> LOGOPOEIA, 'the dance of the intellect among words', that is to say, it employs words not only for their direct meaning, but it takes count in a special way of habits of usage, of the context we *expect* to find with the word, its usual concomitants, of its known acceptances, and of ironical play. It holds the aesthetic content which is peculiarly the domain of verbal manifestation, and cannot possibly be contained in plastic or in music. It is the latest come, and perhaps most tricky and undependable mode.
>
> (Eliot 1954: 25)

Pound makes some interesting observations. He underlines how poets can exploit the associations of words, the knowledge of the kinds of contexts in which particular words occur and how such 'manifestations' are unique to verbal art and are not therefore readily translatable as such. Logopoeia is a specifically modern mode and is to be found both in the poetry of modernist poets, including Pound himself, and in the poetry of poets 'between languages'. The poets 'between languages' sometimes develop a creative tension between order in syntax and the more disordered poetic language of logopoeia.

Hardy's syntax in this poem contrasts markedly between the first two stanzas and the last two stanzas. The patterns of syntactic choice are controlled to allow such contrasts. The syntactic contrasts underscore differences in the way of life experienced by the poet in the past and in the present. Thus a further contrast is set up between syntax and lexis. The syntax connotes order; the lexis connotes fragmentation. Hardy is a poet writing at a time of dislocation of beliefs, of uncertainties of faith, and of ambiguities of action. His syntax does not break up to reflect this and in this respect he is unlike poets such as Gerard Manley Hopkins or T.S. Eliot or Dylan Thomas who are more modernist in orientation and whose regular deviation from rules embodies their vision of a social, cultural, and spiritual world which cannot hold together. Such poets likewise mix lexical layers, even, in the case of T.S. Eliot, to the extent of juxtaposing phrases from different world languages. They go beyond all accepted norms of poetic language.

Hardy remains between languages, holding to a syntax which reflects a commitment rationally to decipher the world while at the same time unfolding a set of discordant and incongruous lexical patterns.

In 'The Oxen' Hardy has produced a transitional poem. It is balanced between beliefs, between experiences, between past and present, between languages, and, in the transition between Victorian and modern worlds, between centuries. Although stylistic analysis cannot claim to point unequivocally to such meanings and although the analysis of lexis is less precise than that of grammar, stylistic analysis can lay a basis on which further interpretations can be built and point to patterns of language use which in such a process cannot be ignored.

SUGGESTIONS FOR FURTHER WORK

1 It may be helpful for studying Hardy's poetry in general and 'The Oxen' in particular to analyse other poems in which there are similar internal grammatical contrasts. Good examples are Ted Hughes's 'Hawk Roosting' and Robert Graves's 'The Legs'. Read these poems carefully and work out what you feel the poems to be about. Then, analyse the poems' grammar and discuss the relationship between the syntactic choices and the kinds of meanings you discern in the poem. A further stylistic contrast for analysis is between poems which hold to syntactic order and patterning and poems in which normal syntactic relations are not upheld. Good examples are: T.S. Eliot's 'Preludes' and 'Marina'; G.M. Hopkins's 'No, I'll not carrion comfort' and 'The Windhover', the latter of which also provides interesting thematic contrast with Hughes's 'Hawk Roosting'. A useful stylistic commentary to read on 'Prelude' I by T.S. Eliot is by M.H. Short in Carter (1982: 55–64).

2 Other poems by Hardy which in their lexical choices appear caught 'between languages' and which may therefore be interestingly compared with 'The Oxen' are 'The Darkling Thrush' and 'After a Journey'. The latter poem is remarkable for its contrast between syntactic control and lexical diffusion. There is a lexical mixture of words and phrases drawn from a wide range of domains including: archaisms and poeticisms: 'hereto'; 'wherein'; 'older'; 'Whither, O whither ... .'; 'Summer gave us sweets but autumn wrought division'; formal, almost technical vocabulary: 'ejaculations'; 'Time's derision'; colloquial spoken lexis: 'There's no knowing'; 'the seals flop lazily'; romantic, almost pop-lyric style expression: 'when you were all aglow'; unusual, possibly dialectal or neologistic expressions: 'I mind not, though Life lours,/The bringing me here'. The use of a word such as *flop* in 'the seals flop lazily' is paralleled in Yeats's 'The Second Coming' where formal vocabulary choices mix with similarly colloquial, informal lexis as in:

What rough beast, its hour come round at last
Slouches towards Bethlehem to be born?

Such juxtapositions are lexical forerunners of the kinds of styles of vocabulary developed by W.H. Auden and Philip Larkin, the latter in particular characterized by a large number of demotic, even scatological expressions which sit alongside more formal choices. Good examples are W.H. Auden's 'Consider', 'Oxford', and 'The Unknown Citizen' and Larkin's 'Poetry of Departures', 'Toads', 'High Windows', and 'A Study of Reading Habits'.

At the same time as exploiting lexical disharmonies and diffusions, however, both Auden and Larkin adhere to an articulate and patterned syntax and in this respect are inheritors of the Hardy tradition of 'between languages'. Donald Davie (1973: 3) in *Thomas Hardy and British Poetry* points to a line of poetry developed from Hardy. He argues that this tradition of carefully structured poetry on familiar themes is stronger than that introduced by modernists such as T.S. Eliot and has been more influential on the history of modern British poetry. By examining both a range of poems and by analysing a number of poems such as, say, Larkin's 'Poetry of Departures', in particular, it would be valuable to explore the validity in *stylistic* terms of Davie's arguments.

3 Other research possibilities to investigate include:

a The extent to which poetry in English is 'balanced' between formal, Latin-based and informal, Anglo-Saxon-based languages. A valuable article on the topic with reference to several centuries of English poetry is by Sylvia Adamson. It is entitled 'With Double Tongue: Diglossia, Stylistics and the Teaching of English' and appears in Short (1989: 204–40).
b The relevance to stylistic analysis of the theories of Mikhail Bakhtin. Bakhtin's term for the lexical mixing we have identified in the poetry of Hardy is heteroglossia. Much of Bakhtin's work underlines that the idea of a neutral, unitary literary language is limited. Bakhtin demonstrates the essential *dialogic* nature of language with different styles and voices competing for attention and ascendancy and reflecting in the process that there is no single point of view, no unitary perspective from which reality can be interpreted. Useful analyses of modern poems from a Bakhtinian perspective are: Katie Wales, 'Back to the Future: Bakhtin, Stylistics and Discourse' and Helga Geyer-Ryan, 'Heteroglossia in the Poetry of Bertolt Brecht and Tony Harrison' in van Peer (1988: 176–92, 193–221).
c The following statement, defining heteroglossia, is extracted from Mikhail Bakhtin's 'Discourse in the Novel':

> social dialects, characteristic group behaviour, professional jargons, generic languages, languages of generations and age groups, tendentious languages, languages of the authorities, of various circles and of passing fashions, languages that serve the specific sociopolitical purposes of the day . . . .
>
> (1981: 331)

It can be applied with equal validity to poetry. Take two twentieth-century poets and evaluate, with particular reference to the above statement, the extent to which they are heteroglossic. One good example is the poetry of W.H. Auden. Poems such as 'Consider', 'Mundus et Infans', and 'The Unknown Citizen' are useful examples with which to begin any comparison (see Auden 1966).

4 A valuable study of evolution of poetic styles which complements aspects of the discussion in this chapter is Stephens and Waterhouse (1990: 162–4 (on Hardy), 203–7 (on Larkin), 177–9 (on T.S. Eliot), 107–14 (on Augustan/Romantic poetry) are especially relevant).

NOTE

1 See, for example, the hymn 'Gentle Jesus, meek and mild' by Charles Wesley (1707–88) with which Hardy and his readers would be likely to be acquainted.

REFERENCES

Auden, W.H. (1966) *Collected Shorter Poems 1927–1957*, London: Faber & Faber.

Bakhtin, M.M. (1981) 'Discourse in the Novel', in M. Holquist (ed.) *The Dialogical Imagination*, Austin, TX: University of Texas Press.

Carter, R. (ed.) (1982) *Language and Literature: An Introductory Reader in Stylistics*, London: Allen & Unwin.

Carter, R. and Nash, W. (1990) *Seeing Through Language: A Guide to Styles of English Writing*, Oxford: Blackwell.

Creighton, T.R.M. (1977) (ed.) *Poems of Thomas Hardy: A New Selection*, London: Macmillan.

Davie, D. (1973) *Thomas Hardy and British Poetry*, London: Routledge & Kegan Paul.

Eliot, T.S. (ed.) (1954) *Literary Essays of Ezra Pound*, London: Faber & Faber.

Hynes, S. (1984) (ed.) *Thomas Hardy*, Oxford: Oxford University Press.

Short, M. (ed.) (1989) *Reading, Analysing and Teaching Literature*, London: Longman.

Stephens, J. and Waterhouse, R. (1990) *Literature, Language and Change: From Chaucer to the Present*, London: Routledge.

van Peer, W. (ed.) (1988) *The Taming of the Text: Explorations in Language, Literature and Culture*, London: Routledge.

6 The auditory imagination and the music of poetry

Richard D. Cureton

EDITOR'S PREFACE

'Poetry was born, like Beatrice, under a dancing star. There is in the nature of things a law of dancing which, at a crisis of great happiness or exaltation, sets the thoughts and the emotions leaping rhythmically to time' (Lynd 1921: ix). This statement on the close relationship between expressing our emotions and rhythm, which I found in a musty anthology of verse from the early 1920s, appears to be one of the basic assumptions for Richard Cureton's new theory of rhythm formulated in this chapter. He argues that rhythmic cognition is one of our most basic mental capacities and that in the evolution of the human species it almost certainly preceded our ability to use language. However, in spite of its elemental nature, it is far from easy to describe accurately how we experience rhythm and what it is.

Owing to the dominance of the written word in our present-day culture, the rhythmical units of poetry appear in print as lines so that our thinking about verse movement has developed along visual rather than auditive lines. Since we are used to describing what we see in words, we also try to catch our sonic perceptions in metaphorical language. However, through their dynamic and transient character, our auditory experiences escape the materializing workings of the mind, which are so typical of our visual experiences, and therefore refuse to be subjected to the symbolizing power of language.

So our relationship to the visual life-world is radically different from our relation to the sonic life-world. The visual world is relatively stable and can therefore be described and labelled; as a result, it tends to remain outside of ourselves. Our sonic life-world, however, we tend to integrate into our inner life because it is unstable and unnameable. Through this very instability and fleeting nature of our sonic experiences, we include them in our temporal consciousness, which in turn is closely linked with our emotional life. This closeness between time and feeling, Cureton assumes, originates from the fact that we experience our sense of time and our feelings as particular patterns of structured energy. And the comprehensive organizing and stabilizing factor of our temporal consciousness is *rhythm*, which is derived from a Greek word for 'flow'.

Now, traditionally, studies of rhythm have been concerned with *metre*, but Cureton moves beyond this limited focus and suggests that, in addition to metre, there are two more components of rhythm, *viz.*, *grouping* and *prolongation*. In this chapter he shows convincingly how by exploiting these temporal abilities, poets can rouse our deepest emotions.

Indeed, Cureton could not have chosen a better poem for the application of his theory than Robert Frost's 'Nothing Gold Can Stay' because its main theme is the inexorable passing of time as we can sense it in the *rhythmic* changes in nature: the tender green of the spring leaves soon darkens; the blossom's life is pathetically brief, and then the leaves themselves die. Likewise the bliss of Eden turned into bitterness, and even the gold of sunset must die before there can be another day and that will die, too. As Cureton clearly demonstrates in his analysis, the poem is actually all a statement of facts; its emotions must come from the response of the reader.

P. V.

Although there is much discussion devoted to the structural features of rhythmic forms, there has developed no comprehensive theory of the genesis, nature, and function of rhythm. We have, to put it in philosophical terms, neither an ontology nor an epistemology of rhythm . . . . What I hope is that prosodic study will proceed from the grammar of meter to the phenomenology of rhythm: from knowledge of the objective correlative to an understanding of the auditory imagination.

(Gross 1979: 9, 16)

TIME AND THE EAR

Of all the literary genres, poetry has the deepest connection with the oral and the aural – with the human voice, music, and their combination in song; and with those aspects of our human life-world that are experienced and ordered by the mind's *ear* rather than the mind's *eye*. Throughout the history of English poetry, and especially in the twentieth century, our print-dominated culture has encouraged art–verse poets to increase the role of the visual in poetry, weakening the connection between verse and hearing. None the less, even in poetry that is significantly visual, the connection between poetry and (what Harvey Gross calls) 'the auditory imagination' has remained strong.

As Gross suggests, the major roadblock to our development of a strong theory of verse movement has been our inability to achieve a deeper philosophical understanding of *time* – the intuitive centre of the life-world we experience through our 'mind's ear'. Because the medium of philosophy is language, the dominant focus of our philosophizings about poetic movement have been products of the eye rather than the ear: objects rather than subjects, the outer world (nature and society) rather than our inner world (vitality, affectivity, desire, ecstasy, empathy, self). Discursive language has enormous symbolic power, but it can communicate the contours and textures of our subjective life only indirectly, and, in the end, bluntly.[1]

There are deep connections between hearing and our inner life.[2] The dominant source of this connection between sound and feeling is the relative evanescence of sound compared to sight. While sight depends crucially on the relative stability of the perceptual object, sound is here and gone. Because of this, sonic perceptions are not really objects at all but more purely events. We naturally relate these events to our external (visual) world, tracing their sources. Given the great reifying powers of metaphorical language, we even name these events, referring to them as 'points' or 'periods' 'in' our 'lives'. But the essential dynamism and transience of sonic experiences make them less substances than pure happenings – pure fluctuations in our sonic sensibilities that are shaped by an aspect of mind entirely distinct from the objectifying process of vision and its great symbolizing accompanist, language.

Because of this dynamism and transience, sonic experiences are not as naturally compositional as visual experiences. Spatial forms are both qualitatively diverse and simultaneously relational. While we can explore a visual scene and its component objects by directing our attention sequentially to different parts (or qualities) of the scene, this temporal exploration is usually a secondary action. Our primary experience is to see the scene – both its objects and their component relations – at once, in relatively full detail.

Our experience of sound has little of this rich relational fullness, however. As with vision, we can hear diverse sounds simultaneously and, like the component objects of visual scenes, these simultaneous sounds can have an interesting momentary texture. But being essentially transient events, these simultaneous sounds do not normally hold their relational texture for long, and in most cases, even these momentary textures are relatively uninteresting (for example, compared to visual scenes). Rather, to hear significantly complex relations between sounds, some mental process must continually project the structural implications of preceding and following sounds on to the sound we hear in the ever-moving present. The ever-moving present must become a type of mutating vectoral hologram for the sonic experience as a whole.

Our relationship to this sonic life-world is also sharply different from our relation to our visual life-world. Being stable and nameable, we naturally view our visual world as distant and other, as a complex of objects, outside of our selves. Our relation to our sonic life-world is naturally closer and more intimate, however, inherently inner rather than outer. Being unstable and unnameable, our temporal consciousness is closely related to the deep-seated, albeit incoherent and unnameable, forces that govern our affective life: our feelings of well-being and internal connectedness, our movements from desire to satisfaction (and return to desire), and our sense of transcendent unity with other things and persons.

The particular organization of temporal consciousness further supports this closeness between feeling and time. Our sense of time derives primarily from sensitivity to felt intensities, waves of energy that when patterned set up systems of structural equivalences capable of holding the changing present in ever-larger webs of temporal relations. The point is: we experience our feelings as similar sorts of structured energy. If the primary intent of poets is to use language to communicate (express, mime, objectify, index, symbolize) inner life, temporal forms are a natural and powerful means to that end.

The most universal term for the vectoral form that organizes and stabilizes our temporal consciousness is *rhythm*, and for want of a better, I will retain this term here. If we are to achieve an understanding of how poets use language to reflect/embody temporal consciousness, we need (1) a general theory of rhythmic response (independent of language) and (2) a theory of how language can elicit such a response.

Rhythmic cognition is one of our most basic mental capacities.[3] Phylogenically, it almost certainly precedes our ability to use language, and as much work in linguistics has recently argued, it is implicated in a good part of what we traditionally identify as linguistic organization.[4] The problem of describing rhythms and how we rhythmize is anything but easy, however. What is a rhythm? The following considerations are important.

RELATIVE PROMINENCE, HIERARCHY, AND COMPONENTIAL FORM

We often think of rhythms as essentially *repetitive* and/or *periodic*, as the recurrence of the same (perceptually rich) object against a fluctuating background, or the movement of different (perceptually rich) objects through a stable, and therefore measuring, scene. But this conception of rhythm only reflects the strongly spatializing bias of language and discursive thought, and should be avoided. Because the components of our temporal consciousness are not objects at all (but events), in themselves they do not have the stability and perceptual richness to recur, and because time is not a space at all (but a field of relational forces) it does not have a preset, stable form that can provide fixed segments of measure. Rather, for temporal events to be built into a larger organization, they must be *given* a relational value in terms of our more general subjective response to their effect.

The principal mental construct that provides such relational values is the *levelled hierarchy* and the principal effect that we respond to is relative *prominence*. As temporal events occur in the ever-moving present, we (1) weigh the relative salience of proximate events in some short interval, (2) construct a schematic representation of these relational weights, (3) break, and then (4) repeat the procedure. The most productive spatial metaphor for the mental product of this process is a sea of waves. Each rhythmic wave has one point of relative salience/prominence/strength and occurs at a well-defined level in a multi-levelled organization: ripples becomes wavelets, which become waves, which become swells, which become tides, which become the 'sea' of our temporal consciousness.

The contrast in organization between this temporal 'sea' and spatial perception is sharp. While spatial perception is flat, simultaneous, and qualitatively rich, temporal perception is hierarchical, sequential, and qualitatively poor. While spatial perception gives us a collection of different things, juxtaposed, and in a moment, temporal perception gives us an array of similar forces, segmented sequentially, but built up vertically into hierarchies.

Given the qualitative poverty of a rhythmic hierarchy, the experiential richness of our temporal perception depends crucially on (1) the number and variety of rhythmic hierarchies that we construct, (2) the vertical scope of each individual hierarchy, and (3) the qualitative differences in relative prominence recorded by each individual hierachy. Over the course of our mental evolution, we have developed the capacity to construct *three* qualitatively different types of rhythmic hierarchies – what I will call the rhythmic *components*.

METRE

Our most primitive rhythmic ability is *metre*. Metre represents our rhythmic response to relatively physical pulsations in a perceptual medium. Compared to the other rhythmic components, it has a relatively restricted scope and a relatively rigid structure. Theorists connect our metrical abilities closely with our consciousness of deep-seated physiological processes (our heartbeat, breath, gait, etc.) and the affective consequences of our essential biological needs (i.e., for sensory stimulation, food, sex, sleep, etc.).

Metre is best characterized as *beating*, as a hierarchy of continuous, point-action saliences. This beating is best represented graphically by a *dot grid*.

.	Level 5
. .	Level 4
. . . .	Level 3
. . . .	Level 2
. . . .	Level 1

Each column of dots represents a beat, and each row of dots represents a series of metrically equivalent beats, a 'level' of metrical organization.

We can describe the relative rigidity and poverty of metrical perception in terms of numerical limitations on this metrical grid. First, compared to the other rhythmic components, metre is often relatively 'flat'. Unless a perceptual stimulus is organized specifically to elicit metre, our metrical response often extends to only three or four levels; and even when maximally organized, a stimulus can usually elicit from us only seven or eight levels of metrical beating. Second, in its horizontal patterning, metre is limited to twos and threes, with a strong preference for twos. At any level of structure, a beat with a certain level of salience can only be separated by one or two beats at the next lower level of salience. Metre also tends to stabilize its horizontal patterning, preferring that all beats on a certain level be separated by one (and only one) or two (and only two) lower-level beats.

Being internally regulated and relatively insensitive to the quality of external events, metre proceeds by responding to relatively gross edges of stimuli, playing out its structural imperatives as it can (or if it can't, giving up entirely). Consequently, compared to the other rhythmic components, it is (1) only weakly segmenting and (2) relatively retrospective in its orientation. If we perceive a perceptual 'edge', we begin to beat and then continue to elaborate as complex a beating as we can give the inherent constraints on metre and the occurrence of further perceptual edges that we encounter in the fleeting temporal present. Consequently, our impressions of metrical segmentation are produced more by the structure of metre itself than the inherent quality of the perceptual medium.

Each metrical segment, or *measure*, begins with a strong beat and contains some pattern of lower-level beats. When we construct these metrical measures, two processes seem especially important. First, the sensitivity of metre to physical stimulation inherently valorizes certain levels of beating over others. In particular, all metrical response seems to favour a level of beating that spaces beats at about 50–150 beats per minute. Music theorists call this valorized level of beating the metrical *tactus*.[5] If we respond metrically to an event, this level of beating (1) will always appear and (2) will always be more salient than other levels of beating. Second, the internal (rather than external) segmentation of a metrical pattern valorizes patterns based on *three* levels. If we are given only one level of beating, we perceive a pulse: beat, nothing, beat, nothing, beat, etc.:

.   .   .   .

If we perceive two levels of beating, we feel alternations in salience – in a duple patterning, beat, off-beat, beat, off-beat, etc.

.   .   .   .
.   .   .   .

But when we perceive three levels of beating, we hear a natural segmentation of the beating. The beats at the third level obtrude perceptually and therefore are perceived as the beginnings of measures.

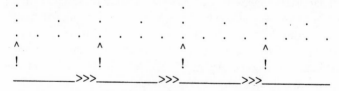

The dynamics of the temporal forces articulated by metre depend crucially on this three-level measuring. In each three-level subset of a metrical hierarchy, we hear the highest level as projecting a measure of two lower levels. This projectional beat is felt as a metrical onset that moves to a metrical close/stand before the next projectional beat at that level. In a metre with a large vertical scope, such measures are nested one inside the other, creating complex impressions of metrical beginning and ending.

In our response to English poetry, the metrical tactus usually responds near the level of lexical stressing (the strongest stress in major-category words: nouns, verbs, adjectives, and adverbs), with lower-level beats responding to subordinate levels of stressing or, at the least, the occurrence of syllables. Higher levels of beating define continuous parts of poetic forms (lines, stanzas, etc.) and respond to coherent higher-level structuring in language: intonation, syntax, and narrative form. Nine levels are adequate to defining most of our metrical responses to English poetry: form, section, stanza, part, line, lobe, tactus, sub-tactus, and pulse. Consider the following poem by Robert Frost.

Nothing Gold Can Stay

Nature's first green is gold,
Her hardest hue to hold.
Her early leaf's a flower;
But only so an hour.
Then leaf subsides to leaf.
So Eden sank to grief.
So dawn goes down to day.
Nothing gold can stay.

In my reading, this text elicits seven metrical levels, with the lowest level being triple and the six higher levels, duple.

Nature's first green is gold,

	section
	stanza
	part
	line
	lobe
	tactus
	pulse

Her hardest hue to hold.

	line
	lobe
	tactus
	pulse

Her early leaf's a flower;

				part
				line
				lobe
				tactus
				pulse

But only so an hour.

			line
			lobe
			tactus
			pulse

Then leaf subsides to leaf.

				stanza
				part
				line
				lobe
				tactus
				pulse

So Eden sank to grief.

			line
			lobe
			tactus
			pulse

So dawn goes down to day.

				part
				line
				lobe
				tactus
				pulse

Nothing gold can stay.

			line
			lobe
			tactus
			pulse

Perceptually, this metrical response has many effects. The most obvious effect is to encase our temporal response to the text in a multi-levelled measuring, a multi-levelled array of projectional, progressional, and terminational events. Even without the other rhythmic components, this measuring has a distinct temporal shape. At the lowest level, the text lilts in a triple pattern, despite the duple patterning of syllables; and while the lines extend to four tactical beats, the language of the lines terminates after three of these beats, producing a firm pause after each line. Higher levels of beating, being duple, support the couplet rhymes, aligning metrical onsets at the part level with the first rhyme-mate and metrical stands at this level with the completing rhyme-mate. The highest levels of metre then shape the metrical relations between the rhymed couplets, (1) making the whole text a four-beat measure based on these paired lines, and (2) making two lower-level four-beat measures based on the lines.

Compared to a non-metrical reading of the text, this metre has several noticeably 'artificial' effects. At the lowest level, the triple metre, which is elicited by the opening triple (*Na-ture's first*) and the many tense vowels and monosyllables on tactical beats, forces us to hold these vowels and monosyllables somewhat longer than we might otherwise, bringing out the vocalic orchestration in the text: N*a*-, gr*ee*n, g*o*ld, h*ar*-, h*ue*, h*o*ld, *ear*- l*ea*f's, fl*ow*-, *o*n-, s*o*, h*ou*-, l*ea*f, -s*i*des, l*ea*f, *au*-, *E*-, s*a*nk, gr*ie*f, d*aw*n, d*ow*n, d*ay*, N*o*-, g*o*ld, st*ay*. Notice that our attempts to hold the first syllable in *Nothing* is frustrated, however, because this syllable is open and has a lax vowel, forcing us to pronounce the word with a relatively awkward gesture.

On the other hand, at mid-levels, lexically stressed syllables that do *not* occur on tactical beats (i.e., *first*, *Then*, and the two line-initial-instances of *So*) are made to move more quickly and tensely. And perhaps most noticeably, the higher-level movement in the second quatrain is severely disturbed by the skewing of structures of meaning against the alternating metre. In terms of the metrical pattern generated by the first stanza, line 5 must carry the projectional beat in the second stanza and line 7 the projectional beat for the last stanzaic part. But line 5 is grouped semantically with the first quatrain and line 7 is grouped semantically with the preceding six lines (rather than the last line). This metrical frustration is disturbing and suspends the higher-level metrical movement, forcing the metre in the second stanza into a 'flatter', more prosaic form (as the text extends the theme of spoiled first fruits beyond nature to humanity and our spiritual 'spoil').

Metre responds to the beginnings of events and registers a few dimensions of an event's contours of prominence, but it is relatively insensitive to the detailed energies presented by the rhythmic medium. For instance, as we have just seen, our metrical response to 'Nothing Gold Can Stay' imposes itself with some force on the language of the text – 'spacing' syllables to maintain the triple pulse, 'spacing' lines to maintain their four-beat composition, presenting declining contours of energy despite the climactic organization of the text, and fighting *against*, rather than responding sensitively to, the relatively asymmetrical shaping of textual meaning in the second half of the poem. Given this restricted responsiveness of metre, it is no wonder that we have developed further temporal abilities to augment our metrical hearing. The central innovation of these other temporal abilities is their more flexible segmentation of the auditory stream; therefore they are often called *phrasing*.

GROUPING

The most radical limitation of a metre is its restriction to the transient present. Like a wound spring, metre searches out a momentary trigger and then winds down according to its own nature and the momentary forces that bear upon it. But in its searching for both this trigger and this course of action, it looks neither forward nor backward. Consequently, the first, and most crucial, contribution of phrasing is to expand the scope of our 'temporal present', to expand the domain within which we can weigh external differences in relative prominence. Towards this end, one phrasal component looks beyond a single temporal point to a small *collection* of points, weighing these points for relative prominence and registering one peak of maximal salience. Unlike metre, this phrasal component *actively* segments the text, repetitively grouping events for inspection. Given this action, this phrasal ability is often called *grouping*.

Grouping actions can inspect as many as six or seven events. Grouping also escapes from the rigid sequentiality of metre. Given events that rigidly alternate in salience, grouping can produce a wide range of patterns according to the segmentation of the temporal continuum it assigns, as in the following (I use 'w' to indicate a relatively weak event and 's' to indicate a relatively strong one).

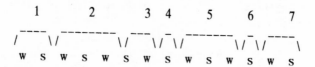

Like all of the rhythmic components, grouping is essentially hierarchical, and because this higher-level grouping is not limited sequentially, it can usually proceed for many levels, as in the following elaboration of our grouping above.

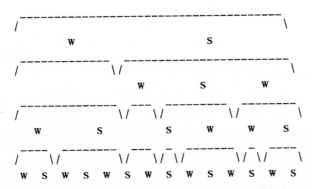

Because of their hierarchical form, grouping structures as a whole can be very complex. In fact, our grouping response to most complex events will be unique.

Two of the major finds in recent work in linguistics have been (1) that all languages grammaticalize a partial grouping hierarchy and (2) that many other aspects of language use are sensitive to our grouping preferences.[6] At the lowest level, syllables are basically groups, surrounding the salient sonorancy of a vowel with a number of less salient consonants. At a second level, relatively unstressed syllables are grouped around lexical stresses, producing what linguists call *clitic phrases*. Clitic phrases are then weighed for relative salience and collected into larger groups, what linguists call *phonological phrases*. And these phonological phrases are then collected into the most basic intonational segmentation, what linguists call *tone units*. For instance, the six syllables in the first line of 'Nothing Gold Can Stay' might be read as one intonational unit, two phonological phrases, and four clitic phrases (I mark three levels of stress: 'v' = weak, '\' = next strongest, '/' = strongest).

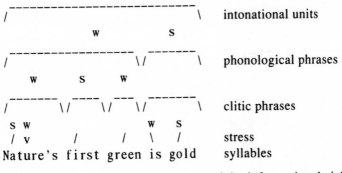

Our grouping response to language weighs informational richness.

The event in a group that carries the most important information is felt as strong. For instance, in the first line of 'Nothing Gold Can Stay' scanned above, the pervasive importance of 'first' fruits to the theme of the text as a whole gives *first* the grouping peak in the line's first phonological phrase. Grouping produces detailed and powerfully modulated temporal representations. It is largely grouping that articulates impressions of relative proportion, expansion/contraction, and rise/fall in our temporal response to a poem.

For example, in 'Nothing Gold Can Stay', much of the dramatic increase in weight and energy in the second stanza is produced by the asymmetrical grouping structures at high levels. The text presents three (progressively deepening) instances of declining first fruits (i.e., natural, human, and cosmic) before delivering the generalizing textual peak in the last line. But these three examples are articulated within textual spans of very different extents. The first example extends for some thirty-two syllables and five intonational units. The final two examples are each delivered in only six syllables and one intonational unit. This 5-to-1 contraction is startling and gives these final examples considerable temporal weight.

```
                                              \     \
Nature's first green is gold,                 !     !
Her hardest hue to hold.                      !     !
Her early leaf's a flower;                    !w    !
But only so an hour.                          !     !
Then leaf subsides to leaf.                   !     !
                                              /     !
                                              \     !
So Eden sank to grief.                        !w    !
                                              /     !
                                              \     !
So dawn goes down to day.                     !s    !
                                              /     /
```

This is not the most dramatic effect at these high levels, either. At the highest level of grouping, the closing generalization, which is also delivered in six syllables, is balanced phrasally against the preceding seven lines and their forty-four syllables.

```
                                              \     \
Nature's first green is gold,                 !     !
Her hardest hue to hold.                      !     !
Her early leaf's a flower;                    !     !
But only so an hour.                          !w    !
Then leaf subsides to leaf.                   !     !
```

So Eden sank to grief.   !   !
So dawn goes down to day.   !   !
                                                  /   !
                                                  \   !
Nothing gold can stay.   !s !
                                                  /   /

PROLONGATION

While grouping and metre can represent our response to events in the
immediate (or slightly expanded) 'present', they cannot represent
qualitative connections between the present and more distant events
(either past or future). The central impression in this additional component of our temporality is our sense of goal-oriented movement, our
sense of 'moving-towards' vs 'moving-away'. We feel the present as an
active anticipation/extension of significant *completions* of our goal-
oriented desires. The major effect of this goal-directed movement is a
sense of prolongation, of delayed satisfaction; therefore, this rhythmic
component is often called *prolongation*.

Like grouping, prolongational forces are hierarchical. Our desires are
not sequential but nested; we regard local satisfactions as parts of more
inclusive satisfactions. Unlike grouping, prolongational forces are only
weakly segmenting, however; they are primarily felt as operating
between/among groups. Given these qualities, prolongational forces are
best represented by annotations on groups. A prolongational anticipation can be represented by 'a', a prolongational extension by 'e', and
a prolongational completion/arrival/satisfaction by 'r'.

In our response to language, the most powerful impressions of
prolongation are created by syntax and discourse organization.[7] At the
highest level, almost all literary discourse is strongly anticipational in
its prolongational contours, while immediately subordinate discourse
levels are usually extensional. Early parts of literary texts usually imply
an existential concern (or 'theme') whose explicit statement we
anticipate. Later parts of the text then explore this theme, extending and
deepening its implications. Then the end of the text explicitly states the
theme. For example, in Frost's 'Nothing Gold Can Stay', we can infer
the theme of the text from his first example (i.e., of natural decline) and
therefore we anticipate its explicit statement. Frost's two subsequent
examples extend and deepen our appreciation of this theme, prolonging
closure. The final line then delivers this closure.

```
Nature's first green is gold.        \    \    \
                                     !    !    !
Her hardest hue to hold.             !    !    !
Her early leaf's a flower;           !    !    !
But only so an hour.                 !    !    !
Then leaf subsides to leaf.          !    !    !
                                     /   !a    !
                                     \    !    !
So Eden sank to grief.              !e    !    !
                                     /    !    !
                                     \    !    !
So dawn goes down to day.           !e    !    !
                                     /    /    !
                                     \    \    !
Nothing gold can stay.               !   !r    !
                                     /    /    /
```

Notice that Frost also mixes anticipational and extensional movement at lower discourse levels. The first five lines present three
statements of the same claim, extending the implications of natural
decline to different images and wordings. But the movement between
the lines in the first two rhyme-pairs is largely anticipational: to
recognize 'early' beauty is to anticipate its decline.

```
Nature's first green is gold,    \    \    \    \    \    \
                                !a    !    !    !    !    !
                                 /    !    !    !    !    !
                                 \    !    !    !    !    !
Her hardest hue to hold.        !r    !    !    !    !    !
                                 /    /    !    !    !    !
                                 \    \    !    !    !    !
Her early leaf's a flower;      !a    !    !    !    !    !
                                 /   !e    !    !    !    !
                                 \    !    !    !    !    !
But only so an hour.            !r    !    !    !    !    !
                                 /    /    /    !    !    !
                                 \    \    \    !    !    !
Then leaf subsides to leaf.      !    !   !e    !    !    !
                                 /    /    /    /   !a    !
                                 \    \    \    \    !    !
So Eden sank to grief.           !    !    !   !e    !    !
                                 /    /    /    /    !    !
                                 \    \    \    \    !    !
So dawn goes down to day.        !    !    !   !e    !    !
                                 /    /    /    /    /    !
                                 \    \    \    \    \    !
Nothing gold can stay.           !    !    !    !   !r    !
                                 /    /    /    /    /    /
```

Syntactic structure is also strongly prolongational. Given a subject we anticipate a predicate; given a transitive verb we expect a complement; given a phrasal modifier we expect a phrasal head; and so forth. For instance, many of Frost's simple clauses in 'Nothing Gold Can Stay' are strongly anticipational, adding a sense of firm arrival/completion to the metrical pauses, grouping peaks, and grouping breaks at line ends, as in line 1 scanned below.

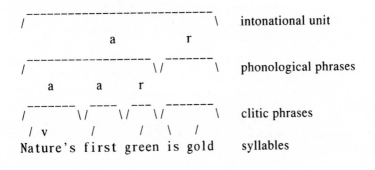

THE MUSIC OF POETRY

While the expressiveness of each of the three rhythmic components is considerable, the 'music' of our rhythmic cognition arises more from their cooperation and/or interaction than from their individual representations. As we have seen above, grouping, metre, and prolongation are elegantly complementary. Metre creates a relatively flat, uniform, and physical time, sensitive to the beginnings of external events but mechanically sequential in its measuring of temporal processes and terminations. Grouping creates a steeply vertical and shapely time, still limited to a relatively local operation but freed from the rigid sequentiality of metre. And prolongation adds a representation of our temporal connectedness to more distant temporal horizons, both past and future, filtering the energies in measured groups through the ears of our temporal desires. In their workings with auditory media such as music and poetry, artists mould their forms so that their creations engage all of these temporal abilities. If their mouldings are careful and crafted, our engagement with their creations can give us some of our rarest (and therefore most cherished) experiences – communion with other temporalities, other subjectivities – heard through the ears that enable our own.

SUGGESTIONS FOR FURTHER WORK

Metre

1 It is also possible to read 'Nothing Gold Can Stay' with a duple pulse. Provide a scansion that demonstrates this. What are some of the aesthetic consequences of reading the poem in this way (vs with a triple pulse)?

2 There is a considerable amount of alliteration in 'Nothing Gold Can Stay'. How does this alliterative patterning relate to tactical beating?

3 What is the relation between metre and rhyme in 'Nothing Gold Can Stay'? What is the effect of this relation?

4 Only two lines in 'Nothing Gold Can Stay' begin with a tactical beat. Which are these? What is the effect of this selective alignment of language and metre?

5 If we give 'Nothing Gold Can Stay' a triple pulse, many pulses are not aligned with syllables. Do most of these unaligned pulses fall (1) within or (2) between clitic phrases? What are some of the effects of these different positionings of unaligned pulses?

Grouping

1 Provide a complete phrasal scansion of 'Nothing Gold Can Stay'. How many levels of phrasing are there in your scansion? How many phrasal units are there at each level? At which levels is the directional movement of groups relatively constant? At which levels is the span of groups relatively constant? What is the effect of these grouping regularities? At which levels is the directional movement of groups varied? At which levels is the span of groups varied? What is the effect of this grouping variation?

2 The clitic phrases in the first and last lines of 'Nothing Gold Can Stay' move their strongest syllable from initial to medial to final position in the phrase in what we might call an 'advancing grade'. Demonstrate this. What is the perceptual effect of a grouping pattern of this sort? Why would this effect be appropriate in the first and last lines of a poem?

3 The first phonological phrases in lines 2–4 have the same shape. Demonstrate this. What is the effect of this similar shaping?

4 Most of the lines in 'Nothing Gold Can Stay' end with an iambic (i.e., ws) clitic phrase. What is the effect of this patterning?

5 'Nothing Gold Can Stay' has many monosyllabic and disyllabic clitic phrases, and it has a couple of clitic phrases with three syllables. But it has no clitic phrases with more than three syllables. What is the effect of this limitation on the spans of clitic phrases in the text?

6 In the first stanza, the first phonological phrase in every line is longer and more complex than the second one. What is the effect of this grouping pattern?

7 'Nothing Gold Can Stay' can be read so that each line is an intonational unit. What is the effect of this alignment of metre and phrasing?

Prolongation

1 In the first stanza, lines move regularly from anticipation to arrival, as does the last line in the poem. The other three lines could be read as having a different prolongational pattern. Demonstrate this. What is the effect of this varied prolongational patterning?

NOTES

1 A good discussion of these matters is presented in Langer (1942, 1953).
2 For a consideration of the relation between hearing and our inner life, see Zukerkandl (1956, 1973) and Seeger (1977).
3 For a detailed argument to this effect, see Fraisse (1963).
4 The most convincing argument for the influence of rhythm on grammar is Gil (1985, 1986).
5 The theoretical tradition I am following is based in music theory. This tradition culminates in Lehrdahl and Jackendoff (1983). Lehrdahl and Jackendoff's major precursors are Schenker (1935/1979), Cooper and Meyer (1960), and Meyer (1956, 1973).
6 For cross-linguistic studies of prosodic hierarchies, see Hayes (1989), and Nespor and Vogel (1986). For further consideration of prosodic hierarchies in English, see ch. 4 in Cureton (1992).
7 Syntactic prolongation has been widely discussed in rhetoric and stylistics. For discussions of discourse prolongation, see Smith (1968) and Haublein (1978).

REFERENCES

Cooper, G. and Meyer, L. (1960) *The Rhythmic Structure of Music*, Chicago, IL: University of Chicago Press.
Cureton, R. (1992) *Rhythmic Phrasing in English Verse*, London: Longman.
Fraisse, P. (1963) *The Psychology of Time*, trans. J. Leith, New York: Harper & Row.
Gil, D. (1985) 'What Does Grammar Include?', *Theoretical Linguistics* 12: 165–72.
—— (1986) 'On the Scope of Grammatical Theory', in S. and C. Modgil (eds) *Noam Chomsky, Nothing Wrong With Being Wrong, Consensus and Controversy*, Barcombe: Farmer: 119–41.
Gross, H. (1979) 'Toward a Phenomenology of Rhythm', in H. Gross (ed.) *The Structure of Verse*, rev. edn, New York: Ecco Press: 5–17.
Haublein, E. (1978) *The Stanza*, London: Methuen.
Hayes, B. (1989) 'The Prosodic Hierarchy in Meter', in P. Kiparsky, and G. Youmans, (eds) *Phonetics and Phonology I: Rhythm and Meter*, Cambridge, MA: MIT Press: 210–60.
Langer, S.K. (1942) *Philosophy in a New Key*, Cambridge, MA: Harvard University Press.
—— (1953) *Feeling and Form*, New York: Charles Scribner's Sons.
Lehrdahl, F. and Jackendoff, R. (1983) *A Generative Theory of Tonal Music*, Cambridge, MA: MIT Press.

Lynd, R. (1921) *An Anthology of Modern Verse*, London: Methuen.

Meyer, L. (1956) *Emotion and Meaning in Music*, Chicago, IL: University of Chicago Press.

—— (1973) *Explaining Music*, Chicago, IL: University of Chicago Press.

Nespor, M. and Vogel, I. (1986) *Prosodic Phonology*, Dordrecht: Foris.

Schenker, H. (1935/1979) *Free Composition*, trans. and ed. E. Oster, New York: Longman.

Seeger, S. (1977) *Studies in Musicology 1935–1975*, Berkeley, CA: University of California Press.

Smith, B.H. (1968) *Poetic Closure: A Study of How Poems End*, Chicago, IL: University of Chicago Press.

Zuckerkandl, V. (1956) *Sound and Symbol: Music and the External World*, Princeton, NJ: Princeton University Press.

—— (1973) *Man the Musician*, Princeton, NJ: Princeton University Press.

7 Teach yourself 'rhetoric': an analysis of Philip Larkin's 'Church Going'

Katie Wales

EDITOR'S PREFACE

It is probably a truism that in their work artists can cut off themselves from their real lives far better than we often suppose. Even so, Katie Wales argues, many Larkin critics overemphasize the poet's personal views and intentions, that is, the producing end of the process of literary signification. Stylistics can redress the balance because its techniques enable the reader to shift to the receiving end of this process and as a result validate his or her responses to the text. (See chapter 4 by Walter Nash in which he also addresses the vexed issue of intentionality.)

To this end Wales proposes an analytical model based on rhetoric, not in the narrow classical sense but as it has recently developed in modern linguistic and literary theory. In particular, she draws on the framework devised by Leith and Myerson (1989), who do not see rhetoric as a rigid code book but as a dynamic process in the production, transmission, and interpretation of utterances. Leith and Myerson (1989: xii) describe the three principles on which their rhetorical approach is based as follows (slightly adapted):

1 *Address*: an utterance is always 'addressed' to someone else, even if that someone is not immediately present, or is actually unknown or imagined.
2 *Argument*: all utterances can be seen as 'replies' to other utterances. The opposing 'voice' can be verified historically but it can also be projected from the utterance itself. All utterances can accordingly be seen as opposing moves in a dialogue which in principle can go on forever.
3 *Play*: the meaning of an utterance will always go beyond the conscious control of the speaker or writer, and there will thus

be a 'looseness' or play of meaning. But the material qualities of language themselves can also be consciously exploited by both addresser and addressee, in the interest of either pleasure or solemnity, and this constitutes another dimension of play.

Wales contends that these principles are highly relevant to Larkin's poems because, contrary to what is generally assumed, they are linguistically most extraordinary and very rhetorical. A case in point is 'Church Going', one of Larkin's best-known poems. Finding the principles of 'address' and 'argument' almost inextricably linked, she first applies these two maxims in a subtle analysis, detecting in the poem a polyphony of 'voices'. The reader can hear how the indifferent and cynical voices of an ordinary cycle-clip-wearing chap gradually give way to the reflective and almost confessional voices of a more imaginative and philosophical persona. Because Larkin appears to permit the voices of his personae to have free play, Wales concludes that the dramatic interplay of these dual-voiced split personalities constitutes 'dialogue' in the Bakhtinian sense of 'internal polemic' uniting the theme and structure of the whole poem.

In the closing stage of her lucid analysis, Katie Wales brings the principle of 'play' to bear on the poem and finds that its suggestive puns, ironic ambiguities, and play of form do not only fulfil the aesthetic function of language, which, for that matter, we have come to expect in poetry. Indeed, these verbal diversions prove to be also an intrinsic part of the poem's overall meaning because they interlock with the elements of 'address' and 'argument'. This unsettling play of language, which induces the reader constantly to reconsider a particular interpretation, artfully undermines any assurances that the poem might provide.

P. V.

It is very easy, for native speakers of English at least, to skip-read Larkin's poetry. The base of his poetic style appears to be common core English, and of his world of reference the common experiences of ordinary suburban men and women, albeit fixed in a period of time and place increasingly alien to the average high-tech student of the 1990s. Yet his poems do warrant rereading, and any methodical framework or scheme of analysis that encourages this can help readers towards a richer understanding and appreciation. A stylistic analysis can show how, even in Larkin's apparently 'plain'-style poems, interpretation is crucially dependent upon features of form: language is not simply a 'medium' for 'content', but a significant part of the whole experience we call literature.[1] Moreover, such an approach, which highlights artefact and artifice, affective language and its effects, can help the reader to avoid the pitfalls of much Larkin criticism, which focuses over-simply on the 'producer' of meaning rather than the 'receiver', on Larkin the poet himself, his views and intentions.

Devices which stress artifice and effect were once the concern of traditional rhetoric, whence modern stylistics can trace its origins; but it is rhetoric in a wider sense which will form the analytical framework here. Following Leith and Myerson (1989) rhetoric is seen not as a static body of knowledge or 'rules' of design, but as a dynamic process in the transmission and interpretation of utterances between author and reader. It is viewed as an activity of perception and reception involving three main principles or 'foci': (1) address (2) argument, and (3) play. Therefore 'all examples of language in use are Rhetorical in so far as they must carry the trace' of these elements (Leith and Myerson 1989: 114). One important consequence is that meaning in rhetorical discourses is not only referential but also comprises 'persuasive force and playful energy' (ibid.: 235). Viewed broadly in this way, Larkin's poems are linguistically quite un-ordinary, highly rhetorical; and a good illustration of these principles is provided by 'Church Going' from *The Less Deceived* (1955) (see Appendix, p. 95). As we shall see, however, it is not easy to isolate these elements in discussion, so subtly and so significantly are they interlinked.

'Address' supposes a 'speaker' and an 'addressee', the latter either explicitly addressed and therefore inscribed within the world of the text; or else existing outside it, implied or, again, directly addressed. Critical attention in the case of Larkin's poetry has most commonly focused on the speaker, who is usually assumed to represent the 'real' poet. I would prefer to talk about the 'persona(e)' in his poetry, from the Latin word for mask; and also to talk about the polyphony of 'voices', the variations of tone and tenor, often indeed within the same poem.

Right from the second word of 'Church Going' the reader is made aware of the dramatic mode of an 'I'-monologue, thrust into the middle of a first-person narrative, with the apparent 'historic' present tense of the informal and immediate account, firmly rooted in a specific situation:

Once I am sure there's nothing going on
I step inside, letting the door thud shut.

In the first two stanzas colloquial features of lexis ('some brass and *stuff*' (line 5); '*God knows* how long' (line 8)) and syntax (ellipsis of conjunction in first line; absence of main verb in the 'listing' sentence, lines 3–8; contractions in *there's* (line 1) and *don't* (line 12)) suggest the voice and persona of an ordinary cycle-clip-wearing chap, not deeply affected by what he sees; and, to judge by the metaphors which occur quite frequently in these two stanzas, rather dismissive in his attitude ('*sprawlings* of flowers' (line 4); '. . . silence/*Brewed* . . .' (line 8); '*Hectoring* large-scale verses' (line 14); 'The echoes *snigger* briefly' (l. 16)). The physical and mental actions described which conclude the second stanza are in harmony, and epitomize the kind of agnostic persona presented so far:

> I sign the book, donate an Irish sixpence,
> Reflect the place was not worth stopping for.
> > (lines 17–18)

Yet is this all to the speaker? I frame this question with the same connective which frames the statement that begins the third stanza, so dramatically changing the tone:

> *Yet* stop I did: . . . .
> > (line 19)

There are hints already of another kind of attitude beneath the mask that seems to prevail in the first two stanzas, and with which the reader has been encouraged to identify. In line 7 the reader is confronted not only by a noun phrase striking in its conjunction of three adjectives ('tense, musty, unignorable'), but also by synaesthesia ('musty . . . silence') and the polysyllabic Latinate 'unignorable'. By such high-lighting or foregrounding upon foregrounding (see also 'play' pp. 93–5) 'unignorable' is certainly not ignorable. The mask has slipped to reveal a personality sensitive to his surroundings, who will take off the cycle-clips 'in awkward reverence' (line 9), who knows his 'pyx' (line 25) from his 'stuff' (line 5), and who is also sensitive to linguistic nuance, presuming his reader will appreciate the stylistic shift from colloquial to formal, not only within the stanza, but also within the phrase: what traditional rhetoricians termed *occupatio*. We can notice another example later in the poem: 'this *accoutred frowsty* barn' (line 53).

In the stanzas which follow the second, the overtly cynical, colloquial voice can still be heard in the projections of a negative future prospect for the church, in both its physical and spiritual dimensions. We can note, for example, further dismissive metaphors and striking neologistic compounds in stanza 5:

Some ruin-bibber, randy for antique,
Or *Christmas-addict*, counting on a whiff
Of gown-and-bands and organ-pipes and myrrh?
                    (lines 42–4)

This fifth stanza, linked by enjambment to the sixth, appears to confirm the cynical persona:

Or will he be my representative,
Bored, uninformed . . . .
                    (lines 45–6)

But again, the connective *yet* qualifies, contradicts, concedes:

. . . knowing the ghostly silt
Dispersed, *yet* tending to this cross of ground
                    (lines 46–7)

Let us consider again line 19 that begins the third stanza, but in full:

Yet stop I did: in fact I often do

It is not only the tone that changes here, but the whole mode of utterance of the poem so far. The narrative changes to reflective monologue, which is almost confessional; the historic present changes to the present of generalization; from simply 'listener' the reader is drawn into the poem as confidant(e). By the end of the stanza, moreover, the reader is more directly involved, jointly addressed, and implicated in the action, as the pronoun shift from *I* to 'inclusive' *we* confirms:

Wondering what to look for; wondering, too, . . .
What *we* shall turn them into, if *we* shall keep
A few cathedrals chronically on show, . . .
Shall *we* avoid them as unlucky places?
                    (lines 21–7)

But the 'inclusive' *we* also has the resonance of the generic and universal: both speaker and reader are part of a collective voice of universal conscience for whom the speaker, in fact, acts as spokesman and 'representative' (line 45).

By the repetition of the verbs of speculation ('wonder') in the third stanza, and the succession of indirect and direct questions which continue into the fourth, fifth, and sixth stanzas, the essentially 'dialogic' nature of the apparent monologue is also revealed: the narrator's addressee is also himself. Such internal argument, but of a more pragmatic nature, is found already in the second stanza, in the form of free direct thought:

Cleaned, or restored? Someone would know: I don't.

But this 'bored, uninformed' persona, by letting his mind run more imaginatively and more philosophically as the poem progresses on a variety of projected speculations, expressed through a complex pattern of self-questioning, is eventually overcome, almost despite himself, by the serious-minded and respectful persona who has the last word in the final stanza.

In the dramatic interplay of the dual-voiced, split personalities, it is 'dialogue' in the Bakhtinian sense of 'dialectic' or 'internal polemic', that is a key structural device in the poem: 'address' inextricably involved with 'argument', the *inventio* of traditional rhetoric.[2] From stanza 3 onwards the hypothetical possibilities of the future ('or . . . or') and the niggling doubts ('yet . . . but') are expressed in an appropriate syntax that is far from plain and simple, and which 'overflows' as it were the confines of the stanzas to suggest, sub-liminally, the power and seriousness of the argument. The blurring of the stanza divisions throughout the poem could almost be seen as a symbolic gesture, suggesting the rationality of prose as against the impressionism of poetry. In terms of syntactic complexity, indeed, the poem builds up to a powerful climax: stanzas 5 and 6 are linked by a sentence at least seven clauses long, followed by two more sentences, equally with at least seven clauses, which actually conclude the poem. Loosely constructed, in rhetorical terms, since they favour 'right-branching' structures dependent on a main clause, these sentences are yet highly indicative of an internal argument that is more and more qualifying, and yet also more and more positive, as the poem comes to an end. The conclusion in structure is a conclusion in argument, however vague and concessive it appears ('If only . . .' (line 63)). A sense of closure is anticipated by the last sentence of stanza 6, which links with stanza 7: in deictic terms it reintroduces the personal voice of the speaker, and brings him physically back to where he started:

> . . . For, though *I*'ve no idea
> What *this* accoutred frowsty barn is worth,
> It pleases *me* to stand in silence *here*;

> (lines 52–4)

So, as for the projected 'someone else' of the last stanza, there is again a 'gravitating to this ground', but with a new seriousness, and a sense of it as a *memento mori*. The word 'silence' in line 54 recalls the 'unignorable silence' of the first stanza, and the full sense of the adjective can now be appreciated. It can in no way be ignored any more than the questions of Faith it symbolizes.

All through the poem the reader is made aware of the physicality of the scene and of the church, and aware also of a transcendent dimension, reflecting both the abstractions of the narrator's train of thought and the supposed spirituality of the church as a symbol of the Christian faith. Many of the lexical items of the poem are strikingly grouped into two main lexical sets. One set, referring to concrete features, parts of a whole (metonyms), reveals the present and future condition of the church, as 'matting', 'seats', 'lectern', and 'roof' give way to 'Grass, weedy pavement, brambles, buttress, sky' (line 36). The other set suggests both perennial theological concerns ('power', 'superstition', 'belief', 'disbelief', 'marriage, and birth,/And death' (lines 50–1), 'destinies') and also individual impulses ('reverence', 'compulsions', 'hunger in himself'). Through the interweavings of the lexis, the physical and non-physical modes of existence are confirmed in their own 'dialectic'.

The final focus for consideration, the principle of 'play', actually heightens the dialogic mode of the poem, as it also heightens the reader's pleasure and stimulates rereadings. The *locus classicus* for double signification as well as semantic play is the pun, and there are some wonderfully subtle yet suggestive ones in 'Church Going'. From the very first line the reader is alerted to the 'echo' of phrase and title, and so is already made sensitive to the possibilities of a kind of distancing between word and referent that will eventually lead to an appreciation of the first line's irony, and of the title's multiple significance:

Once I am sure there's nothing *going on*

On the level of 'plot', in the specific context of situation, this obviously refers to the church's lack of services on weekdays. We realize that the speaker's own visit has nothing to do with attending church regularly, the common meaning of 'churchgoing'. Moreover, by stanza 3, with the apparent conviction of lines like 'When churches fall completely out of use' (line 22), we can reread the verb phrase in line 1 in the more abstract sense of '(not) continuing into the future': cf. line 32 'Power of some sort or other will *go on*'; also line 35 'And what remains when disbelief *has gone*?' In the same way, a reading of the whole poem will draw the reader's attention back to the ironic ambiguity of '"Here endeth"' in line 15: the poem raises the possibility of the demise of the church as a whole, not only the end of the Lesson.

Aware of the temporal progression of beginning, growth, decay, and ending, which the poem raises as a theme, and alerted increasingly to

irony and double meanings, the reader may also wish to go back to the
first stanza and ponder again even the apparently 'ordinary'-sounding
phrase 'Brewed God knows how long' (line 8). Given the situational
context described, the colloquialism jars on the ears just as the cycle-
clips jar visually: it is like swearing in front of the vicar, a social 'gaffe'.
No blasphemy is really intended, although at one stage in its usage the
phrase must have had more force. Etymologically, it reflects an age of
belief precisely in the wisdom of God: God would know how long! And
so its linguistic history nicely reflects in microcosm the ages of belief
that the speaker is to project later in the poem: from 'belief' to
'superstition' and to 'disbelief' (stanza 4).

The play of etymological and current meanings continues in the third
stanza, where here also play of form, through alliteration (and also
assonance), provides foregrounding by sound-repetition against which
the adverb *chronically*, rare in usage, is itself highlighted: [3]

> . . . if we shall *k*eep
> A few *c*athedrals *c*hronically on show,
> Their *p*archment, *p*late and *p*yx in locked cases,
> And *l*et the *r*est *r*ent-fr*ee* to rain and sh*ee*p.
>
> (lines 23–6)

Etymologically, 'chronically' (from 'chronical') would mean something like 'habitually', or 'over a long period of time'; but the
dismissive tone conveyed by the alliterative context reinforces a
pejorative sense associated with the current colloquial meaning of
'chronic', namely 'very bad', particularly associated with illness.

By the final stanza the dismissive, ironic voice has been displaced,
but the etymological word-play remains: perfectly in keeping by this
stage with the sensitive, intellectual persona, and perfectly in harmony
also with the archaisms which themselves mirror the ancient tradition
he is evoking (cf. *accoutred*, (line 53); *blent* (line 56)).[4] Play of sound
through repetition is also found, but no longer ironic:

> A *serious* house on *serious* earth it is . . .
>
> Are *r*ecognized, and *r*obed as destinies.
>
> *S*ince *s*omeone will forever be *s*urprising
> A *h*unger in *h*imself to be more *serious*,
> And *g*ravitating with it to this *g*round,
> Which, he once heard, was proper to *g*row wise in, ...
>
> (lines 55–62)

The polysyllable *gravitating* in one sense simply echoes the native
tending in line 47:

> . . . yet *tending* to this cross of ground

reinforcing, however, more strongly the notion of being drawn by some strong impulse (not specified). Etymologically, like 'gravity', it derives from Latin *gravis* 'serious', the adjective that actually occurs three times in this stanza.

The play of form and meaning is what we have come to expect from and associate with poetry: we talk of the 'aesthetic function' of its language and the effect of pleasure on its readers. But, as Leith and Myerson conclude (1989: 243), verbal play can be 'more than just the acknowledgement of language's material properties'. So the word-play in 'Church Going' is self-reflexive in the deeper sense that it is itself part of the meaning of the poem, contributing to the ambiguities and conflicts of tone and theme, the complexities of address and argument. More generally, the suggestiveness of the language of the poem, which forces the reader to reassess the obvious interpretation of words, works almost unconsciously to reinforce the unsettling of fixed positions and stock attitudes, for which the poem overall is pleading.[5]

APPENDIX

Church Going

Once I am sure there's nothing going on
I step inside, letting the door thud shut.
Another church: matting, seats, and stone,
And little books; sprawlings of flowers, cut
5   For Sunday, brownish now; some brass and stuff
Up at the holy end; the small neat organ;
And a tense, musty, unignorable silence,
Brewed God knows how long. Hatless, I take off
My cycle-clips in awkward reverence,

10   Move forward, run my hand around the font.
From where I stand, the roof looks almost new –
Cleaned, or restored? Someone would know: I don't.
Mounting the lectern, I peruse a few
Hectoring large-scale verses, and pronounce
15   'Here endeth' much more loudly than I'd meant.
The echoes snigger briefly. Back at the door
I sign the book, donate an Irish sixpence,
Reflect the place was not worth stopping for.

Yet stop I did: in fact I often do,

20   And always end much at a loss like this,
    Wondering what to look for; wondering, too,
    When churches fall completely out of use
    What we shall turn them into, if we shall keep
    A few cathedrals chronically on show,
25   Their parchment, plate and pyx in locked cases,
    And let the rest rent-free to rain and sheep.
    Shall we avoid them as unlucky places?

    Or, after dark, will dubious women come
    To make their children touch a particular stone;
30   Pick simples for a cancer; or on some
    Advised night see walking a dead one?
    Power of some sort or other will go on
    In games, in riddles, seemingly at random;
    But superstition, like belief, must die,
35   And what remains when disbelief has gone?
    Grass, weedy pavement, brambles, buttress, sky,

    A shape less recognisable each week,
    A purpose more obscure. I wonder who
    Will be the last, the very last, to seek
40   This place for what it was; one of the crew
    That tap and jot and know what rood-lofts were?
    Some ruin-bibber, randy for antique,
    Or Christmas-addict, counting on a whiff
    Of gown-and-bands and organ-pipes and myrrh?
45   Or will he be my representative,

    Bored, uninformed, knowing the ghostly silt
    Dispersed, yet tending to this cross of ground
    Through suburb scrub because it held unspilt
    So long and equably what since is found
50   Only in separation – marriage, and birth,
    And death, and thoughts of these – for which was built
    This special shell? For, though I've no idea
    What this accoutred frowsty barn is worth,
    It pleases me to stand in silence here;

55   A serious house on serious earth it is,
    In whose blent air all our compulsions meet,
    Are recognised, and robed as destinies.
    And that much never can be obsolete,
    Since someone will forever be surprising

60   A hunger in himself to be more serious,
       And gravitating with it to this ground,
       Which, he once heard, was proper to grow wise in,
       If only that so many dead lie round.

SUGGESTIONS FOR FURTHER WORK

1 Cluysenaar (1982: 313) calls Larkin's diction 'belligerently colloquial'. The informal words and phrases of 'Church Going' certainly seem to need silent quotation marks. Underline the colloquial diction in other Larkin poems, and examine it for potential variety of tones, for register-borrowing, and for the world-views and values invoked. (For example: 'Send No Money', 'Poetry of Departures', 'High Windows'.)

2 Look again at stanza 6 of 'Church Going', in particular the sentence that actually begins in stanza 5: 'Or will he be my representative,' and continues to line 52 'This special shell?'. Do you understand what the nominal relative clause ' what since is found . . . and thoughts of these' in lines 48–51 means:

    . . . because it held unspilt
    . . . what since is found
    Only in separation – marriage, and birth,
    And death, and thoughts of these. . . .
                 (lines 48–51)

The metaphor *unspilt* in the preceding clause may give a clue. Why the ordering of marriage, birth, and death, and not the chronological one of birth, marriage, and death? Look at Larkin's use of nominal relative clauses in other poems. What do they express?

3 Find another poem where you feel differing points of view are being voiced. Is there a neat conclusion? (For example: 'Toads', 'Self's the Man', 'Money', 'Vers de Société'.)

4 Only a few poems in *The Less Deceived* (1955) collection are narrated other than by an 'I'-persona. Are there any differences in tone, style, and theme in these?

5 David Lodge has argued that metaphors in Larkin's poetry are usually characterized by being 'foregrounded' against a predominantly 'metonymic background'. To what extent is this true? What kind or kinds of metaphoric foregrounding do you find?

6 Look at the rhyme scheme in each stanza of 'Church Going'. How regular are the stanzas in this respect? Do any stanzas stand out for this reason? What kind of 'irregular' rhymes appear (for example half-rhyme, eye-rhyme)? What contribution does the metrical patterning make to your appreciation of the poem?

7 Kuby (1974: 19) argues that the poetic impulse in Larkin tends towards 'reduction and condensation rather than expansion and extension'. To what

extent would you agree? How might either of these impulses be manifested linguistically?

8 There have been other stylistic analyses of Larkin's poems, using different approaches and frameworks. Look critically, for example, at Sinclair (1966) on 'First Sight', Trengove (1988) on 'Whatever Happened?', Trengove (1989) on 'Vers de Société', and Verdonk (1991) on 'Talking in Bed'. Or you could make a critical comparison of Cluysenaar and Widdowson, both 1982, and both on 'Mr Bleaney'.

NOTES

1 cf. Fowler (1986: 10):

> the substance of literature is [sometimes] shifted into some obscure, undefined, sphere of existence which is somehow beyond language. But for linguistics, literature *is* language, to be theorized just like any other discourse; it makes no sense to degrade the language to a mere medium.

2 For a résumé of Bakhtin's ideas on the 'dialogic', and other literary principles, with further illustrations from Larkin's poetry, see Wales (1988).

3 'Foregrounding' derives from the Prague School ideas about poetic language, its facility to 'defamiliarize', to exploit language aesthetically. The linguistic sign is thrown into relief against the background of the norms of ordinary language; but within the literary text itself linguistic features can be made prominent against the background of the rest of the text, so particularly inviting focusing points for interpretation by the reader. Two main types of this 'internal' foregrounding are deviation (irregularity) and repetition (regularity): violations of 'norms' by under-frequency and over-frequency, respectively. Metaphors and other *tropes* of traditional rhetoric provide striking examples of semantic (and often grammatical) deviation; alliteration and parallelism, and other *schemes* of traditional rhetoric, striking examples of repetition. See further Wales (1989).

4 *Accoutred*, with its elevated tone and connotations of 'richly attired', is especially interesting. First used by Shakespeare and borrowed from French, its base appears to be *coutre*, referring to the sacristan who robed the clergy.

The first part of stanza 4 is also noteworthy for its archaisms, in keeping with the theme expressed there of a potential reversion in the future to the superstitions of the past. *Simples*, meaning herbs, was a word only in common use from 1580–1750, according to the *OED*; *cancer* with the indefinite article is also archaic. An over-hasty reading of *dubious women* will miss the older sense of 'inclined to doubt' (although there may be an ironic pun here on current usage: the speaker evaluating the women as being 'of doubtful quality').

5 I am grateful to my own first-year undergraduates and MA students for their lively comments on the language of 'Church Going' in seminar discussions; also to Chris Jeffrey (University of Port Elizabeth) and James Whitehead.

FURTHER READING

Latré, G. (1985) *Locking Earth to the Sky: A Structuralist Approach to Philip Larkin's Poetry*, Frankfurt: Peter Lang.

REFERENCES

Cluysenaar, A. (1982) 'Formal Meanings in Three Modern Poems', *Dutch Quarterly Review* 4: 302–20.
Fowler, R. (1986) *Linguistic Criticism*, Oxford: Oxford University Press.
Kuby, L. (1974) *An Uncommon Poet for the Common Man*, The Hague: Mouton.
Larkin, Philip (1955) *The Less Deceived*, London: The Marvell Press.
Leith, D. and Myerson, G. (1989) *The Power of Address: Explorations in Rhetoric*, London: Routledge.
Sinclair, J.McH. (1966) 'Taking a Poem to Pieces', in R. Fowler (ed.) *Essays on Style and Language*, London: Routledge.
Trengove, G. (1988) 'What happens in "Whatever Happened?"?', in W. van Peer (ed.) *The Taming of the Text: Explorations in Language, Literature and Culture*, London: Routledge.
—— (1989) '"Vers de Société": Towards Some Society', in M. Short (ed.) *Reading, Analysing and Teaching Literature*, London: Longman.
Verdonk, P. (1991) 'Poems as Text and Discourse: The Poetics of Philip Larkin', in R.D. Sell (ed.) *Literary Pragmatics*, London: Routledge.
Wales, K. (1988) 'Back to the Future: Bakhtin, Stylistics and Discourse', in W. van Peer (ed.) *The Taming of the Text: Explorations in Language, Literature and Culture*, London: Routledge.
—— (1989) *A Dictionary of Stylistics*, London: Longman.
Widdowson, H. (1982) 'The Conditional Presence of Mr Bleaney', in R. Carter (ed.) *Language and Literature: An Introductory Reader in Stylistics*, London: Allen & Unwin.

8 (Non)-communication in the park

Ruth Waterhouse

EDITOR'S PREFACE

This chapter may be divided into two parts. In the first part Ruth Waterhouse proposes a model theorizing how a poet writes or encodes and a reader interprets or decodes verse language. Encoding and decoding are terms borrowed from communication theory. Encoding refers to the addresser's activity of turning some idea into language, which can be seen as a kind of code, that is, a set of semantic, grammatical, and phonological rules. Decoding is the opposite activity performed by the addressee trying to interpret the linguistic units in which the idea is encoded. This communicative activity is context-dependent because the linguistic codification as well as the decodification are exposed to the impact of all kinds of non-linguistic factors including the sender's and receiver's personal, social, cultural, and ideological contexts.

Waterhouse bases her model on the premise that, given these extra-linguistic factors, a poet is all the same in a position to make particular choices from his or her linguistic repertoire. These choices can be made in two areas of language structure which, following de Saussure's terminology, she calls the paradigmatic and syntagmatic axes. For instance, in her poem 'In the Park', Gwen Harwood may have selected the verb 'whine' from the following set (no doubt, there are more possibilities):

	cry
	weep
	wail
Two children	whine and bicker, tug her skirt
	complain
	moan

So the paradigmatic axis is the vertical one intersecting the sequence of speech or writing. It is the set of related language items from which a selection can be made to fill a particular slot in the sequence. The syntagmatic axis of language is the horizontal one and represents the syntactic order of linguistic elements (words, phrases, clauses) forming a linear sequence. In the above-mentioned example, the poet might also have chosen the order 'Two children tug her skirt, bicker and whine'.

After the paradigmatic and syntagmatic choices have been made, there is a complex interaction between these two axes generating a signifier, for instance, the word 'whine' located in the pattern 'Two children whine and bicker, tug her skirt'. This process is envisaged as taking place in the text, while behind the text, so to speak, it produces a signified for and by the reader, in this instance the 'loaded' image of 'two children whining and bickering, tugging their mother's skirt'. Waterhouse has schematized this intricate process of signification in a three-dimensional model (see Figure 8.1, p. 104).

In the case of figurative language, the primary literal signified (for example, the vehicle of the metaphor 'mouse' in 'He is a mouse') is extended to include a secondary *unstated* signified which the reader must infer from the context (for example, the tenor 'He is a very quiet and shy person'). This extension of the signification process has been included in Figure 8.2, p. 104.

The second part of the chapter is a demonstration of this model. Through a subtle stylistic analysis of the sonnet 'In the Park' by the Australian poet Gwen Harwood, Ruth Waterhouse shows that an understanding of theoretical models of the signification process, like the one she is suggesting, not only makes us much more sensitive to the semantic and artistic potential of verse language but also considerably increases our awareness of the poet's and reader's explicit and implicit attitudes and assumptions.

P. V.

The discourse of English poetry has for centuries challenged poets to experiment with how they can use traditional constraints (such as metric rhythm and rhyme) and yet also the potential of verse form (such as deviation from norms of language choice and ordering within the verse line) to carry signification over and above the usual type of meaning that language carries in ordinary social communication. In the twentieth century poets have deviated from poetic conventions more than in most earlier periods by playing with free verse, with concrete poetry with its emphasis on the visual aspects of language, as well as showing that they can still use traditional forms and even extend them in various ways. Some poets have also gone out of their way to explore sociocultural and ideological as well as literary issues (such as gender and power struggles or how the play of language can initiate but also hamper communication).

The range of issues that twentieth-century poetry addresses has also expanded because English has become the basic language of so many countries, each with physical conditions and a society and culture and ideology that differ in varying respects from those of England itself. But it is not only the encoding of poetry that is influenced by the sociocultural context in which it is written but also its decoding. No reader can avoid his/her environment any more than his/her heredity, and a poem's terms will evoke individual concepts for each reader. For instance, the phrase 'out of date clothes' will evoke a different meaning for decoders in different societies and countries as well as in different decades and even in succeeding years, not to mention in male and female readers!

But decoders' responses to poems cannot remain totally individual. Though poets are inevitably influenced by their society and its language, they set up strategies which expand and yet also exert some control over how their own use of language conveys meaning by setting certain limits upon what it may and may not convey. So how can readers setting out to decode such un-ordinary communication respond to poets' games with language?

In the late twentieth century, any decoder has to come to terms with one obvious aspect of English: the jargons that are constantly cropping up and rapidly changing in all sorts of different discourses, such as that of computers, medicine, pop songs, writing about poetry – the list could be extended almost indefinitely. Jargons have become a way of both facilitating and yet also preventing communication between individuals, depending on whether or not one has a key to what they signify. Sometimes terms from these specialized jargons do filter through into common speech, but to make jargon user-friendly is not always considered necessary, nor is it easy. Yet a jargon is, after all, only a subset of the wider range of language resources available to ordinary speakers and hearers to refer to particular concepts.

So if we are stuck with having to use jargon in order to talk about poetry, what sort should we choose, and, more importantly, what is its function? There are many models which enable us to look at a poem's language and find a way of decoding its meaning, each with its own advantages and disadvantages, its own jargon. Playing round with such models enables us to find one that is user-friendly and on our own wavelength. And of course we do not have to stop at one model only, but can conflate aspects from more than one. Trying out a variety of models sensitizes a decoder to the potential of verse language to signify much more than its mere denotative meaning, including something of both its encoder's and decoder's overt and implied attitudes and assumptions, and that should be at least one main function of any model.

The model I am suggesting starts from the premise that though a poet cannot but help being influenced by the society and culture and period in which s/he lives, within that broad context s/he has various language choices available. What s/he finally chooses to encode carries its own special meaning because of the placement of those particular choices (and no others) within the poem. For instance, a poet who wants to denote the general concept of earth can choose between terms such as 'soil' or 'loam' or 'dirt' or 'silt' (and there are more choices possible, as a thesaurus shows). Each choice not only carries a certain range of denotative information (for example, as compared with, say, 'mud', 'dirt' is signalled as being {+ dry}, though both are {– clean}), but also invites each decoder to formulate from his/her own experiences an individual concept of soil or dirt. Since no decoder can avoid his/her geographical, societal, and cultural context (for example, a farmer may have a different concept of soil from a musician), a poem's word choices will evoke slightly different concepts in each reader.

A poet can provide further constraints by choosing the order in which to encode the bits of information; for example, the order 'she said to the wind' could also be encoded as 'to the wind she said', the inversion of which draws more attention to itself and to the phrase given the unusual initial position, 'to the wind'.

These two areas of choice, whereby there is a vertical paradigmatic choice within a group of words each of which will fit into a particular slot, and a horizontal syntagmatic choice between different orderings of the words, intersect to evoke a signified concept in a process best envisaged as a three-dimensional model, with axes intersecting in the text to produce a sign or signifier, the particular word choice in its particular syntactic ordering, and behind the text concepts or signifieds evoked for and by the reader. Figure 8.1 schematizes this three-dimensional model. However it is not necessarily the denotation of the signified concept that is foregrounded by the context, and although no poet can totally control the signifieds that a decoder brings to a poem's word choices, s/he provides constraints that do limit the decoder's formulations. One of the most obvious ways to do so is to activate a point of view, as for instance in the contrast between the negative

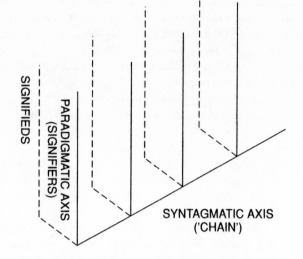

Figure 8.1

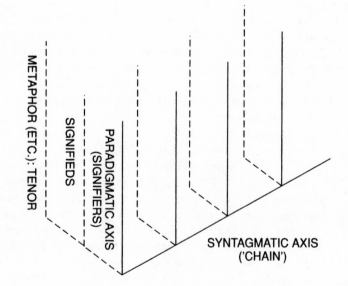

Figure 8.2

connotations of 'whine' and 'bicker' as against the more neutral
associations of 'chatter' in evoking children's communication. To
choose one rather than the other for the paradigmatic axis slants the
point of view and attitude that can be decoded from the choices.

And when a poet uses figurative language, the usual signified of a
metaphor's 'vehicle' such as 'being eaten alive' is displaced by a
further unstated 'tenor' signified (such as being slowly and painfully
destroyed) which a decoder must deduce from the context by an
extension of the referring process, as schematized in Figure 8.2.

The functioning of all these choices is fundamental to the decoding
of signification of meaning, overt and implied, in the discourse. To
demonstrate the model further, then, I should like to look at a sonnet by
an Australian, Gwen Harwood, which uses a traditional sonnet form in
provocative non-traditional ways, as it comments upon one type of male–
female (non-)communication within a framework of twentieth-century
western society and culture:

In the Park

She sits in the park. Her clothes are out of date.
Two children whine and bicker, tug her skirt.
A third draws aimless patterns in the dirt.
Someone she loved once passes by – too late

to feign indifference to that casual nod.
'How nice,' et cetera. 'Time holds great surprises.'
From his neat head unquestionably rises
a small balloon . . . 'but for the grace of God . . .'

They stand a while in flickering light, rehearsing
the children's names and birthdays. 'It's so sweet
to hear their chatter, watch them grow and thrive,'
she says to his departing smile. Then, nursing
the youngest child, sits staring at her feet.
To the wind she says, 'They have eaten me alive.'

An initial strategy for any exploration of verse is to ignore its line-
ends, and to deal with it as with ordinary prose sentences whose
syntagms are arranged in a particular way. I have set out the sonnet
again in this way, in numbered clauses, with capitals indicating the
subjects, verbs, subject complements, direct objects, and object complements of principal clauses, the embedded clause 6 in brackets, with
an added word to assist the sense in square brackets, and with vertical
bars to indicate pairings of verbs and nouns, whether adjacent or

separated. The line divisions of the sonnet itself are marked by a slash, with a double slash to mark the volta or turn within the traditional sonnet form of octet and sestet. An additional broken bracket marks the repetition of a key phrase denoting communication, 'she says'.

In the Park

```
 1   SHE SITS in the park.
 2   HER CLOTHES ARE OUT OF DATE. /
 3   TWO CHILDREN      |WHINE and
                       |BICKER,
                       |TUG HER SKIRT. /
 4   A THIRD           |DRAWS AIMLESS PATTERNS in the dirt. /
5a   SOMEONE
(6   [whom] she loved once
5b        PASSES BY – too late / to feign indifference
               to that casual nod. /
 7   'HOW NICE,' et cetera. 'TIME HOLDS GREAT SURPRISES.' /
 8   From his neat head unquestionably RISES/A SMALL BALLOON . . .
 9   'but for the grace of God . . .' //
10   THEY STAND a while in flickering light,
       rehearsing / the children's |names and
                              |birthdays. /
11   'IT'S SO SWEET / to |hear their chatter,
                     |watch them |grow and
                              |thrive,' /
12                    {|SHE |SAYS |to his departing smile.
13   Then, nursing / the youngest child,
                     |SITS staring
                     |at her feet. /
14   To the wind {|SHE |SAYS,
15   'THEY HAVE EATEN ME ALIVE.' //
```

This defamiliarized format functions to bring out aspects which the decoder might otherwise ignore. Immediately apparent are the parallels, as in the listing of the children's activities in 3 and 4, and again in 11, though with very different terms chosen to denote them; or in the actions of the unnamed woman in 12, 13, and 14, with 'she says' repeated on either side of '[she] sits', which repeats the opening words in 1.

Alerting a decoder to such parallels is, however, only a starting-point, for their function in their larger context is what is crucial for any exploration of their signification. The opening 'She sits' (line 1) is immediately marked by its third-person form as presenting the point of view of an external narrator, who goes on to give her location in a not very specific phrase, 'in the park' (though the paradigmatic choice of 'the' rather than 'a' implies that narrator and narratee share familiarity with the place). When her passivity in 'sitting' rather than in, say, 'walking' is repeated in 13, however, it is preceded and followed by participles which give much more detail as the narrator pans in to provide a close-up of her, as she nurses the youngest child and looks only at her feet, not at the children.

What is omitted can also be a significant choice in verse discourse; in this case, not only is the woman unidentified by anything but the feminine pronoun, but also there is nothing to indicate the gender or age of the children, though five of the fifteen clauses – 3, 4, 10, 11, 13 – include some mention of them. The focus is not upon the children but on the woman, and the loaded term 'mother' does not occur; it is not even 'her' children, but 'the' children, and the choice hints at her distance from them at this moment of self-recognition, of sudden awareness of the devastating experience she has undergone.

Other choices also imply the narratorial point of view: clause 2 gives loaded information about the woman's clothes, evaluating them rather than describing them, in contrast with, say, 'she is not wearing this year's fashions'. It is not until nearly the end of the sonnet that the connotations of that early evaluative phrase are fully activated, the implication that the woman's familial responsibilities prevent her from keeping up to date with her clothes.

The terms chosen to denote the children's actions in 3 are negatively loaded, and though in her direct speech in 11 the woman uses the more neutral 'chatter', the narratorial viewpoint has already hinted that they are unlovable children, and even the less pejorative comment about the third child in 4 includes the judgemental term 'aimless'. That the woman herself in her speech to her former beloved in 11 does not choose such critical terms for the children can suggest that her view of them is less negative than that of the narrator. But it can also imply that her speech is conditioned by the role model that is assigned her by society, something that she acts out, as the choice in 10 of the term 'rehearsing' (instead of, say, 'relating') hints.

The two parallel instances of her tagged speech within the sestet of the sonnet are crucial for its signification. The first statement in 12, syntagmatically placed after rather than before the direct speech of 11, is addressed not even to the former beloved, but metonymically to 'his departing smile', and thereby suggests that the speech in 11 is conventionally stereotyped, with its sugary opening 'It's so sweet' contrasting so strikingly with the bleakness of setting and earlier narratorial comment on the children. By contrast, the final line's inversion in 14, which foregrounds the initial phrase 'To the wind', stresses that it is only to the intangible non-human listener that the woman can in 15 express her real thoughts, in the most important metaphor of the poem: 'They have eaten me alive', where the figure which compares her situation to that of a victim of a predatory animal expresses her pain and despair, while leaving the referent of 'they' unspecific: is it merely the children, or is it a wider comment upon the society and culture which force her into this stereotype and exploit her susceptibility to its pressures so that her attempts at communication are distorted, and what she says and what she really feels are not the same?[1]

Questions such as these that the choices provoke can easily give support to a feminist reading of the poem, which could also focus upon the black comedy in the presentation of the ex-beloved in clauses 5–9. He is identified merely as 'Someone', and the syntagmatic placement of the embedded clause 6 before his response to the woman is given in 5b[2] suggests that her past feelings for him have altered to the extent that they are now signalled by no more than a 'casual nod'. By contrast he is too late to 'feign indifference', and the adjacence of those two negatively loaded terms explains the banal opening gambit of conversation which is cut short by the narrator's cynical 'et cetera', the familiar abbreviation 'etc.' spelled out in full to suggest that the communicative non-exchange between these former lovers is now so purely routine that it need not be spelled out further.

The only information selected for inclusion about the man's physical appearance is 'neat head', but the narrator reduces him to a cartoon character, as the inversion in 8 of the normal order of 'A small balloon unquestionably rises from his neat head' makes clear. His thought in 9 is itself part of a cliché, 'There but for the grace of God go I', but that it is not given in full demands that a decoder supply what is missing. Reader participation thus becomes crucial to the signification of meaning in the poem. While 'et cetera' is spelled out, the cliché in 9 is not, and knowledge of the rest of the phrase allows a decoder to recognize the man's patronizing attitude, which thus becomes an important part of the whole sociocultural context in which the woman is entrapped.

So far I have been using the reformatted version of the sonnet as a basis for discussing some of the choices within the language. But it is important also to perceive the effect of the verse form itself in foregrounding aspects of the meaning. That Harwood has chosen to use a traditional sonnet form accounts in part for the impact of the poem, and especially for the compression that is so characteristic of that verse form. The sonnet is structured on traditional Petrarchan lines, with two quatrains rhyming abba cddc in the octet, and the sestet rhyming efg efg. Words and phrases associated because of the sound link of rhyme are sometimes sharply contrasted, as in the flippant rhyming of 'nod' and 'God' in lines 5 and 8, or the fatuous 'It's so sweet' of line 9 rhyming with the despair symbolized by 'staring at her feet' in line 13, or the 'grow and thrive' of the children in line 11 being rhymed with the final cannibalistic 'They have eaten me alive'.

As interesting as the impact of the rhymes on signification is the use made of the line divisions. The writer plays here with reader expectations, for the end of the line makes for a visual break which can complement or subvert the sense units. The first three lines end with the end of sentences, but the next line runs over into line 5, straddling the conventional division between quatrains, as the man's response to the woman's presence is problematized by the bringing together in these two lines of temporal and relational terms seemingly at odds with one another: 'once' and 'too late', 'feign indifference', and 'casual'. Line 7 also runs over into the next, as the inversion of the sentence leaves in momentary suspension to the beginning of the next line what it is that rises from the man's head, emphasizing the comic effect of the cartoon character's small balloon thought.

There are only the two run-on lines in the octet. In contrast in the sestet all but the last two lines are run-on, and so because of the preceding sense-flow across the line-end four times, it is lines 13 and 14 which are foregrounded by their abrupt conclusions, the woman staring at her feet, and finally verbalizing what has happened to her.

Though the lines are in general ten syllables long (with an extra final unstressed syllable in lines 6 and 7, 9 and 12), the first and the last lines are longer, the first with its two flat statements within the line that situate the woman in a physical location and in terms of superficial societal judgement. The last retrospectively demands that a decoder go back and re-evaluate all that has preceded, to draw out deeper and broader meanings and associations that underlie the spare and compressed language that leads to such a devastating climax.

The poem is about some of the most widespread of all twentieth-century themes: communication and non-communication, the alienation of the individual, the gap between Self and Other. The woman and the man, representing extremes of Self and Other, do not communicate on any meaningful level, even though there has been a closer bond between them in the past. The alienated woman cannot communicate to any but the non-human wind her bitter recognition of the stereotypical role-model in which the male-dominated society represented by the man's patronizing pity has placed her. But the poet has communicated her situation to a decoder who is prepared to look carefully at the choices of language and their structuring.

SUGGESTIONS FOR FURTHER WORK

1 Go through the sonnet, and, not worrying about the rhyme-scheme, choose other terms for some of the paradigmatic slots which will give more neutral, and then more positive, overtones to the evocation of, first, the children, then the woman, and then the man. Then change the ordering of some of the phrases (even sentences) along the syntagmatic axis to weight the information differently; for example, make the first sentence deal with the children rather than with the woman. What sort of impact do the changes have individually and cumulatively on the concepts signified for different classes of readers, and then upon broader significations of meaning in the poem? Can you suggest choices through which the man's point of view could be presented less offensively to a female decoder? Can you devise other metaphors which would present a different attitude to the children's relationship to the woman? Could different cultural assumptions be implied (for example, if the woman wore slacks rather than a skirt and the man were bearded)? Do such changes enable you to comprehend and show more clearly and fully how Harwood's choices interact in the poem as she has encoded it?

2 Choose another short poem (a sonnet, if possible) and set it out in its syntactic units, bringing out any patterning which seems significant for the meaning. Does the reformatting throw any additional light on the original verse form, its rhythm, its line-ends, its rhymes as they interact with broader aspects of meaning?

3 Compare and contrast a poem by a woman and a poem by a man (if possible on related subject-matter), and try to work out whether there is anything in the choices at paradigmatic and syntagmatic level or at the signifier/signified level which enable you to assign each to the appropriate writer. Does the micro-analysis of language choices help you to move on to larger aspects of sociocultural and ideological analysis in such a task?

4 Compare and contrast a poem by a poet from a western cultural background and a poem by a poet from another cultural background and examine various significant choices made by each. How do they point to each poet's cultural presuppositions?

5 Collect a few poems that deal with various types of communication, and explore some aspects of how their encoding and decoding encourages and subverts communication: for instance, William Meredith's 'The Illiterate', Richard Wilbur's 'Praise in Summer', Philip Larkin's 'Talking in Bed', John Ashbery's 'Paradoxes and Oxymorons', W.S. Merwin's 'Odysseus', Adrienne Rich's 'Aunt Jennifer's Tigers', Margaret Atwood's 'Pig Song' (all in Allison 1983).

NOTES

1 Andrew Taylor in 'Gwen Harwood: The Golden Child Aloft on Discourse', in Sellick (1987: 73–91) (reprinted in Taylor (1987: 112–125)), suggests (and rejects the idea) that 'They' in 15 could be the woman's feet. Such a suggestion (ridiculed by Mark Macleod in his review of both books in *Australian Literary Studies* 13 (1988): 393–8) ignores the rhyme link between the children's pelican-like thriving and the woman's recognition of her being eaten alive.

2 Taylor, 'Gwen Harwood', assumes that it is the woman who is surprised before she can 'feign indifference'. This reading seems to ignore the embedding of 6, with the main clause being 'Someone . . . passes by', the added temporal modification elaborating on his reaction. But the choice of the deictic 'that' in 'that casual nod' allows for some destabilizing of the roles at this point.

REFERENCES

Allison, Alexander *et al.* (eds) (1983) *The Norton Anthology*, 3rd edn, New York and London: W.W. Norton & Company.

Carter, R. (1982) *Language and Literature: An Introductory Reader in Stylistics*, London: Allen & Unwin.

Carter, R. and Simpson, P. (1989) *Language, Discourse and Literature: An Introductory Reader in Discourse Stylistics*, London: Allen & Unwin.

Sellick, Robert (ed.) (1987) *Gwen Harwood*, Adelaide: CRNLE Publications.

Stephens, J. and Waterhouse, R. (1990) *Literature, Language and Change: From Chaucer to the Present*, London: Routledge.

Taylor, Andrew (ed.) (1987) *Reading Australian Poetry*, St Lucia, Queensland: University of Queensland Press.

9 Poetry and public life: a contextualized reading of Seamus Heaney's 'Punishment'

Peter Verdonk

EDITOR'S PREFACE

Seamus Heaney is an Irish poet, who writes in English. He was born and educated in Northern Ireland, the eldest son in a Catholic farming family. His life as a poet has coincided with the most recent period of the Northern Irish Troubles, as they are euphemistically called. This mini biography signifies a life lived in a world of cultural, political, and religious division. His poem 'Terminus' from *The Haw Lantern* (1987) contains these lines:

> Two buckets were easier carried than one.
> I grew up in between.

> My left hand placed the standard iron weight.
> My right tilted a last grain in the balance.

In the first instance, 'Terminus' is about what Heaney called his 'in-between boyhood', but in a wider perspective these lines present an appropriate image of his later position between two worlds of experience. Though their double weight means a heavier burden, the poet prefers to carry two buckets so that he can keep his balance. Indeed, in a country like Ireland, it is safer to carry two buckets, otherwise one might end up in one of the camps which keep the country divided against itself. Therefore, Heaney has always been anxious not to become the mouthpiece of either of the contending parties, though much, if not all, of his poetry is deeply affected by this mood of discord. This classic conflict between the artist's autonomy and his dependence is the starting-point of my contextualized stylistic reading of Heaney's much-discussed 'Punishment' from his collection *North* (1975b), which contains some of his most 'committed' poems.

For such an approach it is necessary to treat the poem as a

contextualized discourse, which means in this case a context-bound and interpersonal act of communication. Though aware of the intricacy of the notion of context, I see it as comprising both the wider social, cultural, and historical backgrounds and the narrower context of the immediate situation of utterance. After relating the poem to some of its cultural, political, and artistic contexts, I distinguish the following basic components of its immediate situational context.

First, it is assumed that the actual readers of the poem are an element of its context, in that their interpretations are inevitably affected by their own beliefs and attitudes.

Second, being bent on communicating with the author, readers will search his poem for clues to its context of place and time. Obviously, authors may be expected to provide such clues because they wish to draw the reader into the text's situation.

Third, there is the interpersonal context to consider, i.e., what is the nature of the references to the poem's speaker and to the reader?

The fourth and last contextual component that exerts influence on the language of a text is the genre of discourse. In fact, this element is closely connected with the interpersonal context, because speakers/writers are normally inclined to adapt their style to the discourse genre they are engaged in, for instance, conversation, advertising, journalism, or literature.

Having thus placed the poem in its contextual framework and having assessed Heaney's rhetorical and stylistic strategies, I come to the conclusion that the poet has proved himself a successful performer in his balancing act between his artistic and political commitments.

P. V.

THE DEBATE BETWEEN ARTISTIC AND POLITICAL COMMITMENTS

One of Seamus Heaney's prose books is entitled *The Government of the Tongue* (1988). It is an ambiguous title because it appears to hold a hint of an old conflict: should the tongue (in the sense of the poet's individual talent as well as the common linguistic resource) be governed or should it be the governor? It is the conflict between art's isolation and participation, between its autonomy and dependence, and, more in particular, between poetry and public life. In the title essay of his book, Heaney proposes the following modus:

The fact is that poetry is its own reality and no matter how much a poet may concede to the corrective pressures of social, moral, political and historical reality, the ultimate fidelity must be to the demands and promise of the artistic event.

(Heaney 1988: 101)

This is very much a self-conscious statement and that on two accounts. Though an Irish poet, born and bred in Northern Ireland, he appears to be regarded as a representative English-language poet: witness the inclusion of a generous selection from his poetry in *The Penguin Book of Contemporary British Poetry*, edited by Blake Morrison and Andrew Motion (1982). On more than one occasion, he has expressed his anxiety about this dilemma, for instance, in his inaugural lecture as Oxford Professor of Poetry. Then he said that he always feels the pull of the claims and counter-claims exerted by the terms 'English literature' and 'Irish' or 'Anglo-Irish literature'. Using a forceful image to make his point, he claimed that all writers in his position 'are caught on the forked stick of their love of the English language itself. Helplessly, they kiss the rod of the consciousness which subjugated them' (Heaney 1990: 9).

FINDING A MYTH

The other, probably even more compelling reason for this balancing between the poetic and the political is the fact that Heaney's life as a poet has been virtually coterminous with the most recent period of the Northern Irish Troubles. In the early 1970s when he had become a public figure, he came under increasing pressure to display in his work his concern and involvement, and his artistic anxieties about having to respond in direct terms must have felt relieved when he had been reading a book entitled *The Bog People: Iron Age Man Preserved*, written by the Danish archaeologist P.V. Glob and published in 1969 (Heaney 1980: 57–8, Haffenden 1981: 57)). It reports on the excavations of bodies of Iron Age people buried in bogs in north-western Europe, particularly in Denmark and Ireland. What he found in the book revived his own childhood images of bogland and it provided him with symbols and a mythical background enabling him to put the contemporary political scene in a wider historical and cultural perspective. At about the same time he had moved from Northern Ireland to the south, to Dublin, which must have created a perspective of geographical distance as well.

From these new imaginative and physical viewpoints he was able to look back towards Northern Ireland as a country of the mind and he wrote a sequence of poems published in a limited edition as *Bog Poems*

(1975a), which were subsequently included in a larger collection significantly called *North* (1975b).

One of these bog corpses described and photographed by Glob is that of a girl. Her peat-covered body was entirely naked, her hair was shaved off, a blindfold was tied over her eyes and she wore an oxhide collar round her neck. Probably she had been punished for adultery. The following poem tells us how strongly Heaney identifies himself with this girl, both personally and socially:

Punishment

I can feel the tug
of the halter at the nape
of her neck, the wind
on her naked front.

5 It blows her nipples
to amber beads,
it shakes the frail rigging
of her ribs.

I can see her drowned
10 body in the bog,
the weighing stone,
the floating rods and boughs.

Under which at first
she was a barked sapling
15 that is dug up
oak-bone, brain-firkin:

her shaved head
like a stubble of black corn,
her blindfold a soiled bandage,
20 her noose a ring

to store
the memories of love.
Little adulteress,
before they punished you

25 you were flaxen-haired,
undernourished, and your
tar-black face was beautiful.
My poor scapegoat,

I almost love you
30 but would have cast, I know,
    the stones of silence.
    I am the artful voyeur

    of your brain's exposed
    and darkened combs,
35 your muscles' webbing
    and all your numbered bones:

    I who have stood dumb
    when your betraying sisters,
    cauled in tar,
40 wept by the railings,

    who would connive
    in civilized outrage
    yet understand the exact
    and tribal, intimate revenge.
                    (Heaney 1975b)

THE SHIFTING IDENTITY OF THE POET'S PERSONA

When saying that *Heaney* strongly identifies himself with the Iron Age girl, we touch on the question as to how far the 'persona' or 'speaker' in a poem can be identified with the poet. It is a literary convention that the moment authors start writing they create personae both for themselves and for their intended readers. Obviously, these personae do not flesh out either the writers themselves as they 'really' are, or any of their actual readers. Even so, with regard to the author/persona relationship, it can be held that there is what we might describe as a sliding scale of correspondence between these two. So at one end of this scale, a text may signal to the reader not to assume any correspondence whatsoever between the author and his or her persona, while at the other end, the distance between the two may be practically negligible (Verdonk 1991: 101–2). As a matter of fact, within the poem under discussion there appears to be such a line. Thus, in the first nine stanzas the speaker and the poet need not necessarily be identical. However, in the last two stanzas the identity gap seems to be as good as bridged because the speaker is felt to be very close to the poet's own experience and sensibility. It is even arguable that it is Heaney who is imagining the bog girl of Glob's account as the 'sister' of those Northern Irish girls who were tarred, feathered and tied to railings as a punishment for going out with English soldiers. And, for the same reason, it is plausible that it is Heaney who passes the ambivalent self-judgement. In support of this assumption, I could point to Heaney's own idea of his poetry as a revelation of identities:

> poetry as divination, poetry as revelation of the self to the self, as restoration of the culture to itself; poems as elements of continuity, with the aura and authenticity of archaeological finds, where the buried shard has an importance that is not diminished by the importance of the buried city.
>
> (Heaney 1980: 41)

THE ACTUAL READER AS AN ELEMENT OF THE POEM'S CONTEXT

Whether they are correct or not, it has only been possible for me to draw these particular inferences about the poet's identity and self-definition, because I have played an active role as an actual reader by contextualizing the poem, at least to a certain extent. Thus, I have gathered some information about Heaney's dilemmas arising from his double cultural identity as well as from the tensions between his artistic and political commitments. Furthermore, I have gained an impression of the mythical background which enabled the poet to relate the past to the present and so to universalize sectarian violence in Northern Ireland.

How far my first reaction to the poem differs from what Heaney would have liked to hear from his intended reader, I do not know, but what it does show in general terms is that the actual reader of a text is an element of its context, i.e., the whole complex of factors affecting its meaning and interpretation. To put it differently, in the interactive process between author, text, and actual readers, the latter are not only affected by the text, they can also exert influence on its interpretation (Mills 1992: 182–205). Clearly, this influence differs from reader to reader because they do not bring to texts the same presuppositions and assumptions. They are female or male, belong to a different time or generation, come from different cultural and societal backgrounds, and, therefore, not surprisingly, have different beliefs and attitudes. For instance, some critics have perceived 'Catholic' and 'Republican' attitudes in 'Punishment'. In particular the last two stanzas have raised several eyebrows at Heaney's position on IRA violence. Is the speaker's understanding also a condoning (O'Brien 1975: 404–5, cited in Corcoran 1986: 116)? And Blake Morrison (1980: 109–10), though not wishing to suggest that 'Punishment' in particular and the Bog poems in general uphold the Republican cause, is critical of the mythical framework, which he feels to be a form of 'explanation' (the quotes are Morrison's). In fact he finds that the whole procedure of *North* lends an historical respectability to sectarian killing in Ulster. It will be obvious that these and other criticisms have also become part of the poem's context because readers taking cognizance of them may very well become prejudiced in their interpretation.

These responses as well as my own appear to bear out the assumption offered in this chapter that once readers are drawn into a text's contextual orbit, so to speak, they not only decode or interpret meanings but also encode or create them. On the other hand, this premise does not imply that the interpretation of a text can result in a free-for-all. For though a lot of research has been done on the role of readers, on how they negotiate with a text, i.e., accept or reject it, or respond to it in any other way, the fact remains that the primary impetus for all these responses virtually always comes from the text. So the text is our common starting-point because it is generally acknowledged that there is, as a rule, a considerable interpretative consensus about a great deal of its linguistic features. Therefore, I would like to propose a stylistic analysis of Heaney's 'Punishment' that is conditioned by a dynamic interaction between the poem's text and its context.

THE POEM AS A CONTEXTUALIZED DISCOURSE[1]

Such an approach requires that I should regard the poem as the representation of a discourse. Because this word has become one of the most overworked terms in linguistics, I have to specify that it is used here as a description of the whole complicated process of interaction between people producing and interpreting texts. Furthermore, it is evident that these communicative activities are always pursued in a particular context. What is said, how it is said and how it is comprehended is always partly determined by a wide variety of contextual factors. In actual fact, we can even say that the context or situation precedes the discourse to which it is related.

Though the notion of context is open to many interpretations, I will be using it here in its sense of the whole environment in which a discourse occurs, ranging from the narrower context of utterance, i.e., the more immediate situation of the discourse, to the much wider context of social, cultural, or historical factors. Of course, such a contextual framework is infinitely extendable so that I can only hope to touch on a fraction of it in my discussion of Heaney's poem. Thus, I have so far looked briefly at some of its cultural, political, and artistic backgrounds and will now bring into focus some aspects of its context of utterance. But in doing so I have to make some brief excursions into a few technical matters. In particular I will be examining those features of a text that reflect the major components of its context of utterance, which comprises the physical and temporal situation of the participants in the discourse; the channel or medium of expression; the relationships obtaining between the participants; the genre or type of discourse.

THE SPATIAL AND TEMPORAL CONTEXT

To begin with, we have to distinguish between contexts in which the participants in a discourse are in each other's presence sharing the same place and time, like in face-to-face conversation, and contexts in which the participants are physically separated. For instance, in telephone conversations or live radio or television broadcasts the participants share the same time (unless, of course, there is a time difference), but not the same place, while in the case of letters and most other types of written texts the participants (i.e., the addresser and addressee) share neither time nor place: what is 'here and now' for the addresser becomes 'there and then' for the addressee, and the other way around.

Presumably because they are verbal creatures, readers follow their communicative instincts by searching a text for clues as to how they must visualize or reconstruct a particular context of place and time. In 'Punishment' we can see how the poet provides such clues. For instance, by his use of the definite article the first-person speaker assumes that 'the tug of the halter', 'the nape of her neck', 'the wind on her naked front', 'the bog', 'the weighing stone', etc., are as 'definite' for the reader as they are for himself. Similarly, by using the present tense in 'I can feel', 'It blows', 'it shakes', 'I can see', 'I almost love you', etc., the speaker suggests that his present is the readers' present and that his place is their place. So by creating the impression that poet and reader share a number of contextual factors, this stylistic device has the obvious effect of drawing the reader into the situation.

THE INTERPERSONAL CONTEXT

In addition to this spatial and temporal perspective, a discourse is also related to an interpersonal context, which comprises the identities of the speaker or writer and the addressee, including their social relationship. In everyday face-to-face conversation, as we have seen, speaker and listener can normally identify each other, but in all the other discourse types mentioned the situation is obviously different. So even a simple written message like 'Meet me here tomorrow' cannot be properly interpreted without knowing its interpersonal context, i.e., the identity of the sender hidden behind the pronoun 'me' and that of the addressee implicitly referred to by the imperative 'meet'. (Obviously, we must also know the spatial and temporal context, i.e., the exact place and time, intimated by the adverbs 'here' and 'tomorrow'.)

Poetry, for that matter, shows a wide variety of interpersonal contexts. For instance, poems written in the first person may be addressed to an identified or an unidentified 'you' inside the poem. Other poems are addressed to an outside 'you' or to no one in particular. Still other first-person speakers may address the west wind, a Grecian urn, or a ship. Neither need the first-person speaker be a human being. Thus, we may be hearing a hawk speaking to no one in particular as in Ted Hughes's 'Hawk Roosting'. Then there are also instances in which the first-person narrator, though human, cannot possibly be the poet. For example, the narrator in T.S. Eliot's 'Journey of the Magi', who is one of the three Magi in a reminiscent mood asking an unidentified listener to write down his recollections. Finally, though it would not be difficult to add still other types of discourse situations, there are of course also many poems in which the speakers efface themselves completely by not referring to themselves in the first person at all.

Nevertheless, however bizarre or unorthodox the discourse situation within a poem may be, a 'frame' discourse between poet and reader, a silent communion, so to speak, is always taken for granted. In fact, part of the interest of a poem comes from this double perspective. Thus, as a result of the poet's discoursal strategies the reader may feel estranged from the situation or, conversely, may feel deeply involved with it. It may also be that the identities of the participants in a poem's discourse undergo some change, which makes it necessary for the reader to reassess the situation. In this connection, I have already pointed out the shifting identity of Heaney's persona in 'Punishment'.

Apart from this aspect, the presence of the persona is quite conspicuous and his impact on the poem seems to be very strong. Indeed the poem's first word is the pronoun 'I' and it returns at repeated intervals in equally prominent positions in the opening or closing lines of several stanzas. Up to line 22 the speaker addresses an assumed audience in the outside world, giving a perceptive account of how he imagines the girl's punishment to have been and describing graphically the effects on her body of its long immersion in the bog. Then, about halfway through the poem in line 23, the speaker begins to direct his words at the girl so that the earlier audience now finds itself listening in to what is essentially a very intimate address. Stylistically, this intimacy is greatly reinforced by a relatively high frequency of the second-person pronoun 'you(r)' acting in conjunction with the dominant pattern of the first-person pronoun 'I'. Even so, this reader does not feel left out. On the contrary, all the time I have a feeling that the speaker is working round to his own predicament which he wants to share with me. This impression is supported by textual evidence because the pronoun 'you' addressing the bog girl, which is such a dominant stylistic feature of the preceding stanzas, has vanished from the last. It is here that the speaker expresses the essence of his moral and artistic dilemma.

SPATIAL AND TEMPORAL DEIXIS

Our discussion in the preceding two paragraphs has clearly shown that language contains a category of words and phrases which directly relate an utterance to a speaker's or writer's place and time, and which therefore take their meanings in part from the the situational context in which they are used. For instance, you cannot interpret the meaning of 'here' in the utterance 'The book is here', without knowing where the speaker is situated. These words or phrases are called deictics, while the linguistic phenomenon in general is called deixis (from a Greek word meaning 'pointing').

Some obvious examples of deictics include the spatial terms 'here', 'there', 'in the next village', 'miles from here', etc., the demonstratives 'this/these' and 'that/those', temporal expressions like 'now', 'then', 'today', 'yesterday', 'last Thursday', etc., and the present and past tenses of verbs. Hence the cited instances of the present-tensed verbs from our poem are deictically used because they indicate the time to which the speaker relates the events he describes. In this case, it is of course an imaginary present, which, as we have seen, also 'positions' the reader.

One of the uses of the definite article 'the' can also be called deictic. It does not point to things close to or further away from the speaker, like *this* and *that*, but to things within the speaker's world either already shared or to be shared with the addressee (Traugott and Pratt 1980: 280). For example, *the* in 'Do you remember when we met at the university?' refers back to something already shared by speaker and addressee. On the other hand, from the question 'Have you already visited the castle?' the addressee is to conclude that it must be 'the castle in the speaker's town', i.e., that it is anchored in the speaker's context, and that the addressee is therefore invited to share the speaker's familiarity with it.

Similarly, when the speaker in 'Punishment' uses the definite article in the instances quoted above, he wants his experience and emotions to be absorbed into the reader's world. On the other hand, the speaker's use of the indefinite article *a* in 'she was a barked sapling', 'her blindfold a soiled bandage', 'her shaved head like a stubble of black corn', and 'her noose a ring' seems to signal that he has not yet internalized these observations, in other words, that they have not yet been incorporated in his world of experience.

Though it does not weaken my argument that Heaney's use of the deictic article has the effect of thrusting the reader into the situational context of the poem, there is a more exact if at first sight more prosaic explanation for some of the instances of the article in that, for example, 'the halter', 'the bog', 'the weighing stone', and 'the floating rods and boughs' may refer to certain details in the photographs of the girl illustrating Glob's book on the bog bodies. Of course, Heaney may not have had the actual photographs in front of him when writing the poem and some of the things he describes may very well be the product of his imagination. But, however it may be, this does not detract from the deictic or 'pointing' function of this specific use of the article because the pictures were actually present in the poet's immediate context of utterance.

It was Henry Widdowson (1975: 10–13) who first pointed out this particular use of the article with reference to the poem 'Leda and the Swan' by Yeats, who is presumed to have made use of a reproduction of Michelangelo's picture on the subject. Furthermore, both Halliday (1966: 59) and Widdowson made the interesting observation that this function is a common feature of the English used in tourist guides and exhibition catalogues. In these, too, the article's function is deictic because it points to external objects (for example, paintings, sculptures, altars in churches, gates of castles, etc.) which are supposed to be part of the immediate situation or context when the reader reads about them: 'To reach the battlements, visitors will pass the dungeon head on their right and the guard room of the north west tower' (from a visitors' guide to Saltwood Castle in Kent).[2]

INTERPERSONAL DEIXIS

In addition to the deictics which situate a discourse in a context of place and time, there are other deictic words which mark out the participants in a discourse as speaker or writer and addressee, and therefore indicate the interpersonal context. These interpersonal deictics include the first-

and second-person pronouns *I*, *we*, and *you* and of course their related forms like *me*, *myself*, etc. I have already pointed out the dominant position of these interpersonal deictics in 'Punishment' and gone into their stylistic effect on my reading of the poem.

Furthermore, the interpersonal context of a discourse is filled in by what are usually called social deictics. These can reveal information about the social identities of the participants including their attitudes, statuses, and roles, and the permanent or temporary social relationships obtaining between them. Obvious examples are forms of address, honorifics (i.e., titles given to people as a sign of respect or honour), words denoting kinship, markers of intimacy, and, of course, dishonorifics (Levinson 1983: 89). The latter include, for instance, any kind of address term discriminating against women, race, class or political and religious views. As Kate Clark (1992: 208–24) has recently shown, naming is a powerful ideological tool which also tells a lot about the views and beliefs of the namer. Different names for people point to different ways of seeing them. Clark illustrates her assertion with the example of the varied references to people who use violence to achieve their political aims. Are they terrorists, guerrillas, freedom-fighters, rebels, or resistance fighters? Clearly, these labels suggest different degrees of legitimacy and approval.

So from the socially deictic terms used by the speaker in 'Punishment' we can also make certain inferences about his motives for addressing the bog girl as 'little adulteress' and 'my poor scapegoat'. At first sight, there appears to be affection and compassion in the modifiers 'little' and 'my poor', while in the first instance the name 'adulteress' may have been prompted by the archaeologist's conjectures about the reason for the girl's penalty. At the same time one might wonder whether it is the girl's presumed adultery that incites the perverted sexual thrill which, by his own admission, the poem's speaker derives from the sight of the shrivelled but fully preserved corpse, imagining her nipples hardened by the wind blowing on her naked front. And whether it brings out 'the artful voyeur' in him, gloating over the exposed inner parts of her head and body:

I am the artful voyeur

of your brain's exposed
and darkened combs,
your muscles' webbing
and all your numbered bones:

The allusion in the last line to a Catholic psalm about Christ saying

'They have pierced my hands and feet; they have numbered all my bones', throws into relief the biblical associations of the name 'scapegoat'. It is the scapegoat of the Mosaic ritual (Leviticus 16: 8) which is symbolically loaded with the sins of the people and driven into the wilderness, and therefore used as an allusion to Christ in Catholic worship. Indeed, there appears to be a causal chain involved in this name-giving, because the label 'adulteress' has biblical links too. She figures in the gospel story about the woman who is taken in adultery and is therefore to be punished by being stoned to death. But Jesus says to the scribes and Pharisees: 'He that is without sin among you, let him first cast a stone at her' (John 8: 7). The ensuing silence is of course an admission of their own sins for which they wanted to make the adulterous woman the scapegoat. By now it is becoming clear why it is these names that emerged from the speaker's consciousness. He realizes that, though his pity is close to love, if he had lived at the time of the bog girl he too would have remained silent, and would not have had the courage to defend her:

> My poor scapegoat,
>
> I almost love you
> but would have cast, I know,
> the stones of silence.

The poet's self-rebuke continues and the 'weighing stone' which kept the girl's body down in the bog now weighs heavily on his conscience, because in his own days he also stood by doing nothing when Northern Irish girls, the bog girl's 'betraying sisters', were punished for befriending British soldiers. Their heads too were shaved and tarred by extremists, who then chained them to railings as a deterrent to others. Of course, he used to join in the civilized voices of protest, but in fact he had allowed it to happen, concealing his deep-rooted understanding of the interminable urge for public vengeance:

> I who have stood dumb
> when your betraying sisters,
> cauled in tar,
> wept by the railings,
>
> who would connive
> in civilized outrage
> yet understand the exact
> and tribal, intimate revenge.

The poet must learn to live with his own punishment, which is that his art forbids him to take sides. He must remain 'the voyeur', the prying observer, who must be 'artful', i.e., not only devious but also literally 'full of art'. Yet, it is this very same artfulness which enables the poet to draw the bitter analogy between a victim of tribal retribution in the Iron Age and the victims of sectarian violence in these Christian days.

THE EGOCENTRICITY OF DEIXIS

My final observation about deictics is that they are 'speaker-centred'. Since human beings are inclined to see themselves as the centre of things, speakers locate their discourses predominantly in relation to their own viewpoint. (I hasten to assure the reader that this is of course not intended as a moralizing observation.) Being after all a potential speaker too, the addressee plays the game and relates the meanings of 'here and now' or 'there and then' to the place and time in which the speaker or writer is anchored. In fact, this egocentricity is the quintessence of deixis and of high relevance to literary analysis. Hence authors very often begin a narrative using a number of definite articles. As we have seen earlier in Heaney's poem, this creates stylistically the impression that writer and reader already share some knowledge about the situational context so that the reader is quickly drawn into the narrative. Consider as another example of this stylistic device the opening sentences from D.H. Lawrence's short story *The Shades of Spring* (1985): 'It was a mile nearer through the wood. Mechanically, Syson turned up by the forge and lifted the field-gate. The blacksmith and his mate stood still, watching the trespasser.'

THE GENRE OR TYPE OF DISCOURSE

Yet another contextual feature which the language of a text chimes in with is the genre or type of discourse. Actually, the matter of genre is closely linked with the interpersonal context, because in a discourse situation speakers and writers tend to adapt their language, i.e., their style, to all kinds of conventions imposed by their social roles and settings. This is a reciprocal process, in that also the addressees of a discourse are tuned in to these socialized stylistic conventions. Thus, if we have made ourselves familiar with a particular discourse genre, we have usually also developed a sense of what is stylistically appropriate in a given situation.

In any speech community there are naturally innumerable discourse genres and I will therefore only mention the following widely divergent examples: neighbours having a friendly chat over the garden fence, a journalist interviewing the United States President on TV, managers meeting in the boardroom, a child talking with her grandparents. As these instances show, we can often distinguish various subgenres within a particular discourse genre. So the speech events I have just mentioned would presumably come within the genre of conversation. Likewise, within the discourse genre of the mass media we could distinguish subgenres like television, radio, newspapers, and magazines. Then, of course, further subgenres can be distinguished within each of these: for example news reports, documentaries, quiz shows, etc., within TV discourse.

Since the communicative process I have in mind also produces texts which in a particular culture are recognized as literary, the phenomenon of literature will also be identified as a discourse genre. Here, too, there are broad subgenres like prose, poetry, and drama, each of which can be further classified: for example the novel and short story within prose; lyrical, epic, and narrative genres within poetry; and comedy, tragedy, and farce within drama.

Being imaginative compositions, literary texts are commonly associated with highly individual stylistic expression. However, like most if not all discourse genres, literature is at the same time subject to a great many conventions. Hence the language of poetry is characteristically self-involved, which is most evident in its phonological tissue (metre, rhythm, alliteration, rhyme, etc.), its spatial arrangement in lines and stanzas, particular semantic phenomena like imagery, figures of speech (metaphor, simile, oxymoron, irony, etc.), and parallelistic patterns in its sounds, vocabulary, or syntax. Furthermore, there are of course the specific conventions developed in subgenres such as the epic, the lyric, the sonnet, the pastoral, etc.

As we have seen, learning the genre conventions of non-literary discourses is in fact a matter of socialization. In the same way, we will have to acquaint ourselves with the practices of literary discourses if we wish to establish a satisfactory rapport with their artistic originators.

SOME GENRE CHARACTERISTICS OF POETRY

The form in which I have written the foregoing sections has made me embarrassingly aware that I have separated certain aspects of poetry which in fact cannot be separated. The discourse of poetry is a tightly-knit network of textual and contextual elements which constantly reinforce each other in meaning. Therefore, whenever we examine one or other element individually, we are doing something that is artistically unpardonable. On the other hand, if we wish to communicate with each other about a poem or any other work of art for that matter, we must be practical about it and reconcile ourselves to this inadequacy. In this spirit you are asked to read the following discussion about some formal features which are stereotypical of the discourse of poetry, but should be viewed as part of the complex social and cultural process I have tried to describe briefly in the preceding paragraphs.

In an attempt to track down Heaney's rhetorical or stylistic strategies, if this is at all possible, I must indulge in a certain degree of idealization because in reality language is by no means as neatly organized and partitioned as I am going to make it out here. So it is assumed that, prompted by his artistic talent, and consciously or intuitively, the poet has chosen certain linguistic structures in preference to others which are potentially available in the language he is using. From this we could conclude that the artistically or rhetorically motivated choices he has made together form the poem's stylistic design. Clearly, it is these choices that dominate the structure of the poem's discourse.

Furthermore, it is assumed that the poet has made his choices on particular levels of the structure of language. Though there are various models distinguishing different numbers of levels, in this chapter I shall be making use of the following six-level model of structure:

1	GRAPHOLOGY	(TYPOGRAPHICAL FEATURES)
2	PHONOLOGY	(SOUNDS, RHYTHM, ETC.)
3	LEXIS	(VOCABULARY)
4	SYNTAX	(GRAMMATICAL STRUCTURES)
5	SEMANTICS	(CONSIDERATIONS OF MEANING)
6	PRAGMATICS	(CONTEXTUAL FEATURES)

Needless to say, any choice on any of the levels of graphology, phonology, lexis, and syntax is co-determined by considerations of meaning, i.e., the semantic level, as well as by a wide variety of contextual features, i.e., the pragmatic level.

To begin with, one of the contextual elements I mentioned earlier is that 'Punishment' is included in a collection entitled *North* (1975b), which brings up various associations, especially after reading the other poems. For me it offers evocations of the grimness of the landscape and climate in northern Europe, the northern origin of the Vikings, who invaded and settled at several places in the north of Ireland, the northern homelands of the Anglo-Saxons fighting their endless inter-tribal wars and clinging to their rigid codes of honour and revenge, the supposedly consonantal or guttural accents of the northern peoples, and, of course, there is the allusion to present-day Northern Ireland with its contemporary conflicts and violence, the place where the poet grew up and where his attitudes and beliefs were formed. To bring out this context, the poet has made a specific choice on the phonological level. Instead of using end-rhyme as an organizing device, he has chosen to structure his poem by internal sound patterns in the form of alliteration, which is the repetition of the consonant sound at the beginning of two or more words. The way Heaney handles this verse form is strongly reminiscent of the staple verse line of Anglo-Saxon poetry, which consisted of two half-lines bridged by a pattern of alliterating heavily stressed syllables and was founded on a centuries-old Germanic oral tradition. Presumably, the poet's choice also intimates his idea that the alliterative tradition forced itself upon Irish literary culture. In 'Traditions', a poem included in *Wintering Out* (1972), the first book he published after he had left Northern Ireland to live in the Irish Republic, he wrote: 'Our guttural muse/was bulled long ago/by the alliterative tradition'.

In addition to many alliterative pairs like 'blows', 'beads', 'rigging', 'ribs', 'body', 'bog', and so on, some of the alliterative patterns in 'Punishment' are even repeated: in the first and second stanzas we find 'the halter at the nape', 'of her neck', 'on her naked front', 'it blows her nipples'; similarly, the third and fourth stanzas are linked by the following patterns: 'a barked sapling', 'a stubble of black corn', 'her blindfold a soiled bandage'. Clearly, this patterning has a cohesive function, linking words together at the level of sound. At the same time, these alliterations, in conjunction with the pounding rhythm of the basic system of two or three stresses, reinforce the semantic inter-relationships of many sets of words. Undoubtedly, you will have noticed many disturbing combinations like 'the frail rigging of her ribs', 'her drowned body in the bog', 'her blindfold a soiled bandage', 'the stones of silence', etc.

On the lexical level, Heaney uses yet another stylistic device of Anglo-Saxon poetry, namely the *kenning*, which was also a feature of Old Norse poetry, for that matter. It is a kind of compressed metaphor consisting of a compound of two words used instead of a common word. The sun, for instance, could be referred to as 'world-candle', and a ship, as 'wave cleaver'. In 'Punishment' you will now recognize a similar device in the descriptive images of the parts of the girl's body, which due to their age-long submergence in the bog have become vegetable objects: her nipples are 'amber beads' (amber is a yellowish fossilized resin), her body when it was thrown naked into the bog was a 'barked sapling' (a young tree with its bark stripped off), but when it was dug up her bones were hard as oak ('oak-bone'), her exposed brain resembled a fir cone ('brain-firkin'), and her shaved head was like a 'stubble of black corn'.

If you linger a little longer on the lexical level, you will furthermore notice that these Nordic associations are also accentuated by the poet's preference for vocabulary of Anglo-Saxon origin. Nearly all the concrete and earthy imagery is deeply rooted in the Germanic core of the English language, while a minority of words stemming from its French or Latin influx such as 'connive', 'civilized', 'exact', 'intimate', 'revenge', etc. are employed to refer to the abstractions related to the ambivalent attitude the poet takes in the last stanza.

There is one descriptive term of French origin, though, which deserves our special attention. It is the word 'cauled' occurring in the disconcerting lines 'when your betraying sisters,/cauled in tar,/wept by the railings'. The poet has coined his word from the noun 'caul', which was formerly used for a netted cap worn by women to enclose their hair. The reason why he has chosen this obsolete word must be that it has another meaning which turns out to be bitterly ironic. As it is, a caul was also used to describe the inner membrane enclosing the foetus before birth and which sometimes envelops the head of the child at birth. 'Being born with a caul on one's head' was held to be a charm bringing good luck. The word becomes even more intriguing if we extend it to the Northern Irish girls' 'sister', the Iron Age girl drowned in the bog, because a caul was supposed to be a preservative against drowning. According to *Brewer's Dictionary of Phrase and Fable* (Cassell's edition of 1980), they were once advertised for sale and frequently sought after by mariners. This digression leads me to the maritime imagery used to describe the wind blowing on the bog girl's skeletal body in the opening stanzas: 'the wind blows her nipples . . . it shakes the frail rigging of her ribs'. This description conjures up an image of sails filling out, with the wind shaking a poor arrangement of ropes, shrouds, and stays supporting the mast of a ship, which is eventually wrecked. What is left are some 'floating rods and boughs'.

On the graphological level, which involves the poem's layout, the basic two- or three-stress pattern lends a long and narrow shape to the poem with the short lines often embracing one semantically comprehensible unit, for example, 'I can feel the tug', 'it blows her nipples', 'it shakes the frail rigging', 'body in the bog', 'the weighing stone', and so forth. This peculiar structure appears to be iconic of the process of excavation. Just like the archaeologists have dug up the girl's body by removing the soil layer after layer, the poet, too, in trying to contain his emotions reveals them bit by bit. Interestingly, this implied sense of the poem's shape would be in keeping with Heaney's view of poetry as 'a dig, a dig for finds that end up being plants' (Heaney 1980: 41).

Most of the phonological, lexical, and graphological features I have been able to distinguish tend to show that this particular discourse is a poem, an artefact. Yet there is a counter-force loosening this cohesive structure. This force is the poem's syntax, the grammatical arrangement of its sentences, which in itself is quite regular but all the same disturbs the tight order of the poem by not respecting the line units. In fact, in several places it even exceeds the stanzaic units. Now, in conjunction with the absence of end-rhyme, which would have marked off the line boundaries, the syntactic pull of these enjambed or run-on lines carries this reader steadily through to the end. For me the poem has a strong narrative element and when reading it aloud, I associate it with ordinary speech. In this way the poem becomes a double-edged discourse accommodating both the 'artfulness' of poetry and the 'ordinariness' of everyday human speech, and goes a long way towards fulfilling the poet's artistic ambition to strike a balance between poetry and public life.

SUGGESTIONS FOR FURTHER WORK

1 In this chapter it is argued that there is as a rule a considerable consensus about the interpretation of texts. If this were not the case, communication would become very difficult. On the other hand, it is also arguable that the actual reader of a text is an element of its context, in that s/he actually influences its meaning and interpretation. Read in small groups of students the poem 'Edge' by Sylvia Plath (1965) and try to establish the degree of common understanding and at what points in the text opinions begin to differ considerably. Work out for yourself the reasons for your individual response. Your answers to these questions may well lead to a contextualized stylistic analysis of this poem.

2 Describe the discourse situation in Seamus Heaney's 'Making Strange' from *Station Island* (1984). It appears that the speaker in the poem is caught between two persons. Are there indications in the poem that we need not take this situation literally? If so, could the discourse situation be interpreted as symbolic of the poet's divided self?

You will notice that the poem features a relatively large number of imperatives: '*Be* adept and *be* dialect,/*tell* of this wind', etc. Knowing that the pronouns *I, we,* and *you* are interpersonal deictics, can you work out why these imperatives have a deictic function, too (cf. Leech 1969: 183–4)?

Finally, can you point out some deictics in this poem which draw the reader into the situation of the text?

3 Describe the discourse situation in Tom Paulin's 'A Lyric Afterwards' (in Morrison and Motion 1982), and suggest a contextualized reading. Do you agree with the following critical assessment:

In poems by ... Paulin ..., we are often presented with stories that are incomplete, or are denied what might normally be considered essential information. The reader is constantly being made to ask, 'Who is speaking?', 'What are their circumstances and motives?' and 'Can they be believed?' There is, moreover, leisure to ponder these questions at length.

(Morrison and Motion 1982: 19)

4 In Stevie Smith's poem 'Not Waving but Drowning' (in MacGibbon 1978), the discourse situation is quite complex. We seem to hear several voices. Whose are they? It is said that Stevie Smith was inspired to write this poem by a bizarre and sad newspaper story about a drowning man whose friends thought he was waving to them. Though you have not read the report, you can see in what respect Stevie Smith has changed the situational context of the accident. What is the effect of these changes on your interpretation of the poem?

5 In 'The Tollund Man' from *North* (1975b), Seamus Heaney relates an Iron Age victim of a sacrificial ritual to the victims of contemporary Irish sectarian atrocity. Make a fully contextualized analysis of the poem, using the model suggested on pp. 113–30.

6 In his book *The Haw Lantern* (1987) Seamus Heaney included a sequence of eight sonnets entitled 'Clearances' commemorating his mother's life and death. Reading sonnet four, 'Fear of affectation made her affect', instantly calls to mind Heaney's image of the forked stick on which writers not writing in their mother tongue feel caught because of their love of the English language (see p. 114). From his first collection onwards, language has been a recurrent topic in Heaney's poetry. This sonnet is about language as an instrument of alienation and division. Write a contextualized analysis of this sonnet. I suggest the title 'Betrayal through Language'. Perhaps you could make use of the following statement; 'he [Heaney] delights in language, relishing it . . . as something that embodies politics, history and locality, as well as having its own delectability' (Morrison and Motion 1982: 13).

NOTES

1 For this view of poetry as contextualized discourse, I am deeply indebted to Roger Fowler (1986: 85–101).

2 It is important to distinguish between the notion of *situational context* and that of *linguistic context*. In the case of deictic reference, as we have seen, the identification of the element to which the deictic refers is made on the basis of the *situational context*, which, for that matter, may be quite narrow or extremely wide. For example, in 'He put *the* milk back in *the* fridge', 'the milk' and 'the fridge' are identified in a domestic situation, whereas in 'We all sat in *the* sun', the definite article 'the' refers to something in our general experience of the world. However, in the case of non-deictic reference it is the *linguistic context* that makes identification possible. For instance, in 'I hear you disliked his latest novel. I read his first novel, and *that* was boring, too' the demonstrative 'that' refers to 'his first novel' mentioned earlier in the text. In 'He told the story like *this*: "Once upon a time..."' the demonstrative 'this' refers to the phrase 'Once upon a time' following later in the linguistic context. Similarly, in 'Punishment', the identification of

'*the* nape' in line 2 is based on the following semantic link with the modifying phrase 'of her neck'.

Note that in the case of backward reference, we speak of *anaphoric reference*, while forward reference is called *cataphoric reference* (see *A Dictionary of Stylistics* by Katie Wales (1989) for a systematic and clear overview).

Interestingly, we may also distinguish *indirect anaphoric reference*, which occurs when a reference becomes part of the listener's/reader's knowledge indirectly, i.e., by inference from what has already been mentioned in the discourse, for example, 'John bought *a bicycle*, but when he rode it one of *the wheels* came off.' The definite reference to 'wheels' is possible because a bicycle has been mentioned and we know that bicycles have wheels. Other examples of indirect anaphoric reference often occur when a particular topic has been introduced. For instance, once the topic of an *orchestral concert* has been introduced in the discourse, we may expect definite references like *the programme, the audience, the conductor*, etc. (Quirk *et al.*1985: 267–8).

Furthermore, it is noteworthy that the type of reference may be ambiguous. For example, in a sentence like 'Travel books like *this* do not tell the truth', the pronoun 'this' can perhaps be interpreted as either deictic (with situational reference) or non-deictic (with linguistic reference). It is non-deictic and anaphoric if it refers to 'travel books' mentioned earlier in the sentence. However, if the speaker actually points to a particular specimen of the travel books s/he is talking about, 'this' is used deictically (with situational reference).

Finally, it should be noted that not all present and past tense forms of verbs are deictic. In our foregoing example 'Travel books like this do not tell the truth' the present-tensed verbal group 'do not tell' is not deictic because it is not oriented to the speaker's or writer's temporal *situation*; clearly, it is a general statement.

REFERENCES

Clark, K. (1992) 'The Linguistics of Blame', in M. Toolan (ed.) *Language, Text and Context: Essays in Stylistics*, London: Routledge.
Corcoran, N. (1986) *Seamus Heaney*, London: Faber & Faber.
Fowler, R. (1986) *Linguistic Criticism*, Oxford: Oxford University Press.
Glob, P.V. (1969) *The Bog People: Iron Age Man Preserved*, London: Faber & Faber.
Haffenden, J. (1981) *Viewpoints: Poets in Conversation with John Haffenden*, London: Faber & Faber.
Halliday, M.A.K. (1966) 'Descriptive Linguistics in Literary Studies', in A. McIntosch and M.A.K. Halliday (eds) *Patterns of Language: Papers in General, Descriptive and Applied Linguistics*, London: Longman.
Heaney, S. (1972) *Wintering Out*, London: Faber & Faber.
—— (1975a) *Bog Poems*, London: limited edition.
—— (1975b) *North*, London: Faber & Faber.
—— (1980) *Preoccupations: Selected Prose 1968–1978*, London: Faber & Faber.
—— (1984) *Station Island*, London: Faber & Faber.

—— (1987) *The Haw Lantern*, London: Faber & Faber.

—— (1988) *The Government of the Tongue*, London: Faber & Faber.

—— (1990) *The Redress of Poetry: An Inaugural Lecture delivered before the University of Oxford on 24 October 1989*, Oxford: Oxford University Press.

Lawrence, D.H. (1985) *The Shades of Spring*, in *The Prussian Officer and Other Stories*, London: Granada Publishing Ltd.

Leech, G.N. (1969) *A Linguistic Guide to English Poetry*, London: Longman.

Levinson, S.C. (1983) *Pragmatics*, Cambridge: Cambridge University Press.

MacGibbon, J. (ed.) (1978) *Stevie Smith: Selected Poems*, Harmondsworth: Penguin.

Mills, S. (1992) 'Knowing your Place: A Marxist Feminist Stylistic Analysis', in M. Toolan (ed.) *Language, Text and Context: Essays in Stylistics*, London: Routledge.

Morrison, B. (1980) *British Poetry since 1970*, Manchester: Carcanet.

Morrison, B. and Motion, A. (eds) (1982) *The Penguin Book of Contemporary British Poetry*, Harmondsworth: Penguin.

O'Brien, C.C. (1975) 'A Slow North-east Wind', *Listener*, (25 September): 404–5.

Plath, S. (1965) *Ariel*, London: Faber & Faber.

Quirk, R., Greenbaum, S., Leech, G., and Svartvik, J. (1985) *A Comprehensive Grammar of the English Language*, London: Longman.

Traugott, E. Closs and Pratt, M.L. (1980) *Linguistics for Students of Literature*, New York: Harcourt Brace Jovanovich.

Verdonk, P. (1991) 'Poems as Text and Discourse: The Poetics of Philip Larkin', in R.D. Sell (ed.) *Literary Pragmatics*, London: Routledge.

Wales, K. (1989) *A Dictionary of Stylistics*, London: Longman.

Widdowson, H.G. (1975) *Stylistics and the Teaching of Literature*, London: Longman.

10 The difficult style of *The Waste Land*: a literary-pragmatic perspective on modernist poetry

Roger D. Sell

EDITOR'S PREFACE

As all chapters in this book show, literary stylistics taps the theories and methods of linguistics whenever these appear to suit its primary objective, which is to relate aspects of literary critical interpretation to relevant linguistic features. Thus, moving with the times, stylistics has increasingly developed an interest in socio-linguistic trends in linguistics which seek to integrate the analysis of formal textual structure with a consideration of its relevant situational and sociocultural contexts. In this new orientation it is held that in principle the writing and reading processes of literary texts are not different from those of non-literary texts: they are both communicative interactions, in a particular context, between participants who, in the case of literature, are fictionalized personae.

It is this socially and communicatively oriented direction in literary stylistics that Roger Sell hails in this chapter as a major addition to the literary critical potential of stylistics. He argues, however, that this development should be pushed to its ultimate conclusion: the fictional author and reader should make room for 'real human beings living in particular, though not necessarily shared, historical circumstances'. For literary approaches focusing on the writer's real-world intention and the appropriate or likely response of the real reader, he uses the label 'literary prag-matics', which is obviously twinned with the term 'linguistic prag-matics'. The latter, usually called 'pragmatics' for short, is a relatively recent branch in linguistics which is concerned with the study of those aspects of meaning that cannot be recovered from the text with the help of the formal system of language (phonology, syntax and semantics), but must be attributed to contextual and interpersonal factors. In her *Dictionary of Stylistics* (1989: 369), Katie Wales gives the following clear illustration. The utterance *Can you drive a car?* will have a different 'meaning' if the context and participants vary: spoken by a girl to a young man in a pub, for instance, or by a driver to his passenger when taken suddenly ill.

Similarly, this formal linguistic system cannot account for the pragmatic meanings of the textual disarray of T.S. Eliot's *The Waste Land*, from which Sell has taken Part 2: 'A Game of Chess' to demonstrate his model of analysis. Essentially, pragmatics investigates the social basis of language and, therefore, he proposes to apply Grice's 'Cooperative Principle', which is at work in all linguistic interchanges, with four maxims for ideal communication. As Sell clearly demonstrates, Eliot's breach of these maxims provides explanations for otherwise puzzling elements in the poem's disorderly presentation.

It is perhaps somewhat ironic that Sell should have chosen a section from Eliot's *The Waste Land*, because this poem has frequently been on the dissecting table of the New Critics, whose formalist methods are diametrically opposed to those of literary pragmatics. Though perhaps the poem is now less dauntingly unfamiliar than in 1922, the history of its reception (see, for instance, Cox and Hinchliffe 1968) teaches us that it bewildered many of its early readers. It was found to be disjointed and incoherent, but at the same time this 'rich disorganization' was felt to reflect the modern state of civilization (Leavis 1963: 77). It is precisely this specific make-up of the poem, this collage-like disintegratedness, which appealed to the text-immanent approach of the New Critics. Admitting its lack of logical continuity, they claimed that the poem was an organic whole through strong text-internal associative relationships between a systematic network of metaphors. It is therefore most interesting to compare this 'text-as-text' approach with Roger Sell's fully contextualized reading of what Eliot himself called a 'sprawling chaotic poem'.

P. V.

For many people, *The Waste Land* is the quintessential modernist poem in English, and if asked to comment on its style they would probably say that it's rather difficult. There is now a type of stylistics which can help us discuss this, but the new approach does not focus purely and simply upon the text of the poem itself. Why is this? And how does the approach relate to earlier work in stylistics?

We can start with the distinction often made between literary stylistics and linguistic stylistics. Linguistic stylistics is said to see style as an aspect of all linguistic communication, literary or otherwise, and to discuss it within the framework of some single model of language. Literary stylistics, by contrast, restricts its discussion to literary texts, and is said to use fairly straightforward linguistic terminology drawn ad hoc from various linguistic models. It is generally thought of as less forbiddingly rigorous and more humanistic than linguistic stylistics.

Whereas linguistic stylisticians often go in for a systematic 'stylometrics', compiling comprehensive statistics of overall stylistic regularities, sometimes in very large bodies of materials, literary stylisticians are usually more atomistic, highlighting something here, something there. If, as is often the case, they are dealing with a short lyric poem, they may well end up giving some overall impression of style. But when they do deal with a longer text, their piecemeal approach becomes more noticeable.

Even so, they can capture much of the stylistic character of, say, a play or a novel, and their atomism actually guards against certain pitfalls. Descriptions of overall stylistic tendencies in a text may be misleading since, especially in some literary texts, there can be fluctuations from one part to the next. As Michael Riffaterre (1967) puts it, stylistic 'nonce standards' can suddenly come into play. This may be a matter of just a sentence, of a purple passage, or even of a very long stretch of text – in Leech and Short's terminology, what can come into operation is an internal, 'secondary' norm (Leech and Short 1983: 55). Precisely by comparing fairly short passages here and there, literary stylisticians have been able to pinpoint such contrasts, great and small, and they have sometimes suggested relationships between the stylistic variation and the development of the argument or narrative (for example Sell 1975).

In one respect, however, they have proceeded in just the same way as linguistic stylisticians. They have usually dealt with formal linguistic features, which can be pointed to as words on the page. Most stylistics to date has been 'eyes-on-the-page' stylistics. This may seem so obvious that it could be taken for granted. But it is precisely this which is now beginning to change.

The words on the page will always be important to stylisticians, but over the past twenty years or so linguists have become increasingly aware that surface linguistic form does not, either of itself or in combination with a semanticist's account of meaning, fully explain how people actually communicate with each other. Scholars working in the fields of pragmatics and discourse analysis have shown that language utterances acquire meaning because of the way they are used in specific situational and sociocultural contexts, and that they also become moves in ongoing processes of personal interaction. Nowadays, then, linguistic stylisticians are likely to adopt a pragmatic or discourse model of language communication as their basic framework, and literary stylisticians are no less alert to new possibilities. In particular, it is now much easier to talk about all the things which are not 'there in the words' of dialogues between characters in novels or plays. The analysis of this is sometimes referred to as discourse stylistics (as in Carter and Simpson 1989).

Nor is this all. Literary stylistics can adopt an approach that is even more wholeheartedly contextualizing, in which case it can be spoken of as a type of literary pragmatics. 'Literary pragmatics' is a label used to cover various approaches to literature which take the full consequences of pragmatics and discourse analysis. Such approaches concentrate not only on texts but on the writing and reading of them, seeing writing and reading as processes of genuine communication between real human beings living in particular, though not necessarily shared, historical circumstances. A literary pragmatic stylistics, then, studies pragmatic and discoursal tendencies in the interaction between historically real writers and readers.[1]

In some senses, literary pragmatic stylistics can be seen as part of the natural evolution of literary stylistics. It restricts its attention to literature and has a fairly humanistic feel to it, and it tends to be atomistic rather than systematic and stylometric. The present chapter, for example, will be dealing with just a few aspects of one of the five parts of *The Waste Land*. The hope is that this will suggest something about how we read the entire poem and other high modernist poems as well. If it has any success, this will be partly because the approach is sensitive, like literary stylistics, to stylistic variation, a factor of fundamental importance in modernist poetry.

In another sense, literary pragmatic stylistics comes closer to linguistic stylistics. Its emphasis on literary activity as a contextualized communication process is identical with the long-standing assumption of many linguistic stylisticians that the reading and writing of literary texts do not fundamentally differ from other types of communicative sending and receiving. This concern with real writers and real readers represents a radical departure from some earlier stylisticians' literary formalism. Literary pragmatic approaches reject the idea that works of literature constitute an aesthetic heterocosm, and also the idea that the language of literature is fundamentally different in form and function

from any other kind of language. On the contrary, literary texts work
according to the same linguistic, pragmatic, and discoursal principles
as other utterances. True, literary texts from earlier periods or different cultures call for a special effort from the reader and, as we
shall later see, they may evoke a response which would have surprised
their first readers. But this is true of historical or foreign texts of any
type, and even so the reader is always processing the same text as the
writer's own processing produced under particular circumstances for a
particular potential readership. If the reader has some success in
following interpretative paths similar to those which the first readers
would have followed, a certain amount of genuine communication will
still take place.

As an illustration of the kind of thing that any reader of *The Waste
Land* has always had to do, we can concentrate on the way we process
Part 2: 'A Game of Chess' (see Appendix, p. 152). Part 2 is of course
normally approached from Part 1, but for our present purposes we can
leave this out of account. The transition beween the two parts is abrupt
and mystifying, but we deal with it in basically the same way as the
transitions between the main passages within Part 2.

One of our first concerns with any text is to get some idea of what it's
about. A preliminary impression of 'A Game of Chess' might well be
that it is a rather unpleasant piece of writing. It seems to have two main
female characters, one a lady (or 'lady') placed in a setting with some
claims (or pretensions) to elegance, the other a Cockney in a pub at
closing time. Their moves are restricted by the somewhat sinister 'game
of chess' into which they are both locked, a demeaning sexual determinism of which we see another version in the robot-like copulation of
the typist and the 'young man carbuncular' in Part 3. In the lady the
degraded sexuality expresses itself as neurosis, a fantasy of street-
walking and a strained expectancy, and in the Cockney as prurient
gossip and a predatoriness which made her threaten, not only openly
but self-righteously, to steal an unfortunate friend's husband.

In order to get even this much out of the writing, we have already had
to engage with Eliot's distinctive way of handling his materials,
something which a purely 'eyes-on-the-page' stylistics cannot fully
deal with. A literary pragmatic approach can start from an idea
underlying much work in pragmatics: Grice's suggestion that there is a
'cooperative principle' at work in all linguistic interchanges, with four
maxims for helpful communication (Grice 1975). Eliot plays havoc
with all four maxims and in this way challenges readers to do a lot of
the sense-making for themselves. He does this so consistently that it
can be seen as the superordinate stylistic impulse, but he also flouts

more than one maxim at a time, which means that a cut-and-dried discussion of each maxim in turn will not always be possible. Many pragmaticists would nowadays argue that one of the maxims, the so-called maxim of relation, is in any case more important than the other three, and that they can actually be reduced to it (Sperber and Wilson 1986). But by retaining all four maxims and trying to keep them at least partly separate, we shall perhaps catch more of the interpersonal complexity of Eliot's style.

The maxim of relation states that one thing should have a bearing upon another – that listeners or readers should be able to see why things are relevant. In *The Waste Land*, Eliot tends to write whole passages which, with the exception of a few lines or phrases here and there, seem to hang together fairly well and to be more or less about one and the same thing. The problem of relevance comes at higher levels of coherence, between the poem's five parts, and between the main passages within those parts. Furthermore, the problem is immediately aggravated by simultaneous floutings of Grice's maxim of manner. Among other things, this maxim states that a helpful communicator goes about things in an orderly way. Eliot's presentation is disorderly in the sense that, from one main passage to the next, he switches viewpoint, verse form, stylistic level, and general mood.

'A Game of Chess' seems to fall into three main passages, which on the page are typographically marked by line-spacing. Lines 1–34 are all about the lady sitting at a dressing table in a large room with ornate but possibly tawdry decor – by the time we get to the footsteps shuffling on the stairs (line 31) things are beginning to sound almost sordid. This first passage is a third-person singular description and contains run-on iambic pentameters somewhat reminiscent of late Shakespeare, with fairly elaborate long sentences and a smattering of rare words. The second main passage is lines 35–62. This switches to a partly dramatic method of presentation, with what we can take to be the same lady's words directly reported; more surrealistically, the words are spoken by her hair as she brushes it (see lines 32–34). But there is also what seems to be another voice, though in view of the lack of inverted commas it may not actually speak aloud. Many of the lines are short and colloquial, and there are some decidedly un-Shakespearian rhythms. The third main passage is from line 63 to the end, and dramatizes the pub scene. Interrupted only five times by the barman's calling time, the Cockney woman gives what in effect is a dramatic monologue, printed on the page as verse, but with many short lines, and with the Shakespearian style completely forgotten amid the non-standard syntax and colloquial stress and intonation patterns.

The transition from the first main passage to the second is somewhat puzzling. The lady herself provides some continuity, but whose is the 'other' voice? Is she replying to her own questions? Is it perhaps a male visitor, who will not tell her what he really thinks about her situation? Is it the poet, and if so, during an earlier visit to her, or as he now describes her to us in retrospect or imagination? But the break between the second and third main passage is even sharper. There is an abrupt change of both physical location and social class, with no apparent continuity in the characters involved.

Grice's idea, however, was not simply that there are maxims which a communicator can either observe or flout. Even if the maxims do appear to be flouted, the recipients of a communication nevertheless tend to assume that its sender is still trying to be cooperative. They conclude that the flouting is actually an economical or powerful way of making some kind of point, for instance by irony or understatement. Flouting the maxims can thus be a way of *implying* such a meaning, a meaning which listeners or readers have a natural curiosity to ferret out. This is precisely how Eliot's abrupt transitions work. They are not cooperative in the usual way, but challenge us to make connections for ourselves.

My earlier summary has already suggested one kind of overall relation which we can impose on 'A Game of Chess', and also one of the links that can be made with the typist and her lover in the next part. In moving from the lady to the Cockney in the pub, we see no immediate connection, but assume that in fact there must be one, even though the two women belong to completely different worlds and stories. Given this generous assumption on our part, the sordid sex issue is what we are probably most likely to take as a common denominator. Many of the allusions, such as that to the rape of Philomel (lines 22–7), seem to be in key with it, and the title of Part 2 supports such an interpretation by suggesting what can be read as an all-encompassing metaphor for the sexual determinism. Eliot has a note explaining that the title is based on the chess scene in Middleton's *Women beware Women*, and this in itself is enough to tune us in to the sinister sexual undertone, and to the Cockney woman's designs on Lil's Albert. Such a use of Eliot's notes in interpretation may break the strict literary formalist's rule that one should attend only to the actual text of the poem, but for a literary pragmaticist Eliot's notes hold a central place in the readers' engagement with *The Waste Land*, being part of the circumstances of publication and reading.

The note on *Women beware Women* is *enough* to help us establish a relevance, but both here and throughout we do have to be active. What we do can be discussed partly in terms of Grice's maxim of quantity, which says that a helpful communicator gives neither too much nor too little information, but just the right amount for the purpose in hand. Eliot's abrupt transitions at first make us feel that he has left things out, and the main tendency of his revisions to the manuscript, many of them proposed by Ezra Pound, was indeed to make cuts; elsewhere, the modernist concern for eliptical economy resulted in the minimalist art of imagist poems and haikus. But as with relation, so with quantity: despite the unusual demands made upon us, we are still prepared to assume that Eliot is trying to communicate. If necessary we supply things ourself, making such use of his footnotes as we can. Most obviously, he never really gives us much of a story. What about the two women's previous history? Does the knock on the door (line 62) usually come? Does it come today? Who is it who knocks? Where do the gossipers go when the pub closes? What happened after the gammon dinner? Did Lil lose her Albert to the speaker? All Eliot does is to place the two women in certain settings and let them talk. Yet we can make the rest up for ourselves.

Not that much of our energy goes to embroidering on the stories. We venture our own guesses, but we quickly begin to assume that Eliot has already given what from his own point of view is the most important part, and that the characters' own spoken words, as in a dramatic monologue by Browning, encapsulate the significance of their entire lives. In the end we may take Eliot's hint in one of the notes that the Fisher King myth provides a kind of master narrative, but we come to see this as a thematic cohesion in terms of the sterility motif. It is not a framing plot for tightly interconnected sub-plots, and we soon stop asking 'What happened next?'

Rather, by expanding such information and hints as Eliot does supply we begin to create-or-discover significances and patterns that are rather different from a straightforwardly coherent argument or narrative. My hyphenated expression 'create-or-discover' signals that in any interpretation, and pre-eminently in interpretations of modernist poems, there is a pragmatic reciprocity between reader and text. As a compensation for Eliot's apparent shortfall on quantity, we bring to the text our own familiarity with other texts and with many different spheres of real life. The poem can be read as full of both intertextual and extratextual allusions, and it is our own imaginative-or-recognizing 'ear' which helps us find a path through it.

One of the configurations we create-or-discover involves some blatant enough Shakespearian allusions. The very first line is an almost exact quotation of the beginning of Enobarbus's famous speech describing Cleopatra coming on her barge of state to meet Antony for the first time. The very last line is the last words of Ophelia. And line 49, almost the very middle of 'A Game of Chess', is from Ariel's song to Ferdinand, alluded to in other parts as well. Yet although in this numerological (first–middle–last) sense Part 2 has a clear Shakespearian framework, the fate of the Shakespearian pentameter, as already noted, is rather precarious. 'The Chair she sat in, like a burnished throne' is firm enough, but even in the first passage there are very obvious breakdowns with the short lines (lines 27, 31, 33). In the second passage even the central Shakespearian line itself ('Those are pearls that were his eyes') is trochaic and a tetrameter, and there are further short lines. In particular there is the burlesque rhythm of the 1920s-style rag (lines 51–3), which comments on bardolatry as if from the lips of a flapper. In the third passage the iambic pentameter is vaguer still, and the rhythms of Ophelia's last words could almost be a reminder that even in Shakespeare it could give way under psychic strain to something very different. As we process the verse, then, we are structuring a kind of formal correlative to the increasingly unsettling subject-matter. Though 'A Game of Chess' has no argument or sustained story in the conventional sense, it can be experienced as moving towards its own kind of climax, and this is partly thanks to the verse form's apparently disorderly flouting of the maxim of manner. The flouting, one might say, helps to set up affective implicatures.

Our sense of the same movement is reinforced by our simultaneous processing of another aspect of Eliot's discourse. Here again his disorderliness flouts the maxim of manner: there is no stability in the relationship between his own voice and those of the two women characters. At the beginning we realize that we are dealing with a piece of third-person description; we may remember Homeric descriptions of warriors offering prayers at an altar on the morning of battle, or Pope's description of Belinda at her dressing table. In the second passage, the lady's or the hair's direct speech suddenly forces her and her predicament upon us with much greater immediacy, but there is still the 'other' voice, which could be the same narrator's, even though the running commentary is now more openly cynical and even macabre. And in the last passage, the extensive dramatic monologue confronts us with the callousness of predatory lust in all its naked ugliness, as if making any narratorial comment supererogatory, and leaving us to draw our own sickened conclusions. Once again, then, we can recuperate the presentational disorderliness as a kind of affective crescendo.

Various other patterns emerge as well. We shall never know how many patterns Eliot expected us to find. We may miss much that he intended, but there is also the possibility that we find some things which would have surprised him. All we can say with certainty is that countless things do register with our literary memories and general life experience, and that we do pattern them. All the time we are making things fit, not only from one line to the next but within the larger affective dynamics as well. The 'strange synthetic perfumes' (line 11), for instance, with its parody of 'the strange invisible perfumes' mentioned by Enobarbus, is one of the first sly suggestions that this modern Cleopatra may be not quite so amazing as her great predecessor, and 'drowned the sense in odours' (line 13), though it still sounds Shakespearian enough, could also be a decadent poet from the 1890s, thereby harmonizing with the Beardsleyesque imagery of the boudoir. The instability of the iambic pentameter, then, is only one of several hints on several different levels that the twentieth century represents an unhealthy falling away from pristine certainties.

Other patterns strengthen the links between the three main passages. We can work out, for example, that the lady's jewels, perfumes, and cosmetics (lines 7–13), and poor Lil's false teeth (lines 67–70) – if she didn't spend the money on food for the five kids or on the abortion pills – are simply the accoutrements of different pieces in the same old 'game of chess', and at several points there is a connection between tawdry or frustrated love, and war or a post-war era. The love of Antony and Cleopatra was interwoven with thoughts and deeds of war. If we follow up Eliot's note, we shall find that 'laquearia' (line 16) is borrowed from Virgil's description of the ceiling of Dido's hall, where, already falling in love with Aeneas, she invites him to tell of his experiences of the fall of Troy. Lil is a woman whose husband has been away at war, presumably in the trenches of France. Given all of which, we perhaps supply the idea that the neurosis of the lady is connected with the absence or death of an officer husband.

Yet the main passages never coalesce, and much of our patterning work has to do with strong contrasts between them. Some of these arise when intertextual and extratextual echoes combine with iconic or quasi-onomatopoeic effects. Just as the lady's 'My nerves are bad to-night' (line 35) and the Cockney woman's 'Oh is there, she said. Something o' that, I said' (line 74) belong to two completely different sociolects, so the lady does not speak much, but her repetitions and rhythms precisely suggest, not only her physical movements in brushing her hair, but her nervous agitation, while the Cockney woman has all the volubility of her nasty self-righteousness.

Eliot does not rub things in, but there is still plenty for readers to pick up on. To take one small example: he rejected a suggestion that

'Something o' that' should be spelt 'Somethink o' that' (V. Eliot 1971:
13). Except in 'Goonight' (lines 94–5), Eliot avoided showing pronunciation by spelling, and in this he differed from writers such as George
Eliot, Kipling, Conrad, and Lawrence. On the one hand, no readable
writing convention will ever capture every aspect of speech, and Eliot
may have feared that an attempt at phonetic accuracy would distract from
the things actually being said. On the other hand, his uncanny replication
of the rhythms, idiom, and syntax of Cockney speech strikes us with the
same more-real-than-real quality of non-standard speech in Dickens.
Given these fundamentals, we hear the rest for ourselves.

The comparison with Dickens is worth dwelling on. Whereas some
present-day British poets, beneficiaries of the meritocratic Education
Act of 1944, sometimes fuse 'educated' and 'non-educated' speech in a
single phrase, both Dickens's novels and *The Waste Land* keep different idiolects and sociolects sharply distinct from each other. One can
even speak in Bakhtinian terms of a 'heteroglossia' (see Sell 1986): the
texts acquire a 'many-tongued' life by holding the different ranges of
speech in tension with each other, just as they are within society and
culture generally. Eliot is forever quoting or alluding to other people's
texts, and adopting other people's styles; the poem has various characters of its own, some, like the two women here, with their own
voices; and it has its narrator or narrators, with their own voices as well.
One of the notes says that all the voices somehow belong to the bisexual
old Tiresias, and like the note on the Fisher King myth this may point to
some unity of mood or theme. Yet no theme or mood can ultimately
assimilate all the different voices to each other.

Where Eliot and Dickens differ is in their reporting conventions.
Even though Dickens's late novels make frequent use of free indirect
speech, the transition from the words or thoughts of one character to
those of another is usually obviously motivated, sometimes with
explicit authorial remarks. In *The Waste Land*, the abruptness with
which the voices are introduced is yet another flouting of the maxim of
manner, and was one of the things which caused the first readers most
difficulty.

The problem is all the greater because there are simultaneous
floutings of Grice's fourth maxim, the maxim of quality, which states
that one should only say that which one believes to be true. Now in a
story, whether told in casual conversation or in the form of a literary
work, this maxim applies in a particular way. Even though some of the
people, places, and events mentioned may be real, many others will
most probably not be. We accept fiction on the understanding that it has
its own kind of interest and even truth; for instance, it may suggest

something typical of life in general, or it may mark a moral point. But we can certainly speak of a story as flouting the maxim of quality, if we feel that the teller is not being entirely frank about his or her own personal judgement and feelings as regards the story, and it is precisely here that *The Waste Land* has always seemed such a riddle. How much do we hear of Eliot's own 'true' voice? On the one hand, Eliot himself is presumably the narrator of the first passage in 'A Game of Chess', and only Eliot could have made the poem's juxtapositions. They are often juxtapositions of allusions, but the paradox is that Eliot's own voice is nothing if not allusive. On the other hand, whose *is* the 'other' voice in the second passage? *Could* it be Eliot himself in some sense? If so, he would be no less intrusive than Dickens, but the point is that you can never be in much doubt that Dickens is addressing you. Similarly, what do we do with the last line of Part 2? The gross inappropriateness of 'sweet ladies' as a description of either of this part's two main characters, or of the other denizens of the pub, can be taken as a flouting of the quality maxim on Eliot's part, setting up an ironic implicature. But whether we hear the words as actually spoken by Eliot himself, by Ophelia or her ghost, or by somebody else is a matter of choice. All in all, then, now we hear him, now we don't.

I say 'we', but it is time to examine this usage. So far I have been emphasizing that much of the business of reading Eliot's text still occurs in precisely the same way as for the first readers in 1921. As I hinted at the beginning, however, there is rather more to it than this and I can now apologize if the universalizing 'we' has seemed a bit too authoritarian. The poem, including its manifold voices and various other difficulties of style, may no longer make quite the same impact as it did once. My 'we' has merely been the first stage of a literary pragmatic argument which must now move on to embrace the insights of hermeneutics and reception aesthetics.

Work in these traditions differs from most linguistic and literary stylistics in that its perspectives are not purely synchronic and universalizing. Instead it emphasizes that the act of reading often takes place under very different historical and sociocultural circumstances from those of the act of writing. In all such cases, readers still try to perform the task I have just been illustrating, as much as possible contextualizing a literary text within the original world of the writer in order to get at what they can think of as the writer's meaning. But they will often be ignorant on some points, and they will inevitably bring to bear their own frames of reference as well, so that the full human significance of the text – their general way of relating to it – changes (cf. Hirsch 1976: esp. 1–13).

Two examples. Many present-day readers of *The Waste Land* know that in 1971 Eliot's widow, his second wife, published the original typescipts of the poem (V. Eliot 1971). From these it emerges that an earlier title Eliot had thought of for Part 2 was 'In the Cage', an allusion to the passage from Petronius which subsequently became the epigraph for the entire poem – in English: 'I saw with my own eyes the Sybil at Cumae hanging in a cage, and when the boys said to her: "Sybil, what do you want?" she answered: "I want to die".' Knowing this, it is almost impossible for a reader not to see ways in which it too suggests an organizing metaphor for the whole of Part 2. Second, in our ceaseless efforts to pin down the poem's voice or voices, the parenthesis of line 5 –

> ... fruited vines
> From which a golden Cupidon peeped out
> (Another hid his eyes behind his wing) . . . .

– almost inevitably reminds us of the pawky humour of *Old Possum's Book of Practical Cats*, first published in 1939. Neither of these references was available to the first readers, then, and neither of them is really all that important. But in the 1990s they both seem so entirely natural that it would be absurd to try and stop ourselves using them as at least part of the way in which we relate to the poem.

The same kind of point can be generalized to the entire interpersonal dynamics of a writer's style. Not only is this not straightforwardly 'there on the page' – as we have seen, it never has been. During the course of time, or as the text passes from one culture to another, it actually comes to work in different ways. Readers' reactions to a literary style are bound up with their taste in aesthetic matters generally, which has a very powerful psychological reality. People genuinely believe that certain things are beautiful, shapely, artistic, special. Such convictions, however, are not unaffected by cultural conditioning, and important consequences stem from the simple fact that all new styles, and even styles as radically revolutionary as the modernist ones, are only new until the next new style is introduced.

The difficult style of a high modernist poem such as *The Waste Land* is something experienced by readers of the poem, just as the difficulty of modernist music or painting is something experienced by listeners or observers. But in the 1990s, such a style may actually seem not quite as difficult as it did in the 1920s. Even if, in order to take in and make sense of modernist styles, readers still have to perform the operations just illustrated in much the same way as the first audience did, their minds may do the job more quickly. Modernist styles, like other styles, have been part of the general cultural environment for a very long time now, so that the kind of mental task entailed is simply more familiar.

Attitudes towards the task are also likely to have changed. When people learn to do something difficult they enjoy a sense of achievement, and often the mastery of a difficult skill – whether it be playing the violin or downhill skiing – brings with it a pleasure that is quite specific to the skill in question. Sometimes it is only the anticipation of such delights which can persuade people to slog on with the business of learning. Especially now that modernist poetry has been around for over seven decades, the difficulty of its style may similarly yield up its own kind of pleasure. Despite the profoundly disturbing subject-matter of some modernist poetry, the act of reading it is potentially hedonistic.

To many of the first readers of *The Waste Land* this claim would have seemed simply mad. They could never get as far as finding the difficult style delightful because they felt not only very confused, but much offended. As far as they were concerned, a text which claimed to be a poem yet was so unclear and chaotic as to need footnotes was taking a liberty, and Eliot's perfunctory footnotes merely added insult to injury. One critic complained: 'A poem that has to be explained in notes is not unlike a picture with "This is a dog" inscribed underneath. Not, indeed, that Mr Eliot's notes succeed in explaining anything, being as muddled as incomplete' (Lucas 1923). In short, *The Waste Land* was not a poem but a practical joke in the worst possible taste.

Nowadays, people have to make a considerable effort of historical imagination if they are to grasp this sense of personal outrage. *The Waste Land* has been in print for seventy years, and Eliot himself has been dead for thirty. For nearly two decades, then, young readers have been coming to the poem who have never been its author's contemporaries, and the poem is as distant in time from them as *In Memoriam* was from Eliot's earliest readers. Under these circumstances it really makes very little difference what Eliot wrote: nobody is going to get upset.

Nothing has happened to the poem on the page, but 'off the page' things could hardly be more different. Even from very early on, there were aspects of the communicative situation between Eliot and readers which soon began to modify first impressions of the shocking inconsiderateness of his style (see Sell 1992). Eliot was a living legend. He was held in considerable esteem as the editor of *Criterion*, and through his job with the Fabers' publishing house he became the single most important arbiter and patron of contemporary poetry. With a more than Johnsonian authority of tone, he was forever throwing out hints for a new literary history according to his own criteria. Nor was he slow to associate himself with conservative and even reactionary sentiments, deliberately cultivating an old-fogey persona to boot. Jokes about him flourished freely. Virginia Woolf once wrote to her brother-in-law: 'Come to dinner. Eliot will be there in a four-piece suit' (Gordon 1977: 83–4). How, then, could anybody so important, so old-fashioned, so absurdly proper, be impolite?

Over the years any such idea came to seem even less tenable to the many readers – including schoolteachers, university teachers, and their pupils' pupils – who became well acquainted with Eliot's own critical essays. His most seminal idea about poetry was that it was impersonal – therefore incapable, one would think, of full-blooded rudeness – and his more specific comments on other poets, especially on the difficult Metaphysicals, suggested three justifications for the difficulty his own work (Sell 1992).

First, there was the idea that the difficulty was the only way of capturing the variety and complexity of modern life as experienced by a refined sensibility. Yvor Winters (1959) was to attack this argument as a case of the fallacy of imitative form ('The content is difficult. Therefore the form must be difficult.'), but many readers certainly did come to feel that the fragmentary style of *The Waste Land* was a kind of natural consequence of its theme; the abrupt transitions from one thing to the next were comparable to a collage technique like that used, for similar reasons, in the visual arts of high modernism.

Second, the apparently strange juxtapositions could actually result from the poet's unusual ability to make new wholes out of ordinary experience. This idea, which echoed Coleridge's claim that the poetic imagination works by reconciling opposite and discordant qualities, was to influence American New Critics such as Cleanth Brooks, who himself was influential in his treatment of *The Waste Land* in precisely these terms (Brooks 1939).

Third, the difficultness, and in particular the lack of normal narrative or argumentative coherence, could be seen as the expression of deeper, non-cerebral modes of being and knowing. This line of thought was the more acceptable in that it harmonized with psychoanalytical and Surrealist accounts of the unconscious, but Eliot himself gave more weight to analogies with music: the music of poetry could originate, before words, in a rhythm, and the reader did not need to understand the words in order to appreciate it. My own commentary has itself been influenced by musical thinking. I have suggested that conventional narrative and argument are replaced by dominant motifs, associations, and affective dynamics, and I have used 'harmonize', 'in key with', 'tune in', and 'crescendo' as descriptive terms.

Eliot's critical writings helped to start a tradition of commentary on his own work which subsequently assumed massive proportions, as the study of twentieth-century poetry came to occupy an important place in the syllabuses of schools and universities. It also brought profitable business to publishers. Nowadays many readers read *The Waste Land* for the first time in a student's edition which offers not only a helpful introduction but notes that are much more detailed than Eliot's own. There are many other study aids available as well.

In this situation, new readers can be forgiven for thinking that, no matter how difficult Eliot's style may seem at first, it probably just had to be that way, and that once they get the hang of things it will all be plain sailing: they will easily find some explicator who can sort it all out for them, just as they could buy a reliable guide to home-brewing. Most explicators speak in tones of such disarming matter-of-factness, and with such a flattering confidence in readers' ability to get the point, that readers may even imagine that they have done so without noticing – Eliot without tears, as it were. In other words, there may be a possibility that modernist difficultness will become, not only not shocking – which is inevitable – but not really arresting in any way at all. Just more examination fodder.

Middle-aged and older readers who have always admired Eliot and other modernists may find this a distressing prospect, but it is best to be philosophical about it. The overkill delivered by the twentieth-century 'lit. crit.' industry has merely accelerated the normal progress of fame. New writers have always had to win acceptance. Established writers usually become less fashionable after a time. And after a further lapse of time, they are sometimes rediscovered. Readers approaching them with the preconceptions of an entirely different world-view may find a new significance in them.

For some time now there have been signs that this is already happening in the case of Eliot. Despite the elusiveness of his own voice in *The Waste Land*, despite his own theory of the impersonality of poetry, despite his efforts to keep his own private life private, despite literary structuralists' accounts of the illusoriness of authorial subjectivity, readers are nowadays reading large numbers of excellent author biographies, including biographies of Eliot. We may even wonder whether author biographies are not perhaps making more money than traditional criticism, student aids, and literary theory put together. Be that as it may, it is certainly now widely known that Eliot was very unhappy in his first marriage. Confronted with his wife's mental illness, Eliot was loyal and long-suffering, but the strain was enormous, and he drafted the final sections of *The Waste Land* while himself undergoing psychological treatment in the clinic of Dr Roger Vittoz in Lausanne. Whatever else the writing of the poem entailed for him, it was also therapeutic. Even today it does not allow itself to be read in the way he warned against in 'Tradition and the Individual Talent', as a straightforward expression of the personal sufferings of its author. But present-day readers' knowledge of those sufferings inevitably adds a reverberation to the depiction of the early twentieth-century's sterility and hopelessness. There is a new sense that *The Waste Land* is somehow 'for real'.

And perhaps, despite the overhelpfulness of the 'lit. crit.' industry, the style of the poem will retain or require its conspicuousness, so that its difficulty, no longer insulting, will come to release more of its hedonistic potential. Eliot's floutings of Grice's four maxims may increasingly seem like a cat-and-mouse game with the reader, which readers will readily indulge, and the poem's manifold voices may soon be relished as a ventriloquistic *tour de force*, reminiscent of a fast-changing series of cabaret sketches. The original joint title for Parts 1 and 2 was 'He do the Police in different voices', and perhaps Eliot cut this only because he didn't wish to make such interpretative possibilities too readily apparent; maybe some tastes have to be acquired. As it happens, this particular piece of Cockney speech had itself already been made literary, by Dickens. It is spoken by old Betty Higden in *Bleak House* (chapter 16), who has adopted Sloppy, a foundling. 'I do love a newspaper', she says. 'You mightn't think it, but Sloppy is a beautiful reader of a newspaper. He do the Police in different voices.' Throughout *The Waste Land*, Eliot himself, no less than Dickens in the empathetic public readings he gave of his own works, is forever doing people in different voices, echoing, quoting, parodying. At the same time, his virtuoso performance is also shoring their words against his ruins (see the very last lines of the poem). In part, then, his style is an amazing feat of verbal and vocal conservation. For readers hearing it in this way, such increasingly evident pleasurability may suddenly enter into fascinating relationship with the new perceptions of the poem's subject-matter.

To explain what I have in mind, I shall to all intents and purposes behave like a traditional literary critic. At one and the same time I am prophesying a change of taste and trying to speed it up, by drawing on my own experience of the poem. Even in the work of eyes-on-the-page literary stylisticians, such a move is not without precedent. They have always had educational aims, hoping to raise general levels of language awareness and literary appreciation, and they have always brought their own experiences of literature to bear on their work. They have had to have a 'feel' for the best place to start – what text? what passage of the text? – and their basic mode of argument has been to relate impressions *a*, *b*, and *c* to linguistic features *x*, *y*, and *z*. If they had used linguistic analysis simply as a positivistic camouflage for a fundamental lack of response, their readers would have complained, 'Yes, you have accurately described the linguistic features of this text, but they do not cause the impression you claim for it.'

Similar educational aims and impressionistic sources are no less central for literary pragmatic stylisticians, whose explicit concern with readers' behaviour gives them even stronger reasons for bringing in their own experience of texts. For one thing, that experience is the readerly experience with which they are most intimately familiar. Even more to the point, their grounding in the hermeneutic tradition leads them to say that literature is not a natural, but a human phenomenon, whose mode of existence is within human minds. This means that the only scholars who can approach it are those who are prepared to go on record as to what it means for them, scholars for whom, demonstrably, it is real. Frank Kermode, judging by some of his recent pronouncements (for example, Kermode 1991), may now believe that an interest in literature as a cultural phenomenon is irreconcilable with a genuine literary sensitivity. If he does, this is surely too bleak a view. But it is certainly true that a cultural analysis of literature – including a literary pragmatic analysis – which is not based on a sensitive literary response has no value as scholarship. It cannot know what it is talking about.

If I am right, then, readers finding their way into, or back into, *The Waste Land* during the 1990s may discover-or-create a moving relation between the increasingly relished bravura of style and the newly acknowledged personal reverberation in the poem's portrayal of sordid sterility and blank hopelessness. Readers may begin to assume that, despite all his private anguish, Eliot arrived at the stylistic pleasures before them, that he must have known he would shock his first readers, but that he must have hoped they would eventually come out on the other side of shock. This new reading, though still tracing the poem's non-cerebral dynamics by means of the Eliotian musical analogies, would no longer see the difficulties as setting up an aesthetic heterocosm of non-communication, and would qualify the view that difficult modernist styles are somehow homomorphic with the modern world. There is also a sense in which the style of *The Waste Land* is resistant, oppositional, a point that can be illuminated by a rather different set of Eliotian apothegms. In the essay on Marvell, for instance, he meditates upon a wit which is 'a tough reasonableness beneath the slight lyric grace', an 'alliance of levity and seriousness (by which the seriousness is intensified)' (Eliot 1951: 293, 296). *The Waste Land*, and quite possibly other high modernist poetry as well, may soon be seen as no less nobly paradoxical. On this view, the delightful difficulty of style would have the edifying exemplariness of playfulness in a stoic or, to echo the poem by Empson (1955), of a style learnt from despair. Eliot would be not only a great artist but a great man.

APPENDIX

A Game of Chess

The Chair she sat in, like a burnished throne,
Glowed on the marble, where the glass
Held up by standards wrought with fruited vines
From which a golden Cupidon peeped out
5   (Another hid his eyes behind his wing)
Doubled the flames of sevenbranched candelabra
Reflecting light upon the table as
The glitter of her jewels rose to meet it,
From satin cases poured in rich profusion;
10   In vials of ivory and coloured glass
Unstoppered, lurked her strange synthetic perfumes,
Unguent, powdered, or liquid – troubled, confused
And drowned the sense in odours; stirred by the air
That freshened from the window, these ascended
15   In fattening the prolonged candle-flames,
Flung their smoke into the laquearia,
Stirring the pattern on the coffered ceiling.
Huge sea-wood fed with copper
Burned green and orange, framed by the coloured stone,
20   In which sad light a carvèd dolphin swam.
Above the antique mantel was displayed
As though a window gave upon the sylvan scene
The change of Philomel, by the barbarous king
So rudely forced; yet there the nightingale
25   Filled all the desert with inviolable voice
And still she cried, and still the world pursues,
'Jug Jug' to dirty ears.
And other withered stumps of time
Were told upon the walls; staring forms
30   Leaned out, leaning, hushing the room enclosed.
Footsteps shuffled on the stair.

Under the firelight, under the brush, her hair
Spread out in fiery points
Glowed into words, then would be savagely still.

35   'My nerves are bad to-night. Yes, bad. Stay with me.
'Speak to me. Why do you never speak. Speak.
    'What are you thinking of? What thinking? What?
'I never know what you are thinking. Think.'

    I think we are in rats' alley
40   Where the dead men lost their bones.

    'What is that noise?'
                The wind under the door.
'What is that noise now? What is the wind doing?'
                Nothing again nothing.
45   'Do
'You know nothing? Do you see nothing? Do you remember
'Nothing?'

    I remember
Those are pearls that were his eyes.
50   'Are you alive, or not? Is there nothing in your head?'
                But
O O O O that Shakespeherian Rag –
It's so elegant
So intelligent
55   'What shall I do now? What shall I do?
'I shall rush out as I am, and walk the street
'With my hair down, so. What shall we do tomorrow?
'What shall we ever do?'
                The hot water at ten.
60   And if it rains, a closed car at four.
And we shall play a game of chess,
Pressing lidless eyes and waiting for a knock upon the door.

    When Lil's husband got demobbed, I said –
I didn't mince my words, I said to her myself,
65   HURRY UP PLEASE IT'S TIME
Now Albert's coming back, make yourself a bit smart.
He'll want to know what you done with that money he gave you
To get yourself some teeth. He did, I was there.
You have them all out, Lil, and get a nice set,
70   He said, I swear, I can't bear to look at you.

And no more can't I, I said, and think of poor Albert,
He's been in the army four years, he wants a good time,
And if you don't give it to him, there's others will, I said.
Oh is there, she said. Something o' that, I said.
75   Then I'll know who to thank, she said, and give me a
          straight look.
HURRY UP PLEASE IT'S TIME
If you don't like it you can get on with it, I said.
Others can pick and choose if you can't.
But if Albert makes off, it won't be for lack of telling.
80   You ought to be ashamed, I said, to look so antique.
(And her only thirty-one.)
I can't help it, she said, pulling a long face,
It's them pills I took, to bring it off, she said.
(She's had five already, and nearly died of young George.)
85   The chemist said it would be all right, but I've never been
          the same.
You *are* a proper fool, I said.
Well, if Albert won't leave you alone, there it is, I said,
What you get married for if you don't want children?
HURRY UP PLEASE IT'S TIME
90   Well, that Sunday Albert was home, they had a hot
          gammon,
And they asked me in to dinner, to get the beauty of it
          hot –
HURRY UP PLEASE IT'S TIME
HURRY UP PLEASE IT'S TIME
Goonight Bill. Goonight Lou. Goonight May. Goonight.
95   Ta ta. Goonight. Goonight.
Good night, ladies, good night, sweet ladies, good night,
          good night.

(from T.S. Eliot, *The Waste Land, 1922*)

SUGGESTIONS FOR FURTHER WORK

1 The first main point made in this chapter is that present-day readers of modernist poetry still have to perform the same tasks as its first readers, and that one such task has always been to find ways of compensating for the lack of conventional argumentative or narrative structure. One main strategy is to try to link passages together by some overall theme or mood. Another is to create-or-discover various kinds of patterning.

See if you can trace how you yourself tackle this task as you read Part 5 of *The Waste Land*. Some of the questions you might ask yourself are:

a Into how many different main passages does this part seem to fall?
b To what extent are the main passages different from each other stylistically as 'words on the page'? Think about points such as: range of vocabulary, degree of syntactical complexity, figurative/non-figurative language, questions/statements, longer lines/shorter lines, rhythm.
c Where does narrative come in?
d Are there narrative links between some of the main passages, for instance in a continuity of characters or setting?
e Are there places where there is coherent, non-narrative argument?
f What theme or mood do you create-or-discover in order to link all the main passages together? How does the title of this part, 'What the Thunder said', support you here? And what help do you get from Eliot's notes on this point?
g How does this general mood or theme compare or contrast with the one you use when you are reading Part 2, 'A Game of Chess'?
h Does the metrical variation seem to make a kind of psychological or emotional structure?
i Does the variation in person deixis (from third-person narration or generalization to the use of 'I' or 'you') fall into any kind of pattern?
j How do the words of the poem call on you to activate your extratextual knowledge of types of situation? Are the types of situation distinguished from each other in social terms as they are in 'A Game of Chess'? And how do your extratextual linkages work within your overall reading of this part?
k How do the words of the poem call on you to activate your intertextual knowledge of other written works? What is the role of Eliot's notes here? Is there any kind of overall patterning?
l Does the poem call on associations with other art forms? If so, how do you process these?
m Give arguments in favour of the view that this part must be taken as impersonal.
n Give arguments in favour of the view that Eliot is himself a presence in this part and that it has personal reverberations.
o What do you think about points (m) and (n) on balance?

2 The other main point made in this chapter is that although the words on the page do not change and readers still have to perform the same kinds of task, the total interpretation achieved by readers of different sociocultural backgrounds may nevertheless be different. Partly this may result from ignorance of the state of the language and of the original circumstances in which the text was first written, in which case editorial notes may be called for. But partly it is because fashions and values and frames of reference change. The chapter points out that although Eliot's difficult style once seemed a gross insult to many readers, nowadays it is more likely to seem either just a matter of routine or positively delightful in its own right.
2.1 In order to get some idea of your own sociocultural position as a reader, and of its implications for your reactions as a reader, think carefully about yourself and one other person. The other person should be somebody whom you experience as significantly different from yourself. For example, it might be one of your grandparents, somebody of the opposite sex, somebody from a different background. The kind of points you could focus on are:

a Date and place of birth?
b Sex?
c Social background?
d Family?
e Religion?
f Politics?
g Education?
h Work experience?
i Knowledge of other languages and cultures?
j Knowledge of 'canonical' English literature?
k How was any such knowledge of English literature come by, and why?
l Favourite reading?
m Would normally read *The Waste Land*? Why?/Why not?
n Knowledge of early twentieth-century Britain?
o How was such knowledge come by, and why?
p Hobbies and interests?
q Favourite music?
r Anything else relevant to reactions as a reader?

2.2 Take your two answers on point (l) in question 2.1. What kind of feelings do you and the 'other' person have about each other's favourite reading? Why? What arguments would each of you use in order to try to change each other's taste?

2.3 Do you and the 'other' person differ in the way you would read modernist poetry?

3 Group experiment and discussion. For this you will need to work in a group of three to five people.

3.1 Each person in the group should try to write a text in the manner of a modernist poem. Don't spend too much time and effort on this. It doesn't have to be a great work of art, and it certainly doesn't matter if you don't see how it hangs together. Among other things each text should have: three or more main passages which are *not* clearly linked to each other by argument or narrative; a title; variations in line-length, in syntactical complexity, in range of vocabulary; some intertextual allusions (why not to Eliot?); some extratextual allusions.

3.2 Read each other's texts on the usual assumption that they *are* written in an effort to be cooperative. Discuss with each other particular points at which the maxims of relation, quantity, quality, and manner seem to be flouted, and try to see how, as readers, you nevertheless attempt to make sense of the text. One way to do this would be to adapt points (a) – (o) in question 1 above to the texts you have produced.

3.3 Discuss together your general feelings about the modernist style of poetry. You can draw examples from Eliot or from the texts you have produced yourselves. Does the modernist style really seem terribly difficult? Does it seem old-fashioned? How does it compare with that of television commercials and rock videos? Is reading it at all like reading a detective story or science fiction? Is it fun?

NOTE

1 For a general introduction to literary pragmatics, see Sell (1991b) or Sell (forthcoming). For applications of literary pragmatic stylistics to writers from earlier periods of English literature, see Sell (1985a, 1985b, 1987, 1991a).

REFERENCES

Brooks, C. (1939) *Modern Poetry and the Tradition*, Chapel Hill, NC: University of North Carolina Press.

Carter, R. and Simpson, P. (eds) (1989) *Language, Discourse and Literature: An Introductory Reader in Discourse Stylistics*, London: Hyman.

Cox, C.B. and Hinchliffe, Arnold P. (eds) (1968) *T.S. Eliot: The Waste Land*, London: Macmillan.

Elliot, T.S. (1939) *Old Possum's Book of Practical Cats*, London: Faber & Faber.

—— (1951) *Selected Essays*, London: Faber & Faber.

Eliot, V. (ed.) (1971) *T.S. Eliot: The Waste Land: A Facsimile and Transcript of the Original Drafts including the Annotations of Ezra Pound*, New York: Harcourt Brace Jovanovich.

Empson, W. (1955) 'This Last Pain', in *Collected Poems*, London: Chatto & Windus.

Gordon, L. (1977) *Eliot's Early Years*, Oxford: Oxford University Press.

Grice, H.P. (1975) 'Logic and Conversation', in P. Cole and J. Morgan (eds) *Syntax and Semantics*, vol. 3, *Speech Acts*, New York: Academic Press: 45–54.

Hirsch, E.D. (1976) *The Aims of Interpretation*, Chicago, IL: University of Chicago Press.

Kermode, F. (1991) 'The Old Criticism', plenary lecture at the Inaugural Conference of the European Society for the Study of English, University of East Anglia.

Leavis, F.R. (1963) *New Bearings in English Poetry*, Harmondsworth: Penguin in association with Chatto & Windus.

Leech, G.N. and Short, M.H. (1983) *Style in Fiction: A Linguistic Introduction to English Fictional Prose*, London: Longman

Lucas, F.L. (1923) Review of *The Waste Land*, *New Statesman* (3 November).

Riffaterre, M. (1967) 'Stylistic Context', in S. Chatman and S.R. Levin (eds) *Essays on the Language of Literature*, Boston, MA.: Houghton & Mifflin: 431–41.

Sell, R.D. (1975) 'Two Types of Style Contrast in *King Lear*: A Literary–Critical Appraisal', in H. Ringbom (ed.) *Style and Text: Studies Presented to Nils Erik Enkvist*, Stockholm: Språkförlaget Skriptor: 158–71.

—— (1985a) 'Politeness in Chaucer: Suggestions towards a Methodology for Pragmatic Stylistics', *Studia Neophilologica* 57: 175–85.

—— (1985b) 'Tellability and Politeness in *The Miller's Tale*: First Steps in Literary Pragmatics', *English Studies* 66: 496–512.

—— (1986) 'Dickens and the New Historicism: The Polyvocal Audience and Discourse of *Dombey and Son*', in J. Hawthorn (ed.) *The Nineteenth-Century British Novel*, London: Arnold: 62–79.

158 *Roger D. Sell*

—— (1987) 'The Unstable Discourse of Henry Vaughan: A Literary-Pragmatic Account', in A. Rudrum (ed.) *Essential Articles for the Study of Henry Vaughan*, Hartford, CT: Archon Books: 311–32.

—— (1991a) 'How Can Literary Pragmaticists develop Empirical Methods: The Problem of Modal and Evaluative Expressions in Literary Texts', in E. Ibsch, D.H. Schram, and G.J. Steen (eds) *Empirical Studies in Literature*, Amsterdam: Rodopi: 137–45.

—— (1991b) 'Literary Pragmatics: an Introduction', in R.D. Sell (ed.) *Literary Pragmatics*, London: Routledge: xi–xxiii.

—— (1992) 'Literary Texts and Diachronic Aspects of Politeness', in R.J. Watts, S. Ide, and K. Ehlich (eds) *Politeness in Language: Studies in its History, Theory and Practice*, Berlin: Mouton de Gruyter: 109–29.

—— (forthcoming) 'Literary Pragmatics', in R.F. Asher *et al.* (eds) *The Encyclopedia of Language and Linguistics*, Oxford and Aberdeen: Pergamon Press and Aberdeen University Press.

Sperber, D. and Wilson, D. (1986) *Relevance: Communication and Cognition*, Oxford: Basil Blackwell.

Wales, K. (1989) *A Dictionary of Stylistics*, London: Longman.

Winters, Y. (1959) *On Modern Poets*, New York: Meridian.

11 The poem and occasion

Balz Engler

EDITOR'S PREFACE

After stating the simple fact that the very term 'context' appears to imply that the 'text' comes first in the reading process, Balz Engler proposes to reverse this order, and since the aims of literary pragmatics have often been described as 'recontextualization', his chapter neatly dovetails with the previous chapter by Roger Sell.

Presumably because the word 'context' inevitably conjures up the word 'text' and, consequently, is still often used in its narrow sense of 'the actual surrounding language items in a text', Engler introduces the term 'occasion' to designate certain contextual aspects of time and situation that play a role in our making sense of texts. Apart from including our confrontation with the 'text', such an occasion presupposes at least three other significant factors: (1) consciously or unconsciously we are always conditioned to a text; (2) our reading takes place in a specific situation; and (3) our reading activity shows a particular pattern. Since the text can never be severed from these pragmatic preliminaries (nor will our ultimate reading of the text blot them out), Engler argues for the primacy of 'occasion'. To support his contention and indicating that there are numerous other possibilities, he gives a brief outline of three imagined occasions:

1 Before you start your first job, your father gives you a text about the depression of the 1930s, advising you to remember it when you are bored with your job or when you are about to lose it.
2 You read the text in a book, which you have bought after you have been to an author's reading. You may even have asked the author to sign your copy.
3 You are asked to read the text from a teaching anthology for a course in twentieth-century literature.

As a matter of fact, all these instances show convincingly that it is impossible to distinguish between the effects on the result of our sense-making activity ('the work of literature') of the as yet uninterpreted signs on the page ('the text') and of the other factors of the occasion. Furthermore, he emphasizes the point that, like the above cases, all occasions represent specific uses of literature, which have to be differentiated for the very reason that the poem which comes into existence on each occasion is a different poem.

Having thus established the priority of the occasion, Engler turns things round again, starting with the text and moving from there towards the 'paratext' ('the fringe of the text') that extends meaning to the occasion. In a series of challenging experiments with a poem by the American poet Dave Etter, he makes us aware of various types of paratext which affect our reading such as the text's visual presentation, its title, the author's name, knowledge of the author's biography, its place in a collection alongside other poetic texts by the same author, and links with the American poetic tradition.

In a final edifying experiment, Engler alerts us to the fact that his chapter, written in conformity with the policy of the editor of this book, also creates yet another, quite different, occasion for Dave Etter's poem. Furthermore, this occasion invited us to look at the text as part of different imagined occasions and together with different paratexts. Then there is the occasion created by the specific circumstances in which you studied this book. Ultimately, so the experiment makes us realize, we have an accumulation of occasions as a result of which a poem has come into being that is again different from any of the poems emanating from each individual occasion.

If there is one thing this chapter has made abundantly clear it is that there is no way of our going 'innocently' to a text, including of course the texts in this very book.

P. V.

Like the other chapters in this collection, this one deals with a single text. As an experienced reader you will probably want to read this text first, to judge critically the argument that follows. In proceeding like this you would be following established practice, summarized in the advice offered in one of the most influential teaching anthologies, Brooks's and Warren's *Understanding Poetry*. There we are told to 'begin with as full and innocent an immersion in the poem as possible'

(1976: ix), and, even when we have consulted critical material, to keep in mind that 'criticism and analysis ... is ultimately of value *only insofar as it can return readers to the poem itself* – return them, that is, better prepared to experience it more immediately, fully, and shall we say, innocently' (ibid.: 16; emphasis in original).

In literary stylistics we find a similar commitment to the text as something that can be singled out as the object of study. With the help of linguistic insights 'language effects' are analysed so as to offer a basis for 'a fuller understanding, appreciation and interpretation' of literary texts (Carter and Simpson 1989: 7; cf. also Short 1991: 1082–3).

In privileging the text in the manner indicated, certain other linguistic insights are neglected, in particular those of pragmatics, i.e., those concerning language use. Either the pragmatic dimension is suppressed, as in Brooks and Warren, where we find the notion of *the poem itself*, clearly marked off, isolated, autonomous. Or pragmatics is reduced to something secondary, as in Carter and Simpson, where its task is 'to account for those aspects of meaning which cannot be recovered by straightforward references to the semantic properties of the sentences uttered' (1989: 289).

But there is no innocence of the kind postulated by Brooks and Warren; instead of positing it as an ideal to be striven for (can we strive for innocence?), we should rather consider the implications of its absence. And there are no 'straightforward references to the semantic properties', as posited by Carter and Simpson. What is straightforward, and what is not, is itself determined by language use, i.e., by what is considered secondary in their definition. Such attitudes are reflected in the terms that are employed in discussion; the word *context* presupposes the primacy of *text*. Here, however, I shall argue for the primacy of context.

EXPERIMENT 1

Think of poems and songs that you are fond of. What do you associate them with? Certain other texts? Certain moments in your life? Try to remember when, under what circumstances, you got to know them? Does this affect what they mean to you (in both meanings of the word)?

Certain important moments and situations play a role in determining what texts mean to us – texts always convey some meaning to somebody. This suggests that it may be useful to introduce the term *occasion* for these, in the sense of a '(particular time marked by) special occurrence'

(*Concise Oxford Dictionary*), the specialness of the occurrence consisting partly in the role of the *text* in it. At least three other factors
contribute to such an occasion. It presupposes certain forms of preparation; it takes place under certain conditions; and it follows certain
patterns.

Even before we start reading a literary text what it will mean has
been fixed to a considerable extent, no matter whether we are aware of
this or not. We have learnt certain rules according to which we deal
with various types of texts, rules which are usually passed on in the
family (where children, for example, learn from their parents to
consider literature something worthwhile) and, to a more limited
extent, at school and university.[1] According to these rules, much will
depend on where or from whom we get the text, from an airport
bookstall, a university bookshop, or as a gift from a friend, etc. (cf.
Pratt 1977: 116–25). And much will depend on what we got it for; we
may be curious, seeking comfort, looking for a thrill, or preparing a
course, etc.

We also read texts in specific situations, which not only sharpen or
blunt our perceptions, but also shape them, and thus contribute to what
we make of them. We may be sitting in an evening class in November,
or resting under a blossoming apple-tree; we may just have fallen in
love, or we may have lost a good friend. We may see the texts in the
light of specific other texts, for example, those in the same collection or
anthology.

Finally, and most importantly, we follow certain patterns in reading.
Beginning to read we leave our everyday activities behind; in Yeats's
memorable phrase, the reader 'lays away his own handiwork and turns
from his friend' (1906: 207). And afterwards we return to them seeing
the world, however slightly, in a different light; and, to the extent that
we define ourselves in relation to the world, we also emerge as,
however slightly, different people. As such this process shows striking
parallels to an initiation ritual (Engler 1990: 72–9).

There is one further important point. As we always encounter texts
as part of a particular occasion, never in isolation, there is no way of
distinguishing between what has been contributed to the result ('the
work of literature') by the as yet uninterpreted black marks on the page
('the text'), and what by the other factors of the occasion. A stylistic
analysis of the type described above does not, therefore, give us a
fuller, but a specific type of understanding, which may be new, more
sophisticated, and more satisfying to us, but which cannot claim to be
'closer to the text' and therefore of intrinsically higher value than
other readings.

I should like to illustrate the primacy of occasion with a series of imagined examples. The occasions sketched can, of course, only represent a selection from all those possible.[2] Having established the primacy of occasion and the way it brings a work of literature into being, I shall then continue by moving in the opposite direction, as it were, from the text to the 'fringe of the printed text which in reality, controls the whole reading' (Leujeune in Genette 1991: 261), from the text to what Genette, who still accepts the primacy of the text, has called the *paratext* (Genette 1987).

Let us assume then that, at a family gathering on the Sunday before you begin your first job, your father gives you a text, which he has typed out for you (without indication of its author or its title), and he comments: 'This tells you how things were during the Depression in the 1930s. Remember this, when you are fed up with your job, or when you lose it.' The text will then be important to you because it embodies *a general truth* validated by somebody whom you trust in this matter, and who, by being related to you, also gives you yourself a place in history.

Now let us assume that you are reading the text in a book, which you bought after an author's reading, because you liked what you had heard; you may even have asked the author to sign your copy. The same text is now associated with a voice; it has itself a personal signature, as it were. In reading it you are reminded of another occasion. The poem you are reading is important to you because it says something about *the work of the author*, his or her 'making', the relationship between the privacy of writing and the writer's public role.

Finally, let us assume that you are reading the text from a teaching anthology, in the meeting of a course on twentieth-century literature.[3] You will most probably study it as an artefact, one validated by the authority of literary criticism. It is important to you as *representative of a certain period*, its style and its preoccupation with certain themes. You are interested to a considerable extent in its place in literary tradition and the skilful use it makes of poetic devices. Your teacher may also want to introduce you to specific ways of reading, if a formalist by emphasizing the role of imagery, if an adherent to a certain type of stylistics to the problem of textual coherence.

In all three examples it is the authority of the occasion rather than that of the text which has formed the basis of the result ('the work of literature'); in all three cases, by the way, this authority is also closely associated with that of a personality dominating it.

But we may still have a nagging doubt. What if three people who, having read the same text as part of the occasions sketched, meet and discuss 'the text'? Does not their agreement on what they are discussing

confirm the authority of the text that has remained unchanged throughout the three occasions? The poems resulting from the three occasions
will largely complement each other, but not simply because the three
have read the same text. For one thing, they have a shared social and
cultural background, otherwise they would not have met, and would not
have read the same text. They share interests, otherwise they would not
be discussing poetry. In discussion they will all give up part of what
they have associated with their readings in some cases, and try to insist
on their views in others. Together, they create a poem that is acceptable
to all. As such, it has the authority of this new occasion, the kind of
authority we traditionally ascribe to the text.

None of the occasions sketched (and, as has been indicated, there are
many more) deserves to be privileged over others. None of them is
intrinsically *better* than the others, even though some of them may be
valued more highly than others by those who study and teach literature.
Rather, the occasions are all representative of certain uses of literature. It
is important that we are aware of the differences between them, precisely
because the poem that comes into being on each occasion is different.

But let us turn things around, and, instead of beginning with the
occasion, in which texts are embedded, start with the text, the black
shapes on the page, and move, in more traditional fashion, from there
towards the 'paratexts' that contribute to the occasion.

EXPERIMENT 2

Read the following text and try to 'make something of it'. What kind of
text is it? Take down your observations, and try to group them. What
criteria have you been using in grouping them?

Here is the text, in what Genette would call its 'naked state' (1991: 261):

> On sticky summer Sunday afternoons there would be lots of people
> standing around in the yard, mostly relatives and neighbors in cotton
> dresses and white shirts. They would come and go until dusk, talking,
> talking, talking, talking about jobs, bread lines, foreclosures, about
> Hoover and Roosevelt, about the latest layoff or suicide. Someone,
> usually my father or one of my unemployed uncles, would be
> scratching in the dirt with half a hoe or ragged rake, not to plant, not
> to cultivate, but to do something, to be busy, as if idleness was some
> kind of dark shame or red pimple of embarrassment. I was there, too,
> a silent child with my blue wagon and blue spade, making little
> mountains of dirt and patting them down with my fist. When the
> lemonade ran out, my mother or a maiden aunt would bring out a

pitcher of water and someone would always say, 'You can't beat good old water when you have a terrible thirst.' The Ford in the driveway was ours. It was leaking oil, drop by drop, and the battery was dead. We were obviously going nowhere.

Trying to make something of a text we immediately attempt to place it according to as many criteria as possible, for example, author, addressee, genre, period, tone, style, etc., all the criteria we have learnt to apply. This text looks like a section from an autobiography, which describes with how much patience and dignity unemployed people spent their days in the Depression of the 1930s. English readers will find certain Americanisms fitting, like 'yard', 'layoff', 'wagon', 'driveway', etc. People well-versed in literature may be reminded of James Agee's *Let Us Now Praise Famous Men* (1941), a documentary account of the life of southern sharecroppers. The text does not look like oral history, mainly because there is something literary about it, like the alliterations in '*s*ticky *s*ummer *S*unday afternoons' or in '*h*alf a *h*oe or *r*agged *r*ake', the repetition of 'talking', and the *would*-forms, or the metaphor of the 'red pimple of embarrassment'.

The text is actually a poem. This is how it is visually presented in the source from which it has been taken:

On sticky summer Sunday afternoons
there would be lots of people
standing around in the yard,
mostly relatives and neighbors
in cotton dresses and white shirts.
They would come and go until dusk,
talking, talking, talking, talking
about jobs, bread lines, foreclosures,
about Hoover and Roosevelt,
about the latest layoff or suicide.
Someone, usually my father
or one of my unemployed uncles,
would be scratching in the dirt
with half a hoe or ragged rake,
not to plant, not to cultivate,
but to do something, to be busy,
as if idleness was some kind of dark shame
or red pimple of embarrassment.
I was there, too, a silent child
with my blue wagon and blue spade,
making little mountains of dirt

patting them down with my fist.
When the lemonade ran out,
my mother or a maiden aunt
would bring out a pitcher of water
and someone would always say,
'You can't beat good old water
when you have a terrible thirst.'
The Ford in the driveway was ours.
It was leaking oil, drop by drop,
and the battery was dead.
We were obviously going nowhere.

Our reading is affected by the presentation. It will be slower, more deliberate, slightly drawn out at the end of the lines.[4] The use of pure colours, in 'white shirt', 'blue wagon', 'blue spade', 'red pimple', will acquire a stronger symbolical dimension. What seems to be slightly unusual, 'literary', when the text is read as autobiography will now have its place. Obviously, it is the visual arrangement of the text that indicates to us what kind of reading we should be practising, and it is this practice that produces the effects (cf. on this Fish 1981). The visual presentation may therefore be considered the first type of paratext.

The poem was first published in the *Ohio Review*, the literary magazine published at Ohio University. It appears in an anthology of twenty, usually single new poems by contemporary American authors, presented without any commentary. Only the names of the authors and the titles are indicated.

EXPERIMENT 3

(a) Think of different titles for this poem, for example: 'Dead End', 'Sunday Afternoons', 'Scratchings', 'A Silent Child', 'Talking'. How do they affect the poem? (b) What difference does it make that the author's name is indicated? How important is it to know who he is?

Titles are *about* the text and as such have a status different from what is usually called 'the body of the text'. They create expectations and make us read the text in a certain manner. As such they are a particularly powerful thematization device (Brown and Yule 1983: 139–40);[5] as Genette points out, 'How would we read Joyce's *Ulysses* if it were not called *Ulysses*?' (1991: 262).

The title of the poem quoted is 'Summer of 1932'. It indicates a precise moment in the past, and by doing so suggests a relationship with the present, between the silent child introduced in the second half, and the present of the person speaking. As there is no specific indication that the speaker is not the author, we tend to read the text as a personal statement of the author, as autobiographical.[6]

The author is Dave Etter, as the *Ohio Review* indicates. He is a highly respected poet of the American Midwest, who has published more than twenty volumes of poetry, most of them dealing with the everyday experience of people in contemporary Midwestern towns. He was born in 1928; he was 4 years old in the summer of 1932.

We find the poem again in *Electric Avenue*, published by the Spoon River Poetry Press in 1988. The title of the collection is taken from a poem in it, which is about a man mowing his lawn (or rather cutting the grass) and observing the kind of unusual occurrence typical of a small community. Here, the text appears along with others by the same poet. Additionally, all the texts have been assigned speakers, their names indicating various ethnic, often German or Scandinavian, origins. The title of the text we are discussing now runs: 'Elwood Collins: Summer of 1932' (1988b: 15). This clearly assigns the text to somebody who is not the poet, and makes an autobiographical reading difficult. The speaker is rather characterized as one member of the community among the many others who appear in the collection.

To somebody familiar with the American poetic tradition the new version of the title links the text with one of the great poetry collections of the American Midwest, with Edgar Lee Masters's *Spoon River Anthology* (1915), which documents, along with Sherwood Anderson's *Winesburg, Ohio* (1919), Sinclair Lewis's *Main Street* (1920), and the poems of Vachel Lindsay, the belief in a latent utopian community in the small town, one inherited from the Puritan tradition (Engler 1990: 110–21). The Midwest, it should be added, is a cultural area that has often been misunderstood and misrepresented by East Coast people and Europeans, because its features look all too familiar (like the ones that one despises in one's own culture), and what is original, even exotic about its traditions, is often overlooked (see Atherton 1966).

But Etter's use of Masters's model also emphasizes differences: now none of the figures is defined by its role in the community ('Justice Arnett', 'Dippold the Optician', etc.). Now the names of people no longer serve for full titles as with Masters's epitaphs, which make a single, definite statement on the fates of individuals in the town community. Rather, the combination of a speaker's name, the title, and the account of a single experience creates a sense of postmodern fragmentation and randomness.

In conclusion, I should like us to turn to an occasion where we need not rely on reporting and on our imaginations.

EXPERIMENT 4

You have got to know Dave Etter's 'Summer of 1932' in the course of reading this chapter. Compare this occasion to those you recalled in Experiment 1. In what respects has this occasion been different, and how has it affected the poem?

Again, this occasion has been quite specific. Personal factors have been at work, which are difficult to gauge for the author of this chapter, but which are not, therefore, less important. You have opened this collection of essays in a specific situation, at a specific moment in your life, with specific intentions, and with specific other texts in mind. Probably you would like to learn about new and better ways of understanding, discussing, and teaching poetic texts. And perhaps you are emerging from it as seeing things, however slightly, in a different light.

'Summer of 1932' has therefore been used as part of an occasion that is quite different from the ones discussed earlier. The selection of a single text for discussion was a stipulation of the editor, one that makes excellent sense for such a collection of essays. But it has also focused your attention on the one text in a way which is not in accordance with its publication elsewhere.

You have been asked to consider the text repeatedly, as part of various imagined occasions and together with various paratexts. The ensemble of these, together with the occasion as part of which you were asked to consider them, has produced a poem that is quite different from any of the ones described earlier.

What I have just said about Dave Etter's poem is, of course, valid for all the other poems in this volume as well, and certain general conclusions can be drawn. They concern the fundamentals from which we should start, and the questions that we should be asking ourselves as readers of poetry. First, we have to acknowledge the primacy of occasion and, therefore, the limited and elusive authority of the text. As we only have the occasions, it is impossible to determine what the black marks as such have contributed to the poem. If critics reckon with the possibility of straightforward references to semantic properties, or of the reader's innocence, they *project* authority into the text, which it does not have.

This means that we first have to pay attention to the occasions of reading and their possible effects on results, i.e., the poems. We may then become aware of literature as an activity rather than a body of texts, of a culture of using literary texts with its own rules and rituals. We will become aware of how limited, even limiting, the reading of poetry in the classroom may be; and we may again become aware of what place the experience of poetry deserves in our lives.

NOTES

1 These conventions, which authors and readers share (or rather assume that they do), may in some cases leave marks in the texts – marks like deictic words, the ones that have often been studied by discourse-analysts (cf. Lewis 1972). But these marks are themselves impossible to interpret without reference to an occasion posited by the reader.
2 The differences between reading and listening, for example, cannot be discussed here. Material on this can be found in Engler (1982).
3 The third example of a possible occasion is deliberately introduced last here, even though or just because, unfortunately, it has for many become representative of the experience of literary texts in general.
4 The form of the poem, which favours a conversational tone in delivery, is unusual; the author writes: 'I count syllables when I write poems and they almost always make some kind of pattern, as well as enhance the rhythms in the poem . . . . I have 32 lines. Half of those lines contain eight syllables; then eight lines have seven syllables; four have nine; two have ten; and two lines have eleven syllables' (private communication).
5 There is the interesting case of anthologies where we find editors supplying titles to passages from long poems that they have selected for inclusion. cf. Helen Gardner's titles for her selections from Milton's *Paradise Lost* in *The New Oxford Book of English Verse* (1972): 'Immortal Hate' (I.76–124), 'Holy Night' (III.1–55), 'Evening in Paradise' (IV.598–656), 'The Banishment' (XII.624–49). None of these selections (and their titles) emphasize the narrative character of the poem.
6 In this case such an assumption is correct, as the author confirms in a letter.

FURTHER READING

Etter, D. (1983) *Alliance, Illinois*, Peoria, IL: Spoon River Poetry Press.
—— (1988) *Midlanders*, Peoria, IL: Spoon River Poetry Press.
Levinson, C. (1983) *Pragmatics*, Cambridge: Cambridge University Press.

REFERENCES

Anderson, S. (1919/1960) *Winesburg, Ohio*, ed. M. Cowley, London: Penguin.
Atherton, L. (1966) *Main Street on the Middle Border* (1954), repr., New York: Quadrangle Books.
Brooks, C. and Warren, R.P. (eds) (1976) *Understanding Poetry*, 4th edn, New York: Holt, Rinehart & Winston.
Brown, G. and Yule, G. (1983) *Discourse Analysis*, Cambridge: Cambridge University Press.
Carter, R. and Simpson, P. (eds) (1989) *Language, Discourse and Literature: An Introductory Reader in Discourse Stylistics*, London: Unwin Hyman.

Engler, B. (1982) *Reading and Listening: The Modes of Communicating Poetry and their Influence on the Texts*, Berne: Francke.

—— (1990) *Poetry and Community*, Tuebingen: Stauffenburg.

Etter, D. (1988a) *Electric Avenue*, Peoria, IL: Spoon River Poetry Press.

—— (1988b) 'Summer of 1932', *Ohio Review* 42: 80.

Fish, S. (1981) *Is There a Text in This Class?* Cambridge, MA: Harvard University Press.

Gardner, H. (ed.) (1972) *The New Oxford Book of English Verse*, Oxford: Clarendon Press.

Genette, G. (1987) *Seuils*, Paris: Edition du Seuil.

—— (1991) 'Introduction to the Paratext', *New Literary History* 22(2) (spring): 261–71.

Lewis, D. (1972) 'General Semantics', in D. Davidson and G.H. Harman (eds) *Semantics of Natural Language*, Dordrecht: Reidel.

Lewis, S. (1920/1961) *Main Street*, Signet Classics edn, New York: The New American Library.

Masters, E.L. (1915/1962) *Spoon River Anthology*, New York: Collier Macmillan.

Pratt, M.L. (1977) *Toward a Speech Act Theory of Literary Discourse*, Bloomington, IN: Indiana University Press.

Short, M. (1991) 'Literature and Language', in M. Coyle, P. Garside, M. Kelsall, and J. Peck (eds) *Encyclopedia of Literature and Criticism*, London: Routledge.

Yeats, W.B. (1906) 'Poetry and the Living Voice', in *Explorations*, London: Macmillan (1962): 202–21.

12 'Yo soy la Malinche': Chicana writers and the poetics of ethnonationalism

Mary Louise Pratt

EDITOR'S PREFACE

This chapter by Mary Louise Pratt is about the way an historic figure is raised to the status of a cultural symbol, and about the ways this symbol permeates social thought and finds expression in literature as a powerful instrument to assert cultural meaning and national self-awareness.

In a fascinating account we are told the life story of La Malinche, a young Aztec woman, who played a key part in the Spanish conquest of the Aztec empire by Hernán Cortés in the early sixteenth century. Was she traitor or victim? Whatever the historical truth may be, popular mythology attributed evil intentions to her, which found their expression in the language. Even in present-day colloquial usage in Mexico her name is semantically encoded in derisive words denoting 'traitor' and 'treason'. In recent years the myth of La Malinche was given a new lease by the Chicano ethnic minority movement of Mexican-Americans in the American states north of the Mexican border. Like many other Mexican and Aztec symbols, La Malinche was 'transculturated', as a result of which the myth was adjusted to a different cultural and ideological value system.

In her chapter Pratt focuses on how this resymbolization is reflected in the poetry of some women writers in the Chicano movement, who have tried to rehabilitate La Malinche. She argues that resymbolizing La Malinche has grown into a powerful poetic medium to query the often conflicting interests of the champions of gender equality and racial equality, and of feminism and ethnic nationalism.

Her probing analysis of a few Chicana poems (NB Chicana is the feminine form, while Chicano is masculine) reveals several artistic practices which are characteristic of contemporary Chic-ano/a poetry. For instance, since these poets are bilingual speakers of Spanish and English, they shift easily between one language and the other. This 'code-shifting' appears to be a rich source of meaning because it reflects social reality and it is aesthetically highly productive.

Though she does not state it in so many words, Pratt apparently does not regard literature as an autonomous phenomenon but as part of a complex social, political, and cultural system of values. Furthermore, the type of literature she has focused on does not appear to be primarily mimetic (or a mirror of society): in stronger terms, it is not a product of history but rather a producer of it.

As we have seen in the two chapters by Sell and Engler (chapters 10 and 11), pragmatics is commonly taken to be the study of meaning generated beyond the linguistic structures of a text, that is, by its context or non-verbal environment. To put it in somewhat extreme terms, *communication* is not brought about by the addresser's linguistic act, but by the addressee's successful interpretation of its intent (Green 1989: 1).

The nature of the contextual data needed for this interpretation is multifarious and so is the area of investigation of pragmatics. Perhaps we could say that, as long as the boundaries of its domain are not yet clearly drawn, the scope of pragmatics can be narrow or wide. If it is narrow, the context is limited, for example, to features of the immediate spatial and temporal situation in which the text is actually functioning. If it is wide, the context may be extended to include, for instance, aspects of the sociocultural, historical, and psychological background of the text. Thus defined, pragmatics intersects with a number of other fields such as, for example, sociolinguistics, psycholinguistics, and cultural anthro-pology.

Practitioners of literary pragmatics are likely to endorse the view that the study of literature is bound to benefit from the narrow as well as the broad (or perhaps even the broadest) interpretation of pragmatic theory (Watts 1991: 26–7). This way of thinking definitely places this chapter by Mary Louise Pratt in the realm of literary pragmatics so that it naturally follows those by Roger Sell and Balz Engler.

P. V.

It was towards the end of the year 13-Rabbit in Tenochtitlan when Motecuhzoma, ruler of the Aztec empire, first received news of the strange-looking foreigners arriving on the coast of his domains. (In Christian terms, it was August of 1519. Unbeknownst to Europeans, Tenochtitlan – later named Mexico City – was the biggest urban centre in the world.) 'The strangers' bodies are completely covered,' reported Motecuhzoma's messengers,

> so that only their faces can be seen. Their skin is white as if it were made of lime ... Their deer [for so the Aztecs saw the Spaniards' horses] carry them on their backs wherever they wish to go. These deer, our lord, are as tall as the roof of a house ....
>
> (Leon-Portilla 1962: 30)[1]

Were these peaceable visitors? Invaders? The god Quetzalcoatl whose return had been prophesied by the ancients? As the newcomers made their way inland, news of their power left Motecuhzoma 'distraught and bewildered'. At first, so the chroniclers report, it was hoped the emperor would be encouraged by news that a fellow Aztec was travelling with the strangers – 'a woman from this land, who speaks our Nahuatl tongue. She is called La Malinche, and she is from Teticpac. They found her there on the coast' (Leon-Portilla 1962: 35). This young woman, 14 years old and of noble birth, was acting as translator and mediator for the bearded newcomers and concubine to their leader, Hernán Cortés. Why, Motecuhzoma must have wondered, was she serving these pale visitors with their metal clothes and deadly, inexplicable weapons? Why was she helping them forge an army of his own conquered peoples? Why did she save them from ambushes, attacks, misunderstandings likely to prove their undoing? Was her presence, and her role as Cortés's lover, proof of his divinity? Or was she simply a traitor?

Exploration, imperial invasion, and conquest are endeavours overwhelmingly associated with men. Yet this young Aztec woman, known variously as Malintzín, La Malinche, and Doña Marina, became a key participant in the struggle between the Aztec and Spanish empires, as it played itself out in Mesoamerica over the two and a half years between Cortés's arrival and the fall of Tenochtitlan. The subject of this chapter, however, is her present-day status as a symbol in Mexican and Mexican-American culture. Four and a half centuries after her death, La Malinche continues to function in literature and thought as a vital site for the negotiation of cultural meaning and national self-understanding. After some remarks on her traditional meaning in vernacular culture, this chapter will go on to examine some contemporary poems about her.

In Mexican popular mythology, La Malinche, as she is called, is the quintessential symbol of betrayal, the indigenous woman who sold out to the Spanish conquistadores. She plays a negative role opposite two powerful positive symbols from Mexico's history: Cuauhtemoc, the last Aztec ruler and a symbol of heroic resistance to the invaders, and the Virgin of Guadalupe, the national saint created out of the intersection of Christianity and Aztec religion. La Malinche is associated with the common derisive expression *hijo de la chingada*, 'son of the screwed/raped woman', an insult, understood to allude to the illegitimate son she bore by Cortés. By extension, some interpreters have seen her role as that of symbolic mother of an ill-fated Mexican nation, born out of conquest, violence, rape, and betrayal.[2] Others have contested this negative interpretation, often underscoring her status as victim rather than villain.

In colloquial usage in Mexico the words *malinche* and *malinchista* today survive as derisive terms meaning 'traitor', especially suggesting betrayal of the nation. A *malinchista* is person who adopts foreign values, assimilates to foreign culture, or serves foreign interests. The semantics here are worth commenting on, for they exemplify how history gets coded in language. On the one hand, this popular usage of *malinche* encodes the story of Malintzín Tenépal (her Aztec name) in the national language in a particular moral and ideologically loaded way: she sold out to the enemy and her action was a betrayal. On the other hand, the term ties the concept of betrayal to Mexico's own history of colonialism and Indian–European relations, embedding that history in the lexicon. Notice too the inherent sexism: whether committed by man or woman, betrayal is coded in the language as female. To be a traitor is by implication to become female, while to be female is to be inherently a potential traitor. Of course by no means all speakers of Mexican Spanish are conscious of the specific history encoded in the term *malinche*, yet, as in all languages, the cultural attitudes that produced the usage also hold the term in place in the language, and vice versa. Linguists have not yet designed adequate theories for expressing such historical and ideological dynamics.

North of the Mexican border in the United States, the myth of La Malinche came into play in recent years with respect to a different national identity: that of the Chicano ethnic movement that consolidated itself in the 1960s in the states of Texas, Arizona, New Mexico, Colorado, and California. All of these states were part of Mexico until 1848, and in all very large proportions of the populations are of Mexican descent. Influenced profoundly by its ties to Mexican culture, the Chicano movement evolved a distinct identity and politics within the United States, based around resistance against subordination by the Anglo-American majority. La Malinche, like many Mexican and Aztec

symbols, was *transculturated* into the symbolic repertory of the
Chicano movement.[3] In other words, the symbol and myth of La
Malinche were appropriated and inserted into a different cultural and
ideological complex. This transculturation involved a process some
have called *resemanticization* or *resymbolization*, that is, the reworking
of established meanings in response to changing fields of values. The
rest of this chapter is about Chicano resymbolizations of La Malinche,
as exemplified in a few of the many poems about her. More generally,
the discussion exemplifies the kinds of issues that arise in the study of
minority and ethnic literatures, and of what one might call the poetics
of ethnonationalism.[4]

Initially it was in its traditional meaning as 'traitor' that La Malinche
first entered the vocabulary of the Chicano movement. In a usage that
undoubtedly evolved much earlier, Chicana women who married Anglo
men or took Anglo lovers were derisively labelled 'malinches'. The
label was also applied to Chicanas[5] who sought higher education, a
move regarded as assimilating to white culture, and to those who allied
themselves with feminism (Enríquez and Mirandé). The meaning seems
self-evident, but again it is interesting to examine the semantic transfer
involved: the sixteenth-century relation between an indigenous woman
and a Spanish man in Mexico is 'mapped' on to the twentieth-century
relation between a Mexican-American woman and an Anglo-American
man in the United States. Spanish colonialism in Mexico is paralleled
by what was often called the 'internal colonialism' (Acuña 1981)
suffered by the Chicano people under Anglo-American domination.[6]

The sexism in this usage of La Malinche again is obvious, and has
not gone uncontested. Over the years, women writers, poets, and
thinkers in the Chicano movement have sought to reclaim and re-
vindicate La Malinche, partly as a way to challenge the male-
centredness of traditional nationalisms. For Chicanas the figure of La
Malinche has provided a vital, resonant site for defining and symbolizing themselves and formulating women's ethnic history and struggle.
In particular, resymbolizing La Malinche became a means for exploring
the often conflicted relations between struggles for gender equality and
struggles for racial equality, between feminism and ethnic nationalism.
Two such resymbolizations are discussed below, and others appear in
the exercises.

In what may be the first Chicana poem using the Malinche figure,
Adaljiza Sosa Riddell (1973) laments – and at the same time embraces
– the Chicano image of the Malinche/traitor, that is, the Chicana
woman married to a white man. 'My name was changed, por la ley', this
bilingual poem begins: 'My name was changed, by the law'. Right from

its outset, then, the poem alludes to the gendered asymmetries of intermarriage: Chicana women who married Anglo men often 'lost' their Spanish surnames, the public badge of Chicano identity. This was not so, however, for Chicano men who married Anglo women and 'gave' them Spanish surnames. Masculinist nationalism unjustly read the woman's action more negatively than the man's. Sosa Riddell challenges this unjust view head on in her first line by noting that her name was something she was obliged *by law* to change, not something that she willingly gave up. The law that makes her a Malinche derives from a patriarchal privilege shared by Anglo and Chicano men alike!

The poet goes on to recount the pain of leaving her Chicano childhood behind while retaining her ethnic identity, and being criticized for betrayal. She exclaims:

> Malinche, pinche,
> forever with me;
>> I was born out of you,
>> I walk beside you.
>> bear my children with you
>> for sure, I'll die
>> alone with you.

(*Pinche* is a slang expression roughly equivalent to English 'damned' or 'damn it'.)

These lines take a bold initiative which the speaker's male detractors cannot take: rather than reject 'Malinche' as an epithet unfairly ascribed to her, the poetic 'I' embraces the symbol and bonds herself to it. She claims Malinche as her mother ('I was born out of you'), and as her companion or perhaps her sister ('I walk beside you, bear my children with you'). Indeed, by the end of the stanza ('for sure I'll die alone with you'), Malinche seems to become the primary relationship in her life, a soul mate or perhaps a spiritual companion. The relationship is not to be idealized, however. The poem closes with a reminder of the pain of the speaker's cultural predicament, the pain both of having married out of her culture and of being criticized for it:

> Pinche, como duele ser Malinche,   [Damn, it hurts to be Malinche]
> Pero sabes, ése,   [But you know, man]
> what keeps me from shattering
> into a million fragments?
> It's that sometimes,
> you are muy gringo, too.   [very Anglo]

With a wry twist characteristic of Chicano humour, in the final lines the speaker turns the derision ironically back on her male accuser.

Sosa Riddell attempts not so much to redefine the figure of La Malinche, as to claim it. The 'I' of the poem speaks *from within* the position of traitor assigned to La Malinche and claims that position as an autonomous space of being rather than a negative space ascribed from the outside by others. She seizes voice as Malinche, to depict her own situation and point up the contradictions of her accuser. This taking of voice is an act common to minority and ethnic literatures, especially in their emergent phases when writers must carve out positions of speech, often by recoding the very images that have been used to exclude or silence them. In her final lines, Sosa Riddell seems to be warning her fellow Chicanos against excessively purist forms of ethnic identity, suggesting that all to some degree participate in the dominant Anglo culture.

The passages quoted from Sosa Riddell's poem exemplify several artistic practices characteristic of contemporary Chicano/a poetry: Spanish–English bilingualism, to begin with, or rather the practice called *code-switching*, in which speakers switch spontaneously and fluidly between two languages. Code-switching is a linguistic practice highly characteristic of Mexican-American speech, and of other kinds of bilingualism as well.[7] Linguists have been very interested in its grammatical, social, and creative dimensions. From a grammatical or syntactic perspective, for example, analysis shows that code-switches most often happen at syntactic breaks, as in the first line of Sosa Riddell's poem ('my name was changed, *por la ley*'). One of the most frequent code-switches involves terms of address (such as *ése* above), and exclamations (such as *pinche*). Sometimes code-switching involves only phonology, that is, switching between English and Spanish pronunciation, as when proper names are pronounced with Spanish phonology to indicate Chicano ethnic identity.[8] (The word *Chicano* itself sounds very different pronounced with English and with Spanish phonology, so that one's pronunciation of it easily establishes one's ethnic affiliation.)

In the context of fiercely monolingual dominant cultures like that of the United States, code-switching lays claim to a form of cultural power: the power to own but not be owned by the dominant language. Aesthetically, code-switching can be a source of great verbal subtlety and grace as speech dances fluidly and strategically back and forth between two languages and two cultural systems. Code-switching is a rich source of wit, humour, puns, word play, and games of rhythm and rhyme. Many Chicano poets show dazzling virtuosity at such bilingual/

bicultural play. Consider the irony, for example, in Sosa Riddell's switch to Spanish in her last line (*muy gringo*, 'very Anglo', 'very assimilated') to point out that her Chicano accuser also shows signs of assimilation.

One of the most aesthetically effective interlingual strategies in Sosa Riddell's poem is her use of assonance and rhythm to harmonize the Spanish and English phrases. Notice how the rhythm of *Mălínchĕ pínchĕ* is repeated exactly by the English of the following line 'fŏrévĕr wíth mĕ'. In the final stanza, a rich alliteration works across the two languages, while rhythmic parallels link the second and third lines ('Pĕrŏ sábĕs, ésé/Whăt keéps mé frŏm sháttĕrĭng'). In the final line on the other hand, *múy gríngo*, with its repeated *i* sound and its two stressed syllables in a row, deliberately interrupts the rhythm and assonance, thus acquiring emphasis. Such interlingual dynamics are not artificial or contrived, but rather constitute a profound and productive dimension of bilingual linguistic consciousness, here put to effective artistic use.

The presence of colloquial language also characterizes much Chicano poetry, affirming its links to oral expressive culture, where parody and a witty, slightly self-deprecating sarcasm are highly developed and valued. In Sosa Riddell's final stanza, a wry humour, carried by the colloquial expressions *pinche*, *ése*, and *gringo*, mitigates an otherwise poignant statement. Internal rhyme, as with name: changed, *pinche*: *malinche*, *muy gringo*, is also a value in Chicano oral aesthetics.

Some five years after Sosa Riddell's poem, another composition on La Malinche appeared that undertook an entirely different resymbolization. In a poem entitled 'La Malinche' (1978), Carmen Tafolla vehemently rejects traditional interpretations of La Malinche. Her poem returns to the historical record and rewrites Malinche's story in an entirely new light. The text, given below in its entirety, is best read aloud:

La Malinche

Yo soy la Malinche.

My people called me Malintzín Tenépal
The Spaniards called me Doña Marina

I came to be known as Malinche
5   and Malinche came to mean traitor.

They called me – *chingada*
           ¡*Chingada*!

(Ha-Chingada! Screwed!)

Of noble ancestry, for whatever that means, I was sold into slavery
10 by MY ROYAL FAMILY – so that my brother could get my inheritance.
... And then the omens began – a god, a new civilization, the
downfall of our empire.

 And *you* came.

  My dear Hernán Cortés, to share your 'civilization' – to play
a god,
... and I began to *dream* ...
15   I *saw*,
  and I *acted!*

I saw our world
 And I saw yours
  And I saw –
20   another.

And *yes* – I helped you – against Emperor Moctezuma Xocoyotzin
himself!
I became Interpreter, Advisor, and lover.
 They could not imagine me dealing on a level with you –
  so they said I was raped, used,
25   *chingada*
    ¡*Chingada!*

But I saw our world
 and your world
  and another.

30 No one else could *see!*
  Beyond one world, none existed.
 And you yourself cried the night
 the city burned,
  and burned at your orders.
35 The most beatiful city on earth
  in flames.
You cried broken tears the night you saw your destruction.

My homeland ached within me
  (but I saw *another!*)

40 Another world –
  a world yet to be born.
And our child was born ...

and I was immortalized *Chingada!*
Years later, you took away my child (my sweet mestizo new world
child)
45   to raise him in your world.
         You *still* didn't see.
             You *still* didn't see.
     And history would call *me*
                 chingada.
50   But Chingada I was not.
         Not tricked, not screwed, not traitor.
     For I was not traitor to myself –
         I saw a dream
             and I *reached* it.

55   *Another world* . . . .

                 la raza.
                 la raaaaaaaa-zaaaaa . . . .

                                     (Carmen Tafolla)

(The final phrase *la raza* is a term used to refer to the Chicano people or
to all Latino peoples collectively. Its literal meaning in Spanish is 'the
race'.)

Perhaps, says Tafolla's (re)visionary interpretation, Malintzín Tenépal was operating not in the service of Cortés (or anyone else), but
towards independent goals of her own. Perhaps she had a project as
global and hegemonic as that of both Spanish and Aztec imperialisms.
Perhaps she too was embarked on a world-historical mission to found a
new society – though not through the destructive, masculinist practice
of conquest. Let us trace out the argument by 'walking through' the
poem stanza by stanza.

The opening line, 'Yo soy la Malinche', 'I am Malinche', has a
powerful resonance for readers familiar with Chicano literary tradition,
for it echoes the opening line of one of the foundational texts of both
Chicano literature and Chicano nationalism, the powerful poem 'Yo soy
Joaquín' written by Roldolpho 'Corky' Gonzales in 1967, and made
into a classic film by Luis Valdés.[9] By invoking these landmark texts,
Tafolla identifies her poem as an analogous foundational project, but in
this case she is founding a specifically female Chicana identity, and
perhaps a female, or even feminist, nationalism. She explicitly responds
to the masculinist nationalism of the Gonzales and Valdés texts, which
excluded women from the core of Chicano identity and relegated them
to secondary roles as supporters and reproducers of men.

As with Sosa Riddell's poem, Tafolla uses the first person, giving voice to the historically silent female subject. In the first ten lines La Malinche introduces herself through various identifications and symbolizations, including her Aztec name, Malintzín Tenépal. She alludes to the terrible experiences that led to her encounter with the Spaniards. Born into the Aztec nobility, her father died when she was a small child, and her mother remarried, bearing a son with her new husband. Wishing her family's wealth to pass on to her new son rather than her daughter, Malintzín's mother, so the accounts go, sold her daughter in slavery to some Maya traders, and feigned her death. Eventually it was as a slave that she was turned over to the Spanish, and it was through her life in slavery that she acquired the bilingualism that made her so valuable to them.[10] This early history undermines myths of Malinche as traitor to her people, for it makes clear that 'her people' in an important sense betrayed her first. Many have redefined La Malinche as a victim – oppressed by patriarchy well before she was oppressed by Eurocolonialism.

Tafolla builds in a different way on this biographical information, however. Her poem goes on to propose a radical reinterpretation of the entire Spanish conquest. Her Malinche boldly claims that the very injustices done to her by her family are what brought the Spaniards to Mexico's shores. The downfall of the Aztec empire *resulted from* the wrong done to her by Aztec patriarchy. So she places herself at the centre of history, rather than on its margins. The mention of omens in line 11 refers to Aztec accounts of the period, according to which the arrival of the Spaniards was preceded by a number of terrifying omens – a blazing comet in the sky, a temple that spontaneously burst into flames, a woman wailing in the streets at night (Leon-Portilla 1962: 3–12). The arriving Spaniards were initially thought to be the god Quetzalcoatl, whose return in the form of a yellow-haired man from the west had been prophesied among the Aztecs.

In lines 14–17, Malinche establishes herself as the central, world-changing protagonist of the Aztec–Spanish encounter. Cortés, who went down in history as the main protagonist of the conquest, was merely playing god and transmitting a fake 'civilization'. Malinche, on the other hand, is the visionary and the agent: 'I began to *dream*/I *saw*,/ and I *acted*!' Notice how this triplet echoes, and strongly contrasts with, Julius Caesar's famous phrase 'I came, I saw, I conquered'.

What Malinche saw in her dream, she tells us, was another world – a genuine New World – distinct from the patriarchal and militaristic realities of both Aztec and Spanish societies. In lines 17–29 she refutes readings of her as a victim of colonial violence. The victimization story, she argues, is itself paternalistic, denying her status as an independent agent ('They could not imagine me dealing on a level with you'). The derisive term *chingada* 'screwed' is introduced, then repeated with exclamation marks that say 'Humbug!' (The punctuation in line 26 is Spanish.)

In lines 30–9 Malinche describes the razing of Tenochtitlan (Mexico City) in August of 1521. Histories say Cortés did weep as he watched the city destroyed, at his own command. Malinche feels the pain, but unlike Cortés she sees beyond it. The same is true of her anguishing loss as a mother, described in the following two stanzas. During the Spanish occupation of Mexico City she became pregnant by Cortés, bearing a son who was named Martín, and whom Cortés, over her objections, later sent to Spain to be educated. On his return to Mexico, so the story goes, Martín repudiated his Indian mother, breaking her heart. La Malinche mourns the loss of 'my sweet mestizo new world child', but again she sees beyond it. She thus rejects symbolizations that subsume her into her role as mother, insisting that her vision goes far beyond the child she bore and who was taken away from her. Again the emphasis is on Cortés's inability to envision a new and better social order which he could help found. 'You *still* didn't see', she exclaims, 'And history would call *me* chingada ["screwed up"]'.

The poem's final stanza completes the resymbolization of Malinche. By a series of parallel negations, the traditional interpretations of traitor and victim are repudiated: 'Not tricked, not screwed, not traitor'. Malinche's own dream, the 'other world' of which she is founder is at last named concretely: 'la raza', first spoken, then shouted long and loud from the depths of her being: 'la raaaaaaa-zaaaaa . . .'. The final dots carry the echo of the shout into the present, opening the poem onto the new history to which the author and reader are heirs.

Though Tafolla's resymbolization of La Malinche draws on traditional mythology in identifying her as founder of *la raza*, it does so in a way that does not privilege her reproductive role, and does not define her actions as either betrayal or victimization. Tafolla's Malinche claims a vast world-building project of a kind not recognizable to masculinist heroics of orthodox history, a project that subsumes her reproductive powers into political, strategic, and visionary activity. Tafolla thus appropriates Malinche as a cultural or even revolutionary *ideal*. The relevance of this idealization to the search for a women's form of ethnonationalism is clear. The ethnic movement is called upon to recognize women as more than just handmaidens to the men and reproducers of the race. Ethnic women are called upon to claim power as world-makers and social and spiritual visionaries.

In this brief chapter it has been possible to comment on only two of the rather large corpus of contemporary poems around the figure of La Malinche (two others are introduced in the exercises). As the Americas acknowledge the five hundredth anniversaries of their first contacts with Europe, a re-engagement with history provides the chance for self-reflection, redefinition, and renewal. As the texts discussed here might suggest, poetry has a vital role to play in that process.

SUGGESTIONS FOR FURTHER WORK

1 In 1985, Naomi Quiñonez published an interesting poem entitled 'Trilogy' which draws together three female icons all traditionally associated with sexual betrayal: the biblical Eve, Helen of Troy, and La Malinche. The poem devotes a stanza to resymbolizing each of these figures, questioning the misogynist ethics of blame that has traditionally defined them. 'Let your ashes fly into the wind', she writes, 'Perhaps today we [women] can learn to accept ourselves.' Here is the stanza of her poem devoted to La Malinche:

```
     Eve . . . Malinche . . . Helen
     Eve . . . Malinche . . . Helen
     Tu padre te llevó        [Your father screwed
     a la chingada . . .        you (over) . . .]
5    Often we utter the atrocity of Malinche's sin
     as if she had no father
     who ingrained in her absolute obedience
     to men
     as if he had not given her
10   to Cortéz as a gift.
     She, obeying men
     obeyed her father's wish
     to be given
     obeyed Cortéz
15   and gave him Mexico.
```

a State succinctly how this poem reinterprets the myth of Malinche as traitor. Compare Quiñonez's resymbolization with Tafolla's.
b Sosa Riddell's poem, discussed above (pp. 175–8), ended with a wry ironic twist that defused sentimentality and turned an accusation back on the accuser. How would you describe the ironic twist at the end of Quiñonez's stanza? Is it similar?
c Discuss the use of language in Quiñonez's stanza, with attention to code-switching, orality, rhythm, syntactic repetition. Comment on the multiple uses of the verb 'give' in lines 9–15.

2 In her poem 'Malinche Reborn' (1988), Helen Silvas draws on the Malinche myth to describe the experience of a Chicana woman who lets herself be seduced and abandoned by an Anglo lover, ignoring inner warnings of danger:

Malinche Reborn

moon faced woman
eyes of earth brown
seeking wisdom in writing
dreamt of big fat rats
5   grabbing, tearing her throat
throwing premonition away
she danced & twirled
under the lunar light

daughter of darken caves
10   daughter of buried secrets

tossing caution warnings
like white petaled flowers on
morning dew grass
secure well hidden she thought
15   her forest of curtained emotions
lured enticed like her ancient ancestor
by flour faced creatures
only to be found out discovered
in the morning light
20   wet by forest tears
morning moisture brands her
she stands betrayed
a traitor to herself

she is malinche.

(Helen Silvas)

a How does the poem link the protagonist to the indigenous Aztec past?
b In lines 3–8, why is the protagonist seen as dreaming of 'big fat rats tearing her throat', and what is the significance of her throwing this premonition away?
c How are images of whiteness used in the third stanza (lines 11–23)? What connotations do they have?
d In what ways does the poem resymbolize the traditional equation of Malinche = traitor? To what extent is that equation kept intact? Do you think the poem has a didactic message? If so, do you agree with it?
e How does the poem distinguish different modes of knowledge associated with indigenous culture on the one hand and European culture on the other?
f Why do you think the lover never actually appears in this poem?

3 Give some examples of code-switching from your own linguistic experience. If you are a native speaker of a language other than English, or of multiple varieties of English, chances are you use code-switching yourself or live among those who do. Are there similarities or difference with the usages illustrated from Chicano bilingualism?

4 Explain the following bilingual joke (in Spanish, *mariposa* = 'butterfly', *flor* = 'flower'):

'What do a mariposa and an elevator have in common?
– They both go from flor to flor.'

5 Discuss the use of typography and graphic presentation in Tafolla's poem. To what extent is it used to make the poem seem more oral? What other effects do the graphics have?

6 It was suggested above that lines 14–16 of Tafolla's poem echo and contrast with Julius Caesar's famous line 'I came, I saw, I conquered'. Comment on the contrast. How is this motif retained through the rest of the poem?

7 La Malinche is only one example of a female national icon, and of a foundational myth (positive or negative) built around a woman. Describe briefly another such icon or myth that you know about, and discuss briefly ways it might be 'resymbolized' in response to changing values.

NOTES

1 So recorded the Aztec chroniclers some twenty years after Mexico had fallen to the invaders. Their accounts are excerpted and summarized in Miguel Leon-Portilla's *Broken Spears* (1962).

2 This argument was developed in an innovative and controversial study of Mexican national character by the philosopher and poet Octavio Paz in the 1950s (*The Labyrinth of Solitude* 1962). Critics were quick to question misogynist symbolizations of La Malinche. The hostility directed at La Malinche, it was argued, displaces or mystifies the fact that tens of thousands of indigenous inhabitants joined forces with the Spanish against what they had experienced as Aztec domination. In psychosocial terms, blaming it all on La Malinche provides a way of leaving intact a Manichean (and androcentric) myth of noble Aztec warriors victimized by ruthless Spanish warriors, a myth that proved useful to Mexican nationalism as it developed following the revolution of 1910.

3 The term *transculturation* was first proposed in the 1940s by the Cuban sociologist Fernando Ortiz, as a way to discuss the dynamics of cultural interaction between dominant and subordinate groups. It is not, Ortiz argued, simply a matter of the latter assimilating to the former in a straightforward way. Rather, he showed, subordinate groups are *selective* about what they acquire from a dominant culture, and *inventive* about what they do with it. The term transculturation tries to capture the dynamic aspects of the process, and the power which the subordinated exercise in shaping their interaction with the dominant and sustaining a degree of cultural autonomy.

4 I owe this term to the noted Chicana critic, Norma Alarcón. On La Malinche, see her essay cited in the references (Alarcón 1983).

5 Nouns are marked for gender in Spanish. *Chicana* is the marked and feminine form, while *Chicano* is the unmarked masculine form.

6 Just as the indigenous peoples in Mexico were there before the Spanish arrived, so the Mexican-Americans in the south-west were there before the Anglos arrived. The analogy rests on deep historical continuity: until 1848 the United States south-west was Mexico, and the Mexican-Americans were Mexicans. The Malinche myth is in this sense not an import.

7 For an introductory discussion of code-switching, see Elizabeth Closs Traugott and Mary Louise Pratt (1980).

8 Though many Americans from Spanish speaking backgrounds do not speak

Spanish fluently, a great many do have fluent Spanish phonology or
pronunciation. Chicano or Latino identity is thus readily indicated through
speech even when speakers have little fluency in Spanish. Chicano English
is also a distinctive variety, with characteristic phonology, intonation,
lexicon, and gestural features.

9 *I am Joaquin,* produced by El Teatro Campesino, directed by Luis Valdés
and George Ballis, 1969. The phrase 'Yo soy Joaquín' in turn alludes to a
line from the classic Mexican-American border ballad, 'The Ballad of
Gregorio Cortés' whose protagonist, a Mexican-American victimized by
the Texas rangers, repeatedly affirms his identity with the line 'Yo soy
Gregorio Cortés'.

10 Most of this information on Malinche's life is found in Bernal Díaz del
Castillo's classic *Historia de las cosas de Nueva España* (1632). This text
is available in English as Díaz del Castillo (1963). Eventually Cortés 'gave'
Malintzín Tenépal in marriage to his subordinate Juan Jaramillo, with
whom she lived until the latter's death. Cortés also gave her a large tract of
land so that Malintzín ended her life in material prosperity.

FURTHER READING

Bruce-Novoa, Juan (1982) *Chicano Poetry,* Austin, TX: University of Texas
Press.

Candelaria, Cordelia (1980) 'La Malinche, Feminist Prototype', *Frontiers*
2 (summer): 1–6.

—— (1986) *Chicano Poetry: A Critical Introduction,* Westport, CT:
Greenwood Press.

del Castillo, Adelaide R. (1977) 'Malintzin Tenepal: A Preliminary Look
into a New Perspective', in Rosaura Sánchez and Rosa Martínez Cruz
(eds) *Essays on La Mujer,* Los Angeles, CA: Chicano Studies Center,
University of California: 124–48.

Ordóñez, Elizabeth (1983) 'Sexual Politics and the Theme of Sexuality in
Chicana Poetry', in Beth Miller (ed.) *Women in Hispanic Literature,*
Berkeley, CA: University of California Press: 316–19.

Phillips, Rachel (1983) 'Marina/Malinche: Masks and Shadows', in Beth
Miller (ed.) *Women in Hispanic Literature,* Berkeley, CA: University of
California Press: 97–113.

Sánchez, Marta (1985) *Contemporary Chicana Poetry,* Berkeley, CA:
University of California Press.

Zamora, Beatrice (1978) 'Archetypes in Chicana Poetry', *De Colores,*
Albuquerque, NM: 4.3: 43–52.

REFERENCES

Acuña, Rodolfo (1981) *Occupied America: A History of Chicanos,* 2nd
edn, New York: Harper & Row.

Alarcón, Norma (1983) 'Chicana's Feminist Literature: A Re-Vision
through Malintzin/or Malinche: Putting Flesh back on the Object', in
Cherríe Moraga and Gloria Anzaldúa (eds) *This Bridge Called My Back:
Writings by Radical Women of Color,* New York: Kitchen Table Press.

Díaz del Castillo, Bernal (1963) *The Conquest of New Spain*, trans. and intro. by J. H. Cohen, Harmondsworth: Penguin.

Enríquez, Evangelina and Alfredo Mirandé (1978) 'Liberation, Chicana Style: Colonial Roots of Feministas Chicanas', in *De Colores*, Albuquerque, NM: 4.3: 7–21.

Gonzales, Roldolpho (1967) *Yo soy Joaquín/I am Joaquín*, Delano, CA: Farmworkers Press.

Leon-Portilla, Miguel (1962/1992) *The Broken Spears: The Aztec Account of the Spanish Conquest*, Boston, MA: Beacon Press.

Green, G.M. (1989) *Pragmatics and Natural Language Understanding*, Hillsdale, NJ: Lawrence Erlbaum Associates.

Paz, Octavio (1962) *The Labyrinth of Solitude: Life and Thought in Mexico*, trans. Lysander Kemp (originally published 1950), Eng. trans., New York: Grove Press.

Quiñonez, Naomi (1985) 'Trilogy', in *idem. Sueño de Colibri/Hummingbird Dream*, Boulder, CO: West End Press.

Silvas, Helen (1988) 'Malinche Reborn', in Ivan Gordon Vailakis (ed.) *Irvine Chicano Literary Prize, 1985–87*, Irvine, CA: Department of Spanish and Portuguese, University of California.

Sosa Riddell, Adaljiza (1973) Untitled poem, *El Grito* (Berkeley, CA) 7: 76.

Tafolla, Carmen (1978) 'La Malinche', in *idem. Canto al Pueblo*, San Antonio, TX: Penca Books.

Traugott, Elizabeth Closs and Pratt, Mary Louise (1980) *Linguistics for Students of Literature*, New York: Harcourt Brace Jovanovich.

Watts, R.J. (1991) 'Cross-Cultural Problems in the Perception of Literature', in R.D. Sell (ed.) *Literary Pragmatics*, London: Routledge.

Index

Printed in the United Kingdom
by Lightning Source UK Ltd.
106276UKS00001B/75